Energy and Housing

Energy and Housing

Consumer and Builder Perspectives

Edited by

Raymond J. Burby
Mary Ellen Marsden

University of North Carolina at Chapel Hill

 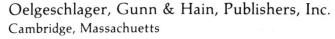

Oelgeschlager, Gunn & Hain, Publishers, Inc.
Cambridge, Massachusetts

International Standard Book Number: 0-89946-030-5

Library of Congress Catalog Card Number: 79-26662

Printed in the United States of America

Library of Congress Cataloging in Publication Data

Main entry under title:

Energy and housing.

    Includes index.
    1. Dwellings—North Carolina—Energy conservation. 2. Dwellings—Energy conservation. I. Burby, Raymond J., 1942-   II. Marsden, Mary Ellen.
TJ163.5.D86E52   696   79-26662
ISBN 0-89946-030-5

Contents

List of Figures

List of Tables

Preface

The research reported here documents the current status of energy efficiency in new and existing housing in one state—North Carolina—with findings that are applicable to other states as well. Two central actors in the process of increasing the energy efficiency of homes—the consumer and the builder—are intensively studied. Although other actors such as financial institutions, investors in the rental segment, and architects also contribute toward the level of energy use in the residential sector, consumers and builders, in conjunction with policymakers, are key decision agents. This report presents a thorough analysis of the trend toward building for energy efficiency in homes from the perspective of both consumers and builders, and it offers policy proposals for state officials. Analyses are based on two parallel studies of households and builders conducted during the fall of 1978, with supplementary analyses based on a survey of energy policy offices in the fifty states and a survey of solar builders.

Raymond J. Burby, Assistant Director for Research of the Center for Urban and Regional Studies, directed the builder survey and analyses, and Mary Ellen Marsden, Research Associate with the Institute for Research in Social Science, directed the household survey and analyses. Additional members of the research team were Michael W. McKinney, Associate Professor, Public Administration Program, North Carolina Central University, and the following faculty and staff members of the University of North Carolina at Chapel Hill: Angell G. Beza (Associate Director for Research Design, Institute for Research in Social Science), Susan E. Clarke (Director of Research Programs, Institute for Research in Social Science), Jeanne T. Hernandez (Research Associate, Institute for Environmental Studies), William W. Hill (Assistant Professor, Department of City and Regional Planning), Edward J. Kaiser (Professor, Department of City and Regional Planning), Duncan MacRae, Jr. (Kenan Professor, Departments of Political Science and Sociology), David W. Orr (Assistant Professor, Department of Political Science), and Carl M. Shy (Director, Institute for Environmental Studies).

We are indebted to the North Carolina Energy Institute, under the direction of Dr. James C. Bresee, for primary support of the research undertaken here. In addition, members of an advisory committee composed of representatives of business and industry, utility companies, state and local policymaking bodies, and the social science research community provided helpful guidance toward sharpening the research hypotheses, designing and implementing the field research, and maximizing the relevance of the research to public policy issues. The committee members included Professor Ray F. DeBruhl (Department of Civil Engineering, North Carolina State University), Nicholas DeMai, Jr. (North Carolina Home Builders Association), Norman Gustaveson (Orange County, North Carolina, County Commissioners), Jonathan B. Howes (Center for Urban and Regional Studies), Daniel A. Koenigshofer (Integrated Energy Systems), John Manuel (Energy Division, North Carolina Department of Commerce), Professor Frank Munger (Institute for Research in Social Science), Jane Sharp (North Carolina Department of Administration), Donald E. Stafford (Duke Power Company). While the research is stronger because of their assistance, they of course bear no responsibility for any shortcomings of the final product.

The research also could not have been conducted without the assistance of several graduate research assistants at the university—Laura Webb (Department of City and Regional Planning), Robert S. Agnew and Marie Guerin (Department of Sociology), and Gary Sidbury (School of Public Health, Epidemiology). In addition, the help of approximately thirty dedicated interviewers, too numerous to name here, is gratefully acknowledged. Frank DiIorio and Edward Bachmann of the Institute for Research in Social Science also provided expert computer assistance in creating the data files.

Our thanks go to Vonda Hogan and Bonita Samuels of the Institute and to Pat Sanford and Peggy Quinn of IRSS Publications for their excellent secretarial assistance, as well as to Barbara G. Rodgers and Carroll C. Carrozza of the Center and Elizabeth Fink of the Institute for their administrative assistance.

Raymond J. Burby
Mary Ellen Marsden
Chapel Hill, North Carolina
August 1979

Energy and Housing

Chapter 1

Introduction: Energy and Housing

Raymond J. Burby and Mary Ellen Marsden

Residential environments account for a major portion—approximately 20 percent nationally—of our total energy consumption. During the 1950s and 1960s, increased consumer purchasing power and the accompanying greater use of inefficient electrical heating, air conditioning, and other appliances pushed the rate of growth of residential energy consumption to over 4.0 percent per year. As energy prices have risen, the rate of growth in demand has slowed. With current energy prices, the demand for energy in housing is expected to rise at an annual rate of 2.3 percent through the year 2000 (Hirst and Carney, 1978). However, even though continued price increases will further dampen increasing residential energy growth, there is general agreement that our nation can do better if energy conservation goes beyond what market forces dictate.

A number of observers have pointed to an array of national benefits from accelerated energy conservation. In 1974, the Ford Foundation's Energy Policy Project team concluded that conservation would provide benefits in every major area of concern, including "... avoiding shortages, protecting the environment, avoiding problems with other nations, and keeping real social costs as low as possible" (Freeman et al., 1974, p. 325). Three years later, President Carter made conservation the cornerstone of the National

Energy Plan issued on April 29, 1977. In fact, an analysis of the plan by the U.S. General Accounting Office (1977) indicated that national energy goals could be achieved only if voluntary conservation were to exceed most estimates of the public's willingness to save energy. In 1979, the Council on Environmental Quality (1979, p. iii) concluded that the United States ". . . can do well, indeed prosper, on much less energy than has commonly been supposed." In addition to reducing the need for costly oil and gas imports, the council suggested that technologically feasible low energy growth could reduce the number of needed coal and nuclear power plants to a small fraction of what otherwise would have been required. This in turn could release capital for other productive purposes while conserving our diminishing domestic fossil fuel resources.

CONSERVING ENERGY IN HOUSING

Because of the enormous amount of energy involved and great potential for conservation,[1] considerable national attention has been devoted to methods of saving energy in the residential sector. Numerous opportunities have been identified for energy conservation in housing. They range from how people run their households to the ways in which housing is arranged to form neighborhoods. They include housing design and construction practices as well as the equipment used for heating and cooling and for other household purposes. Recent studies conducted at Oak Ridge National Laboratories (Hirst and Carney, 1978) suggest that through the implementation of policies to make use of these opportunities, the rate of growth in residential energy consumption can be dramatically slowed—to 1.2 percent per year—and households can save billions of dollars over the costs of their investments in energy conservation.

In 1975 energy use in the average single family detached house in the nation was distributed as follows: space heating, 68.6 percent; water heating, 14 percent; air conditioning 4.9 percent (relatively low because figures include non-air-conditioned homes); lighting, 3.5 percent; and appliances and other uses, 9 percent (NAHB Research Foundation, 1979, p. 7). Significant savings are possible in each of these aspects of residential energy use through changes in the operation and structural characteristics of existing housing and the design and construction of new houses.

Studies have shown that a number of changes in the ways in

which households operate their homes can result in substantial energy savings. Some of the savings that have been suggested include, on average:

a savings of 15 percent by setting back thermostats in winter by an average of 6 degrees to 68 degrees

a 7-percent savings by setting thermostats to 60 degrees at night

a 6- to 12-percent savings by setting back water heat from 145 degrees to 120 degrees

a 10- to 15-percent savings by maintaining furnace and air conditioning units at maximum efficiency by annual checkups (Thompson, n.d., p. IV-228)

In addition, savings achieved through other changes in housing can be virtually nullified by wasteful operating practices. In Twin Rivers, New Jersey, for example, researchers who were experimenting with alternative housing retrofits found that even after adjusting for differences in building orientation and other physical characteristics, twice as much energy was consumed in some three-bedroom townhouses than in some other identical units (Harrje, 1978; Seligman et al., 1978).

Another means of improving the energy efficiency of the existing housing stock is through changes in the nature of the structure (retrofits). For example, an energy conservation study by the U.S. Environmental Protection Agency (1975) indicated that additional insulation—in attics, storm windows, and weatherstripping—could save close to 20 percent in energy consumption in the approximately 18 million older homes in the nation without such insulation. In the case of heating and cooling equipment, a study by Hittman Associates (1973) found that in single-family housing a 21-percent reduction in primary energy consumption could be achieved if electrically heated appliances were converted to their gas-fired counterparts. Or, according to the Council on Environmental Quality (1979, p. 11), almost 1 percent of total national energy demand could be saved if resistive heating systems were replaced with heat pumps. Finally, significant savings are possible through conversion to solar space and hot water heating. Nationally, the U.S. Department of Energy estimates that solar energy will provide from 5 to 15 percent of U.S. energy supplies by the year 2020 (Division of Solar Energy, Energy Research and Development Administration, 1977). To achieve this target, national energy goals call for 2.5 million residential solar installations by 1985.

In new residential construction, research by Hittman Associates (1978) suggests that energy savings between 30 and 60 percent can be achieved through technically feasible modifications in design and construction. Key changes in current building practices that are needed to achieve these savings include reducing the glass area of buildings by approximately 25 percent; using double glazing or reflective glass; installing weatherstripping and caulking; increasing wall, floor, and ceiling insulation; and using more efficient heating and cooling systems. More modest energy savings, ranging from 11.3 percent in single-family dwellings to 42.7 percent for low-rise apartment buildings, will accompany the adoption of the American Society of Heating, Refrigeration, and Air Conditioning Engineers (ASHRAE 90-75) standard for new construction (Arthur D. Little, 1976, p. 5). An economic analysis of the impacts of related standards indicates that by the year 2000 residential fuel bill reductions will exceed additional construction costs by almost $8 billion nationally, with a benefit/cost ratio for energy-conserving residential construction standards of 2.9 (Hirst and Carney, 1978). In the case of appliance efficiency, the same study found that achievement of Federal Energy Administration 1980 efficiency targets for space heating, water heating, refrigerators, freezers, air conditioners, and other appliances would save 11.3 quadrillion Btu (quads) by the year 2000 with a benefit/cost ratio of 1.6 (Hirst and Carney, 1978).

Finally, a number of proposals have been put forward for energy conservation through neighborhood design and the arrangement of housing and other land uses within urban areas. For example, through neighborhood design, buildings can be oriented to take advantage of the heating capability of the sun and cooling capability of the winds. In addition to building orientation, energy can be saved through a variety of other neighborhood design concepts, including reduced street widths, protection of solar rights, bicycling and walking paths, functional landscaping, optimal street light placement, increased density, and district heating (Robinette, 1977; Bainbridge and Hammond, 1976).

At the community level, urban form—the spatial arrangement of urban activities and open space—has been found to be related to energy consumption. Through the manipulation of various aspects of urban form—such as the overall scale and density of a community, configuration of developed and undeveloped land, and location of individual land uses—it has been estimated that community energy consumption can be reduced by 3 to 10 percent by the year 2000 (Leighton, 1977). In the short term, it has been estimated that national energy consumption could be reduced by about 3 percent between 1975 and 1985 through the adoption of energy-efficient patterns of development (Keyes, 1976). Because of the required changes in living patterns and lifestyles, achieving the potential short-term savings would obviously be extremely problematic.

THE POLICY CHALLENGE

Although different analysts will arrive at different estimates of the exact amount of energy that can be saved in the residential sector, depending on their assumptions, two points seem clear: (1) the amount of energy in housing that can be saved is very large, and (2) a number of technical options and a number of elements of housing construction, reconstruction, and operation must be taken into account in the formulation of a comprehensive residential energy conservation program. The public policy challenge is also clear: to translate potential energy savings into actual reductions in the energy used in housing.

Federal efforts to meet this challenge, as exemplified by the Energy Policy and Conservation Act of 1975, the Energy Conservation and Production Act of 1976, and the bills comprising the National Energy Act of 1978, have followed four major thrusts.

1. Mandatory federal appliance efficiency standards are to be established by 1980 for thirteen categories of home appliances, ranging from furnaces to television sets.
2. To promote the installation of additional insulation (the national goal is to insulate 90 percent of all homes by 1985) and other structural retrofits, public utilities are being required to provide home energy audits and conservation advice to households. Weatherization loans and grants for low- and moderate-income families and the elderly have been provided. Also, income tax credits for home insulation are now available.
3. To promote energy efficiency in new residential construction, mandatory standards for new building are being developed by the Department of Housing and Urban Development for implementation through state building codes.
4. To promote more rapid adoption of solar energy technologies, a residential solar demonstration program has been mounted, reduced interest loans for homeowners and builders who use solar are available, and income tax credits for homeowners who install solar energy devices have been adopted.

In combination, these measures and those aimed at other sectors of energy use are expected to result in ". . . reduced oil import needs by

1985, increased use of fuels other than oil and gas, and more efficient and equitable use of energy in the United States" (Office of Public Affairs, U.S. Department of Energy, 1978).

As essential as energy conservation is to our national well-being, meeting the energy policy challenge is equally important at the subnational level. States that lack significant indigenous energy resources face the prospect of a steady transfer of income to energy-producing regions unless conservation and the development of alternative energy sources create new "supplies" of energy to fuel internal growth and development (see Burgraff, 1978; and Miernyk, 1977). Unfortunately, most states have not followed the federal government's lead by adopting vigorous programs to promote energy conservation in housing. Instead, they have assumed that federal policies or the marketplace (rising energy prices) will be sufficient to create a demand for retrofitting, energy-efficient building and neighborhood design and construction, and the rapid adoption of solar energy technologies. As noted by the Council of State Governments (1976, p. 29), however, "Little evidence exists to verify or quantify these assumptions."

In addition to relying on the price of energy to stimulate conservation, state energy policy analysts must consider the relative effectiveness of four other strategies for reducing energy consumption in residential environments. These strategies include: (1) supply restriction/allocation policies; (2) regulatory policies; (3) incentive policies; and (4) information and education policies (Healy and Hertzfeld, 1975).

Supply strategies have most often been suggested as an appropriate course of action in emergency situations. However, they are not viewed as an appropriate long-term approach to reducing energy consumption. As a result, most attention has focused on regulatory, incentive, and voluntary (information and education) approaches.

A number of regulatory policies for promoting energy efficiency in residential environments have been proposed. They include:

1. building codes with provisions to insure that future dwelling units are designed and built with energy conservation features and with controls (such as light switches and thermostats) which make it practical for the occupants to follow energy-conserving life styles
2. disclosure regulations (such as required energy labeling on heating and cooling equipment, and the recording of energy consumption for a previous time period in deeds or other

documents when dwellings are transferred), which make it possible for consumers to make more informed purchase decisions

3. subdivision regulations, which require attention to the energy implications of lot and building orientation and neighborhood design.

Incentive (and disincentive) strategies most often have been proposed as a means to encourage homeowners to undertake retrofitting of existing buildings to make them more energy-efficient and to adopt solar and other energy augmentation devices. The two most common incentive strategies are (1) income tax credits for retrofit and solar investments, and (2) real estate tax exemptions to relieve property owners of increased tax liability due to improvements which increase the energy efficiency of their homes. In addition, a number of states have used low-cost loan programs to encourage retrofitting and have provided direct grants to insulate the homes of lower-income and older households (weatherization programs). Although disincentives have yet to be used, higher utility rates or property taxes presumably could be applied to energy-inefficient homes to encourage property owners to invest in retrofitting their dwellings. The differential in rates would be designed to reflect the social costs of the energy-inefficient dwellings.

Finally, almost every state has pursued voluntary approaches to energy conservation, in which the state uses public education to increase consumers' awareness of the need and techniques for energy conservation. In this regard, they have been joined by the federal government and a host of trade associations and other groups so that a wealth of information on how to save energy in housing is available to consumers and to every sector of the housing industry.[2]

A number of economically and technologically viable options to reduce energy consumption in housing are available. As a result, it now appears, "The major difficulties to reduced energy use in residential and commercial buildings are public inertia and institutional obstacles, rather than technology or building economics" (Council of State Governments, 1976, p. 30). Before more effective policies can be devised and pursued, either at the national or state level, much more information is needed regarding household and homebuilder energy conservation decisionmaking and other targets for future policy initiatives.

THE RESEARCH CHALLENGE

Social science research can contribute to energy policymaking and program formulation for the residential sector in four basic ways.

1. Research can provide policymakers with an accurate picture of the current status of energy conservation in housing. High-quality baseline data are essential as indicators of the need for residential energy conservation programs and as bench marks against which to measure change over time so that the success of various policy initiatives can be ascertained.
2. Research can suggest why particular energy conservation outcomes are occurring. Before methods of producing change can be devised and evaluated, information is needed about key factors associated with the energy conservation decisions of households and homebuilders. If these factors include at least some elements that can be shaped by public policy, then policymakers will have a better understanding of how to achieve national and state goals for energy conservation in the residential sector.
3. Research can isolate existing effects of public policy (both intended and unintended) on energy conservation decisions so that past policy decisions and existing programs can be evaluated.
4. Research can suggest new avenues for energy policy development.

In recent years, the base of knowledge about energy conservation in the residential sector has been expanding rapidly. However, the process of saving energy in housing is extremely complex. As shown in Figure 1-1 taken from a study of decisions involved in the diffusion of residential solar energy technologies, a variety of types of decision agents—performing a highly interrelated set of functions, each subject to influences from a vast array of sources—determine the energy efficiency realized in the residential sector (George Washington University, 1978). To date, most social science research on energy conservation in housing has focused on homeowners' attitudes toward the energy problem in the United States and their actual behavior in reducing energy use and investing in energy conservation features, such as extra insulation and storm windows. Fewer studies have examined consumers' knowledge of energy conservation practices or the degree of acceptance of energy policy alternatives. With the exception of a few studies which have

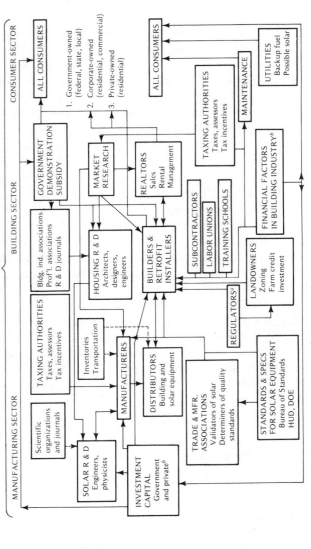

SOLAR TECHNICAL DELIVERY SYSTEM

EXTERNAL FORCES: Media, Public Education & Information, Price of Competing Fuels, Price and Availability of Money

MANUFACTURING SECTOR | BUILDING SECTOR | CONSUMER SECTOR

Scientific organizations and journals

SOLAR R & D Engineers, physicists

INVESTMENT CAPITAL Government and private[b]

MANUFACTURERS

Inventories Transportation

TAXING AUTHORITIES Taxes, assessors Tax incentives

DISTRIBUTORS Building and solar equipment

TRADE & MFR. ASSOCIATIONS Validators of solar Determiners of quality standards

STANDARDS & SPECS FOR SOLAR EQUIPMENT Bureau of Standards HUD, DOE

Bldg. ind. associations Prof'l. associations R & D journals

HOUSING R & D Architects, designers, engineers

BUILDERS & RETROFIT INSTALLERS

REGULATORS[a]

SUBCONTRACTORS

LABOR UNIONS

TRAINING SCHOOLS

LANDOWNERS Zoning Farm credit investment

GOVERNMENT DEMONSTRATION SUBSIDY

MARKET RESEARCH

REALTORS Sales Rental Management

TAXING AUTHORITIES Taxes, assessors Tax incentives

FINANCIAL FACTORS IN BUILDING INDUSTRY[b]

MAINTENANCE

ALL CONSUMERS

1. Government-owned (federal, state, local)
2. Corporate-owned (residential, commercial)
3. Private-owned (residential)

ALL CONSUMERS

UTILITIES Backup fuel Possible solar

appraisers
Federal Reserve Board (interest rates, availability of capital)
insurers

[a]Regulators: building code writers
building code inspectors
city planners
zoning authorities
housing agencies
state & local governments

[b]Financial factors in building industry:
lending agencies (banks, S&L's, etc.)
federal and state building & solar authorities
(e.g., HUD, DOE, State housing authorities)
GNMA, FNMA

Figure 1-1. Residential energy conservation process. *Source:* The George Washington University, 1978.

9

investigated institutional constraints in the diffusion of solar technologies, the new construction segment of the residential sector has to this time been ignored.

In the case of existing housing, much social science research has explored those socioeconomic and demographic factors associated with energy conservation behavior and attitudes, particularly the central role of income in predicting conservation behavior (Newman and Day, 1975; Gottlieb and Matre, 1976; Cunningham and Lopreato, 1977). Other studies have addressed the equity of energy prices on the poor and elderly (Schwartz and Schwartz, 1974; Morrison, 1977; Welfare Research, 1978; Hatch and Whitehead, forthcoming). Less central have been studies of public resistance to energy policy alternatives (Murray, et al., 1974; Bultena, 1975; Zuiches, 1976) or investigations into the influence of the choice of housing structure and retrofitting on energy use (Seligman et al., 1978; Hittman Associates, 1978). Relatively neglected have been studies of the interaction between consumers, policymakers, and key decision agents in the residential sector. In fact, most social science research to date in the field of energy conservation has presented economic modeling and aggregate-level sectorial analyses of energy use and conservation (see critiques of energy research in the social sciences in Landsberg et al., 1974; Wilbanks, 1977). Studies are needed which more adequately examine those social and political factors influencing the drive toward increasing energy conservation and energy efficiency in existing housing.

In the case of new construction, previous research has identified characteristics of the housing industry that produce "self-reinforcing resistance to change" (Schon, 1967) in the industry. In particular, attention has been devoted to

building codes which have frozen outmoded practices into law (Thompson, 1978)

the highly leveraged character of the industry, which leads builders and buyers to be very sensitive to the first costs of housing (Hirschberg and Schoen, 1974)

the sensitivity of lending institutions to risk, which can lead to an aversion to financing innovative housing (Barrett, Epstein, and Haar, 1977)

fragmentation of the housing industry, which increases the number of decision points involved in the diffusion of an innovation (Council of State Governments, 1976)

the orientation of building craft unions to traditional modes of operation (Beyer, 1965; National Commission on Urban Problems, 1968, Pt. III, chapter 4) legal uncertainties regarding "access to the sun," which may result in consumer hesitancy to invest in solar devices (Eisenstadt and Utton, 1976; Miller, Hayes, and Thompson, 1977; Myers 1978).

Improved knowledge of institutional and economic constraints is reflected in the current federal emphasis on energy-efficient building standards (U.S. Department of Housing and Urban Development, 1978), and federal and state efforts to reduce the first costs of energy conservation features through the use of tax credits and abatements (Minan and Lawrence, 1978).

While information about economic and institutional constraints has been valuable in the initial development of policies to promote the adoption of energy conservation features in new housing, as with conservation in existing housing, information at a finer grain is needed if we are to move forward to a second generation of policy development. In particular, we need detailed information about the market (consumer demand) for various energy conservation features and about the builders who are most likely to respond to market signals. For example, to what extent has consumer demand for energy-efficient housing been expanding? What types of home buyers are most likely to consider dwellings in higher than usual residential densities or with particular energy conservation features, such as solar space or hot water heating? What factors have motivated consumer interest in energy efficiency in new housing? Are additional incentives needed? Is additional information needed? How much extra are consumers willing to invest to achieve greater energy efficiency in their future homes? To what extent are builders responding to consumer interest in energy conservation? Which energy conservation features are builders adopting most rapidly? Which types of builders are the "early adopters" of new energy conservation technologies? What sources of information and adoption decision criteria do builders use in deciding to incorporate various energy conservation features in new housing? How can public policy stimulate greater attention to energy conservation in new construction? Answers to these questions will provide a basis for more finely tuned and carefully targeted federal and state policies to increase the market penetration of energy conservation practices and new technology in the new construction segment of the residential sector.

THE STUDY

Energy and Housing provides answers to these and a host of related questions about energy conservation in housing. It reports the results of a pioneering study designed to provide energy policy-makers and program personnel with an improved base of information about two key groups involved in the process of achieving energy efficiency in the residential sector—households and homebuilders. In addition, it reports on energy conservation policies being developed in the fifty states and, based on analyses of household and builder behavior in North Carolina, suggests a number of new directions for state governments to move in order to increase energy savings in the residential sector.

The data reported in the following chapters were collected through three separate surveys of households and homebuilders in the state of North Carolina and a national survey of state energy agencies. To answer questions related to household energy conservation, 604 interviews were conducted by telephone during the fall of 1978 with a statewide probability sample of household heads and spouses. The sample frame of telephone numbers was constructed so that cases were drawn from each county in the state in direct proportion to the county's proportion of the state population. Telephone numbers were then systematically selected from telephone books, and the last two digits were randomized. The response rate of the household survey was 81 percent.

Information about homebuilders was obtained through personal interviews conducted during the fall of 1978 with a statewide random sample of builders. Because an insufficient number of "solar" builders was obtained through random selection procedures, a supplemental sample was drawn and twenty additional solar builders were interviewed during the spring of 1979. The sample frame for the base survey of homebuilders was constructed from two sources: membership lists of the North Carolina Home Builders Association, and the *List of Licensed General Contractors* published by the North Carolina Licensing Board for Contractors. From this sample frame a random sample of firms was drawn; firms were then screened by telephone to determine whether they had constructed a single-family detached house during the past year. After the participation by a firm in homebuilding was verified, an interview was arranged with the entrepreneur or company employee who had ultimate responsibility for the characteristics of the houses built—their location, size, architectural style, room layout, equipment, materials, and special features, including those geared toward energy conservation. In all, interviews averaging sixty minutes each were completed with 100 homebuilders located in sixty-two communities. The response rate for the basic builder survey was 73 percent.

Approximately 400 telephone contacts were required with

knowledgeable persons—architects, N.C. Home Builders Association chapter presidents, solar equipment suppliers, and building inspectors, among others—in order to develop an exhaustive list of firms that had constructed speculative houses with passive or active solar systems. The sample was limited to speculative builders because of our interest in builders' decisions (as opposed to owners' decisions, which would be in effect for custom solar homes built to specifications of the buyer or the buyer's architect). The survey produced a sample frame of only twenty-seven firms; this appears to be the extent of solar speculative builders in North Carolina at this time. Of these firms, interviews using a separate solar builder interview schedule were completed with the principals of twenty companies— a response rate of 74 percent. Characteristics of solar builders are described in Supplementary Analysis II.

The final approach to data collection used in this study involved a national survey of state energy conservation plans for the residential sector. In June 1978, information was solicited from each state through a letter addressed to the administrative head of the state energy office. Information requested included the state's current and intended future use of three types of policies: (1) incentives and disincentives, such as tax credits and low-interest loans; (2) regulatory programs, such as building code provisions applicable to energy-related aspects of residential structures; and (3) public education programs. In addition, states were questioned about their use of surveys and other methods of monitoring and evaluating the success of their programs and were asked to provide copies of annual reports and other material describing their energy conservation efforts. Responses were obtained from forty-four states. The list of state energy agencies which were asked to provide information is provided in the appendix. A state-by-state summary of the survey results is provided in Supplementary Analysis III.

AN OVERVIEW OF ENERGY AND HOUSING

This report of the study findings and policy suggestions is organized into three major parts. Each part examines a different facet of energy conservation in the residential sector. In Part I, "Energy and Existing Housing," chapters are devoted to the energy efficiency of the existing housing stock and to consumer decisions in the operation of their homes and apartments. Information is provided on fuel use, degree of thermal efficiency, and the participation of households in retrofitting tabulated by location, aspects of the structure, and characteristics of the household. Consumer behavior and conservation decisions are analyzed in terms of their implications for energy conservation education programs. Information is also provided about consumers' attitudes toward energy problems and energy policy options, and about their expectations for monetary paybacks from investments which improve the energy efficiency of their homes.

In Part II, "Energy in New Housing," chapters are devoted to three aspects of energy conservation in the production of new homes:

1. characteristics of the market for new housing, and consumers' interest in the energy efficiency of their next home
2. the structure of the housing industry, and characteristics of homebuilders as they affect the potential for the diffusion of new energy conservation technologies in the residential sector
3. builders' individual decisions to construct houses and neighborhoods incorporating various energy conservation features.

The data and analyses highlight consumer demand for energy efficiency in housing and the way in which the homebuilding industry is responding to this demand. By analyzing the attention given by builders to energy efficiency in terms of both the structural characteristics of the homebuilding industry and the decisions of construction firms and private builders, a foundation is laid for the development of policy initiatives addressed to the new construction segment of the residential sector.

Part III, "Residential Energy Conservation Policy and State Government," explores energy conservation policy in the United States and offers suggestions for the next generation of state energy programs and policies. In analyzing the states' experience with conservation policy, particular attention is given to the range of state plans and programs stimulated by the Energy Policy and Conservation Act of 1975 (EPCA) as amended by the Energy Conservation and Production Act of 1976 (ECPA). Based on current policies pursued by state governments and our analyses of consumer and builder attitudes and behavior, we present for consideration and further discussion a set of new policies aimed at both existing and new housing.

NOTES

1. For example, in 1975 total energy consumption in the United States was about 71 quadrillion Btu (quads). In that year, residential energy use was 23.5 percent of the total or about 16.7 quads. Based on a national housing inventory of 78 million dwellings, overall consumption per dwelling unit was about 214 million Btu per year. (See NAHB Research Foundation, 1979.)

2. A number of residential energy conservation manuals and reports have been prepared by and for organizations associated with residential building, development and rehabilitation. A sampling of these includes:

   a. American Institute of Architects
      American Institute of Architects. 1974. *Nation of Energy Efficient Buildings by 1990*. Washington: The Institute.

   b. American Society of Heating, Refrigeration, and Air Conditioning Engineers
      American Society of Heating, Refrigeration, and Air Conditioning Engineers. 1975. *Energy Conservation in New Building Design*. New York: The Society, August.
      Arthur D. Little, Inc. 1976. *An Impact Assessment of ASHRAE Standard 90-75*. Conservation Paper Number 43A, Office of Buildings Programs, Energy Conservation, and Environment, Federal Energy Administration. Washington: U.S. Government Printing Office.

   c. National Association of Home Builders
      National Association of Home Builders. 1978. *Designing, Building, and Selling Energy Conserving Homes*. Washington: The Association.

   d. NAHB Research Foundation, Inc.
      NAHB Research Foundation, Inc. 1979. *Insulation Manual: Homes, Apartments*. Rockville, Md.: The Foundation.

   e. The National League of Cities/U.S. Conference of Mayors
      Jeff Bander, Mel Bergheim, Tara Hamilton, Norman King, and Sarah Wald. 1975. *Energy Conservation in Buildings: New Roles for Cities and Citizen Groups*. Washington: The National League of Cities and U.S. Conference of Mayors, January.

   f. U.S. Department of Commerce, National Bureau of Standards
      Stephen R. Peterson. 1974. *Retrofitting Existing Housing for Energy Conservation: An Economic Analysis*. Washington: Center for Building Technology, National Bureau of Standards, Department of Commerce, December.
      U.S. Department of Commerce, National Bureau of Standards. 1973. *Technical Options for Energy Conservation in Buildings*. Washington: The Department, July.

   g. U.S. Department of Energy
      AIA Research Corporation. 1976. *Decision Making in the Building Process*. Washington: The Corporation, August.
      Eric Hirst and Janet Carney. 1977. *Residential Energy Use to the Year 2000: Conservation and Economics*. Springfield, Va.: National Technical Information Service, September.

National Conference of States on Building Codes and Standards. 1977. *Model Code for Energy Conservation in New Building Construction.* Springfield, Va.: National Technical Information Service, June.

Pope, Evans and Robbins, Inc. 1976. *Building Energy Handbook,* Vols. I and II. Springfield, Va.: National Technical Information Service, December.

h. U.S. Department of Housing and Urban Development.

Abt Associates, Inc. 1975. *In the Bank . . . Or Up the Chimney? A Dollars and Cents Guide to Energy-Saving Home Improvements.* Washington: U.S. Government Printing Office, April.

AIA Research Corporation. 1978. *Phase One/Base Data for the Development of Energy Performance Standards for New Buildings.* Washington: Office of Policy Development and Research, U.S. Department of Housing and Urban Development, January 12.

Hittman Associates, Inc. 1978. *Residential Energy Consumption: Detailed Geographic Analysis.* Summary Report, Report No. HUD-PDR-250. Washington: U.S. Government Printing Office, January.

Hittman Associates, Inc. 1974. *Residential Energy Consumption-Multifamily Housing—Final Report,* Report No. HUD-HAI-4. Washington: U.S. Government Printing Office, June.

Hittman Associates, Inc. 1973. *Residential Energy Consumption—Single Family Housing Final Report.* Report No. HUD-HAI-2. Washington: U.S. Government Printing Office, March.

Real Estate Research Corporation. 1978. *Building the Solar Home: Some Early Lessons Learned.* Residential Solar Program Report No. 2. Washington: U.S. Government Printing Office, June.

Real Estate Research Corporation. 1978. *Selling the Solar Home: Some Preliminary Findings,* Solar Program Report No. 1. Washington: U.S. Government Printing Office, April.

i. U.S. League of Savings Associations

Harold B. Olin and Richard J. Laya. *Energy Conservation & You: A Housing Energy Primer.* Chicago: United States League of Savings Associations.

REFERENCES

Arthur D. Little, Inc. 1976. *An Impact Assessment of ASHRAE Standard 90-75.* Conservation Paper Number 43A, Office of Buildings Programs, Energy Conservation and Environment, Federal Energy Administration. Washington: U.S. Government Printing Office.

Bainbridge, David A., and Jonathan Hammond. 1976. *Planning for Energy Conservation.* Prepared for the City of Davis, California. Winters, Calif.: Living Systems, June 1.

Barrett, David, Peter Epstein, and Charles M. Haar, 1977. *Financing the Solar Home: Understanding and Improving Mortgage-Market Receptivity to Energy Conservation and Housing Innovation.* Lexington, Mass.: D.C. Heath and Company, Lexington Books.

Beyer, Glen H. 1965. *Housing and Society*. New York: The Macmillan Company.

Bultena, Gordon. 1975. "Public Response to the Energy Crisis: A Study of Citizens' Attitudes and Adaptive Behaviors." Ames, Ia.: Department of Sociology, Iowa State University.

Burgraff, Shirley. 1978. "Energy, the New Economic Development Wildcard," Paper prepared for the White House Conference on Balanced Growth and Economic Development. Tallahassee, Fl.: Florida A&M University, January.

Council on Environmental Quality. 1979. *The Good News About Energy*. Washington: U.S. Government Printing Office.

Council of State Governments. 1976. *Energy Conservation: Policy Considerations for the States*. State Environmental Issues Series. Lexington, Ky.: The Council, November.

Cunningham, William H., and Sally Cook Lopreato. 1977. *Energy Use and Conservation Incentives: A Study of the Southwestern United States*. New York: Praeger Publishers.

Division of Solar Energy, U.S. Energy Research & Development Administration. 1977. *Solar Energy in America's Future: A Preliminary Assessment*. Washington: U.S. Government Printing Office, March.

Eisenstadt, Melvin M., and Albert E. Utton. 1976. "Solar Rights and Their Effect on Solar Heating and Cooling," *Natural Resources Journal*, Vol. 16, No. 2, pp. 363-414.

Freeman, S. David; Pamela Baldwin, et al. 1974. *A Time to Choose: America's Energy Future*. Final Report by the Energy Policy Project of the Ford Foundation. Cambridge, Mass.: Ballinger Publishing Company.

George Washington University. 1978. *Solar Energy Incentives Analysis: Psycho-Economic Factors Affecting the Decision Making of Consumers and the Technology Delivery System*. Prepared for the U.S. Department of Energy Under Contract No. Ex. 76-G-10-2534. Washington: U.S. Department of Energy, January.

Gottlieb, David, and Marc Matre. 1976. *Sociological Dimensions of the Energy Crisis: A Follow-up Study*. Houston: University of Houston Energy Institute.

Grier, Eunice S. 1975. "National Survey of Household Activities." Washington: The Washington Center for Metropolitan Studies, December.

Harrje, David T. 1978. "The Twin Rivers Experiments in Home Energy Conservation." In Raymond J. Burby and A. Fleming Bell, eds., *Energy and the Community*. Cambridge, Mass.: Ballinger Publishing Company, pp. 19-23.

Hatch, John W., and Tony Whitehead. Forthcoming. "Increasing Energy Costs and the Poor: New Challenges for Community Organization." In Karen M. Gentemann, ed., *Social and Political Perspectives on Energy Policy*. Chapel Hill, N.C.: Institute for Research in Social Science.

Healy, Robert G., and Henry R. Hertzfeld. 1975. *Energy Conservation Strategies*. An Issue Report. Washington: The Conservation Foundation.

Hirschberg, Alan, and Richard Schoen. 1974. "Barriers to the Widespread

18 / Introduction

Utilization of Residential Solar Energy: The Prospects for Solar Energy in the U.S. Housing Industry." *Policy Sciences*, Vol. 5, pp. 453-468.

Hirst, Eric, and Janet Carney. 1978. "Effects of Federal Residential Energy Conservation Programs." *Science*, Vol. 199 (24 February), pp. 845-851.

Hittman Associates, Inc. 1973. *Residential Energy Consumption—Single Family Housing—Final Report.* Report No. HUD-HAI-2. Washington: U.S. Government Printing Office, March.

Hittman Associates, Inc. 1978. *Residential Energy Consumption—Detailed Geographic Analysis.* Summary Report, Report No. HUD-PDR-250. Washington: U.S. Government Printing Office, January.

Keyes, Dale L. 1976. "Energy and Land Use: An Instrument of U.S. Conservation Policy?" *Energy Policy* (September), pp. 225-236.

Keyes, Dale L., and George E. Peterson. 1976. "Metropolitan Development and Energy Consumption." Land Use Center Working Paper 5049-15. Washington: The Urban Institute, September.

Landsberg, Hans H., et al. 1974. *Energy and the Social Sciences: An Examination of Research Needs.* Washington: Resources for the Future, Inc.

Leighton, Gerald S. 1977. "Statement." *Energy and the City.* Hearings Before the Subcommittee on the City of the Committee on Banking, Finance and Urban Affairs, House of Representatives, Ninety-fifth Congress, First Session, September 14, 15 and 16, 1977. Washington: U.S. Government Printing Office, pp. 208-228.

Miernyk, William H. 1977. "Rising Energy Prices and Regional Economic Development." *Growth and Change*, Vol. 8, No. 3 (July), pp. 2-7.

Miller, Alan S., Gail Boyer Hayes, and Grant P. Thompson, 1977. *Solar Access and Land Use: State of the Law 1977.* Rockville, Md.: National Solar Heating and Cooling Information Center.

Minan, John H., and William A. Lawrence. 1978. "State Tax Incentives to Promote the Use of Solar Energy." *Texas Law Review*, Vol. 56, pp. 835-859.

Morrison, Denton E. 1977. "Equity Impacts of Some Major Energy Alternatives." Paper presented at annual meeting of American Sociological Association, Chicago.

Murray, James R., et al. 1974. "Evaluation of the Public Response to the Energy Crisis." *Science*, Vol. 184, pp. 257-263.

Myers, Barry Lee. 1978. "Solar Rights in Residential Developments." *Practical Lawyer*, Vol. 24, No. 2 (March), pp. 13-20.

NAHB Research Foundation, Inc. 1979. *Insulation Manual: Homes, Apartments.* Rockville, Md.: The Foundation.

National Commission on Urban Problems. 1968. *Building the American City.* Washington: U.S. Government Printing Office.

Newman, Dorothy K., and Dawn Day. 1975. *The American Energy Consumer.* Cambridge, Mass.: Ballinger Publishing Company.

Office of Public Affairs, U.S. Department of Energy. 1978. *The National Energy Act.* Washington: U.S. Department of Energy, November.

Robinette, Gary O., ed. 1977. *Landscape Planning for Energy Conservation.* Reston, Va.: Environmental Design Press.

Schon, David. 1967. *Technology and Change.* New York: Delacorte Press.

Schwartz, T.P., and Donna Schwartz. 1974. "The Short End of the Shortage: On the Self-Reported Impact of the Energy Shortage on the Socially Disadvantaged." Paper presented at annual meeting of Society for the Study of Social Problems, Montreal.

Seligman, Clive, John M. Darley, and Lawrence J. Becker. 1978. "Behavioral Approaches to Residential Energy Conservation." *Energy and Buildings*, Vol. 1 (April), pp. 325-337.

Sonderegger, Robert C. 1978. "Movers and Stayers: The Resident's Contribution to Variation Across Houses in Energy Consumption for Space Heating." *Energy and Buildings*, Vol. 1 (April), pp. 313-324.

Thompson, Grant P. n.d. "The Role of the States in Energy Conservation in Buildings." Paper No. 14 in *Energy Conservation Training Institute.* Washington: The Conservation Foundation, pp. IV-215 to IV-233.

Thompson, Grant P. 1978. "The Law and Energy Conservation." In Raymond J. Burby and A. Fleming Bell, eds., *Energy and the Community.* Cambridge, Mass.: Ballinger Publishing Company. Chapter 8.

U.S. Department of Housing and Urban Development, Office of Policy Development and Research in Cooperation with U.S. Department of Energy. 1978. *Phase One/Base Data for the Development of Energy Performance Standards for New Buildings.* Washington: The Department, February.

U.S. Environmental Protection Agency. 1975. *Comprehensive Evaluation of Energy Conservation Measures.* Final Report, 230-1-75-003. Washington: The Agency, March.

U.S. General Accounting Office. 1977. *An Evaluation of the National Energy Plan.* Report to the Congress by the Comptroller General of the United States. Washington: The Office, July 25.

Welfare Research, Inc. 1978. *The Impact of Rising Energy Costs on the Elderly Poor in New York State.* Albany, N.Y.: Welfare Research, Inc.

Wilbanks, Thomas, J. 1977. "The Role of Social Science Research in Meeting Energy Needs." Paper #5351. Oak Ridge, Tenn.: Oak Ridge National Laboratories.

Zuiches, James J. 1976. "Coercion and Policy Acceptance: The Case of Energy Policies." Paper presented at the annual meeting of the Society for the Study of Social Problems.

PART I

Energy and Existing Housing

Chapter 2

Structural Characteristics and Energy Efficiency of Existing Housing

Mary Ellen Marsden

The structures in which families live account for a larger proportion of the variance in energy use than does the behavior of residents; building design and construction are therefore the most important factors in residential energy conservation. Structural characteristics of the home—such as size, shape, degree of insulation, and type of heating and cooling equipment—are factors over which residents have little immediate control, but which are more important contributors to energy use than consumer behavior (Newman and Day, 1975). Research by Hittman Associates (U.S. Department of Housing and Urban Development, 1977, II-2) also indicates that the type of dwelling—single-family, townhouse, or apartment—strongly influences the level of energy consumed, largely due to differences in exterior surface area, air infiltration, and internal load density. Single-family residences are the most energy-consumptive, followed by townhouses and high-rise and low-rise apartments. Further, the type of heating equipment is a central factor determining the energy intensiveness of the structure. Although consumer behavior in identical structures may double energy consumption (Seligman et al., 1978; Harrje, 1978b), the structure itself exerts important situational constraints on the level of energy consumption and energy conservation.

Estimates from a number of sources indicate that changes in residential structures can result in substantial energy savings. Modifications in the amount of glass area, the use of double glazing, an increase in the amount of insulation, and the use of more efficient heating and cooling systems can result in reductions of 30 to 40 percent of total heating and cooling energy use in homes (U.S. Department of Housing and Urban Development, 1977, II-3; Burby, 1978). Retrofitting of existing structures can result in lowering current heating bills by 20 to 30 percent (Harrje, 1978a), while heating requirements for apartments may be one-third, and for townhouses one-half, that of single-family homes (U.S. Department of Housing and Urban Development, 1977, IV-9). These figures illustrate the significant reductions in energy consumption which can result in the residential sector from structural changes in housing.

Energy use in the residential sector has increased slightly over the last ten years but has remained a fairly constant 20 percent of the total energy bill (U.S. Bureau of the Census, 1978, p. 606). By 1972, the residential sector consumed 20340.35 trillion Btu in the U.S.— 2630.39 in the South Atlantic states, and 440.008 in North Carolina where this study was conducted (Hoch, 1978, p. 75, 79). The per capita rate of consumption for household use in North Carolina of 84.277 million Btu was somewhat lower than the 97.683 rate for the U.S. (Hoch, 1978, p. 84), but it reflects such factors as climate, lifestyle, and the quality of housing. Of the total household energy use, two-thirds was for heating and cooling and one-third for other uses (Darmstadter, Dunkerley, and Alterman, 1978, p. 38). Analyses presented in this chapter explore the extent of energy use and conservation in existing housing by examining structural characteristics and degree of energy efficiency of single-family detached homes, multiple-family homes, and mobile homes. Of particular interest are the type of heating and cooling equipment, the extent of insulation and other energy-saving features, and homeowner improvements to the energy efficiency of existing housing.

EXISTING HOUSING STOCK

While the single-family detached dwelling is the most energy-consumptive type of residence, it is the most preferred and most prevalent in the United States and, in particular, in North Carolina. According to the 1970 Census of Housing (1970, Table 3), single-family detached dwellings accounted for 69 percent of the total housing stock in the U.S. compared to 83 percent for North

Carolina; multiple-family residences for 28 percent and 12 percent, respectively; and mobile homes for 3 percent and 5 percent, respectively. Comparable state figures from this survey of households indicate that 81 percent of the population lives in single-family detached dwellings, 11 percent in multiple-family dwellings, and 8 percent in mobile homes. Although the difference between the 1970 state census figures and the 1978 survey figures may be due to sampling variability, the larger percentage of mobile homes in 1978 compared to 1970 is a reflection of a nationwide trend in which the mobile home is an increasingly far less expensive alternative to the single-family detached dwelling. In addition, these figures reveal the energy-intensive nature of housing both in the United States and in the state of North Carolina.

The nature of existing housing stock is examined first by investigating the location, structural characteristics, and characteristics of residents for single-family detached, multiple-family, and mobile home residences.

Locational Characteristics

An examination of the location of existing housing stock in the last panel of Table 2-1 shows that residences in the state are disproportionately located in the central Piedmont region, nonmetropolitan counties, and places of 2,500 people or more. These tendencies also hold true for the most prevalent single-family detached dwelling, while multiple-family dwellings are strongly concentrated in the densely populated Piedmont region, in metropolitan and urban areas. Mobile homes are more frequently located in nonmetropolitan or rural areas compared with other types of housing. These figures suggest that the more energy-intensive forms of housing—single-family detached houses and mobile homes—are located in less densely populated nonmetropolitan areas. Those areas are also characterized by long driving distances and dependence on the automobile for personal transportation; hence, there is the potential of increasing economic constraints on nonmetropolitan households as energy prices increase.

Structural Characteristics

Of the three types of homes, single-family detached homes tend to be the largest, oldest, most expensive, and most frequently owner-occupied, as shown in Table 2-2. Each of these structural and ownership characteristics is strongly indicative of the current degree of

Table 2-1. Type of Housing, by Locational Characteristics (Percentage Distributions)

	Single-family Detached (N = 488)	Multiple Family (N = 69)	Mobile Homes (N = 46)	Total[a] (N = 604)
Region				
Mountain	15	6	15	14
Piedmont	50	76	46	53
Coastal Plain	25	11	28	23
Tidewater	10	7	11	10
	100	100	100	100
County				
Metropolitan	32	70	33	36
Nonmetropolitan	68	30	67	64
	100	100	100	100
Size of Place				
Urban	70	96	67	73
Rural	30	4	33	27
	100	100	100	100
Total	81	11	8	100

[a]Percentages on this and subsequent tables may not add to 100 percent due to rounding error.

energy efficiency and the likelihood of improvements to the energy efficiency of the dwelling. If 1975 is taken to be a date after which the inclusion of energy-efficient features was prevalent, largely through stricter building codes, mobile homes outdistance single-family and multiple-family dwellings in the recency of existence. Fully 54 percent of single-family homes were built before 1960, while 60 percent of mobile homes were built after 1970. Thus, there is evidence that the extensively used single-family dwelling is not energy-efficient, while the newer mobile homes may be more so. However, the overwhelming proportion of owner-occupied dwellings suggests that residents have an economic investment in increasing the energy efficiency of their structures. These structural characteristics closely approximate those for the total U.S. in 1970 of 5.0 median rooms, 75 percent built before 1960, 63 percent owner-occupied, and $89 median contract rent (U.S. Bureau of the Census, 1970, 1-9, 1-243). However, the current market value of owner-occupied units appears

Table 2-2. Type of Housing, by Characteristics of Structure (Percentages and Values)

	Single-family Detached (N =488)	Multiple Family (N =69)	Mobile Homes (N = 46)	All Housing (N = 604)
Number of Rooms (mean)	6.2	3.9	4.6	5.8
Year Built (percent)				
After 1975	8	7	14	9
1970-1975	17	32	46	21
1960-1970	20	22	30	21
Before 1960	54	39	9	49
	100%	100%	100%	100%
Percent with Attic	58	37	—	57
Percent with Basement	25	29	—	25
Tenure (percent)				
Owner-occupied	88	7	76	78
Renter-occupied	12	93	24	22
	100%	100%	100%	100%
Value of Structure				
Market value, owner-occupied (mean)	$42,772	*a*	$10,346	$40,383
Monthly rent, renter-occupied ($200/mo. or less)	$85	$77	$100	$82

*a*Under 10 cases; subsample size too small to provide reliable estimates.

to be less than in other regions. On the basis of structural characteristics, most existing housing may have been built without the benefit of energy-saving features.

Characteristics of Residents

Relative to other types of homes, single-family detached dwellings tend to have somewhat larger households, occupied primarily by married couples with children and by older and more affluent ,residents. Residents of multiple-family dwellings are most frequently single and younger, less affluent but better educated. Mobile home households tend to be younger families with heads of households less well educated than residents of other types of homes. Overall, residents of single-family homes are the least mobile, with an average length of residence of 13.3 years. (See Table 2-3.)

Table 2-3. Type of Housing, by Characteristics of Residents (Percentages)

	Single-family Detached (N = 488)	Multiple Family (N = 69)	Mobile Homes (N = 46)	Total (N = 604)
Household Type				
Single	7	45	17	13
Married, no children	22	10	20	20
Married, children	49	16	37	44
Single parents	5	11	13	6
Elderly	17	17	13	17
	100%	100%	100%	100%
Size of Household				
Average number of persons	3.1	2.0	4.7	3.1
Socioeconomic Status				
Percent with income over $15,000	47	21	35	43
Percent with more than high school education	35	47	22	35
Race				
White	84	81	85	84
Nonwhite	16	19	15	16
	100%	100%	100%	100%
Average Age of Respondent	47	40	39	46
Average Years Residence in Home	13.3	4.8	5.0	11.7

These patterns of residence for the single-family detached home are indicative of a greater likelihood of energy consumption and a stronger likelihood of energy conservation and investment in energy-saving features for the home. Larger households and families with children are those who often spend significant amounts of time in the home and thus who are more likely to use energy and less likely to conserve (Klausner, 1978). In contrast, the more affluent and better educated are more likely to conserve and engage in the use of innovative energy-saving equipment (Burby and Marsden, 1979; Cunningham and Lopreato, 1977). The extent of current and planned energy saving activities among varied segments of the population is further examined later in this chapter and in those that follow.

ENERGY EFFICIENCY IN
EXISTING HOUSING

Over the past thirty years, North Carolina has changed from dependence on wood for heating fuel to a predominant use of heating oil (U.S. Bureau of the Census, 1978). By 1970, 62 percent of North Carolina homes were heated by fuel oil or kerosene, 15 percent by natural gas, 11 percent by electricity, 5 percent by bottled gas, and only 4 percent by wood (U.S. Bureau of the Census, 1970.) These figures contrast markedly with those for the total U.S.: 26 percent fuel oil or kerosene, 55 percent natural gas, 8 percent electricity, 6 percent bottled gas, and 1 percent wood (U.S. Bureau of the Census, 1970). Figures presented in Table 2-4 illustrate the predominance of heating oil in the state and suggest some changes. Although the sample of North Carolinians interviewed by telephone may be weighted more towards urban, more affluent and better educated respondents and thus more toward those who live in electrically heated homes, Table 2-4 suggests a decreasing dependence on fuel oil and kerosene, with a move toward greater electrification and use of natural gas.

The majority of homes use some form of forced air furnace, with 14 percent using the more energy-intensive electric baseboard heaters and only 5 percent using the more energy-efficient heat pump. Almost one-third use some form of auxiliary heating—fireplaces or woodstoves in single- and multiple-family residences, and room heaters most frequently in mobile homes. Residents of single-family homes and mobile homes spend far more for heating than do their counterparts in multiple-family residences who pay for their heating costs. With little variation by type of home, between two-thirds and three-fourths of households interviewed in the state have air conditioning.

Thermal Efficiency of Owner-Occupied Homes

Since homeowners are much more likely than renters to invest in improvements to their dwellings, the remainder of this chapter examines the thermal efficiency and retrofitting of owner-occupied dwellings, a subsample of 470 of the 604 households interviewed. First, the current status of the energy efficiency of homes is investigated in Table 2-5.

Almost one-half of the respondents interviewed proclaimed their homes "fully insulated," that is, with insulation in the ceiling, floors,

Table 2-4. Type of Housing, by Heating and Cooling Equipment (Percentages)

	Single-family Detached (N = 488)	Multiple Family (N = 69)	Mobile Homes (N = 46)	Total (N = 604)
Major Fuel Used to Heat Home				
Fuel oil/kerosene	50	14	70	48
Electricity	23	56	17	26
Natural gas	20	26	9	20
Bottled gas	1	–	4	1
Coal	1	1	–	1
Wood	5	–	–	4
Other, N.A.	–	3	–	–
	100	100	100	100
Major Heating Equipment				
Room/baseboard heaters	15	14	2	14
Warm air furnace	54	64	76	57
Floor or wall furnace	15	16	12	15
Heat pump	6	–	2	5
Radiator/hot water	2	1	2	3
Fireplace/wood stove	5	1	2	3
Other	3	4	4	3
	100	100	100	100
Percent of Homes Using Auxiliary Heat	36	9	11	31
Room heaters	18	40	80	20
Fireplace/woodstove	78	60	20	76
Other	4	–	–	4
	100	100	100	100
Heating Bill for Previous Winter ($300 or More)	50	22	31	46
Percent of Homes with Air Conditioning	69	74	72	70

and walls. Little variation in this proportion was seen by region. However, metropolitan area homes, newer homes, and those occupied by married couples, whites, and the more affluent and better educated are more likely to be "fully insulated." In fact, 75 percent of homes built after 1975 are fully insulated according to homeowner reports. Similar tendencies are also seen for insulation in the ceiling, floors, or walls, with insulation in the ceiling and floors being more prevalent.

Almost three-fourths of homeowners have storm windows, storm doors, or weatherstripping and caulking, while one-half have all three (Table 2-5). Homes in the Piedmont, newer homes, and those occupied by the more affluent and better educated homeowners, whites, and the non-elderly are more likely to have these improvements. Also, such households more frequently have storm windows, weatherstripping, and caulking. In contrast, older homes and those inhabited by lower-income, less well educated and elderly people are more likely to have storm doors.

Overall, one-fourth of homes can be described as "thermally efficient"—that is, they are fully insulated and have storm windows, storm doors, and weatherstripping and caulking. The energy-efficient structure is more prevalent in the Piedmont and in homes that are newer and occupied by more affluent, better educated, married, and white individuals. Those living in the less energy-efficient structures are nonwhites, the elderly, and single parents—those groups least likely to be able to afford the heating bills associated with poor insulation and weatherproofing. Because an increasing number of researchers and government officials are recognizing the price the poor pay for living in inadequate housing (Hatch and Whitehead, forthcoming), the weatherization of low-income dwellings is part of most state energy plans.

The trend toward increasing energy efficiency in homes is dramatically depicted by Figure 2-1, which shows the extent of use of energy-efficient equipment in homes over the past decades. The use of each feature except attic fans has increased substantially over the period; the decrease in the use of attic fans may be associated with the pervasive use of central air conditioning in new homes. By 1975, over three-fourths of homes had insulation in the ceiling, walls, or floors, or had weatherstripping; over half had storm doors and storm windows or double-paned glass. Fully 43 percent of newer homes have heat pumps, while 47 percent use wood as an auxiliary heat source. Notably absent is the use of alternative energy sources such as solar heating. These figures, however, only partially depict the current energy efficiency of existing housing since they describe the original equipment of the home and omit from consideration the retrofitting of homes to improve thermal efficiency.

Improvements to Thermal Efficiency

Significant proportions of homeowners have made improvements to the thermal efficiency of their homes—44 percent have at some time added insulation, either to the ceiling, floors, or walls; 17

Table 2-5. Thermal Efficiency of Owner-occupied Homes

	Percent of Homes with Insulation[a]			
	Insulated Ceiling	Insulated Floors	Insulated Walls	Fully Insulated
Total	87	87	74	46
Locational Characteristics				
Region				
Mountain	92	53	76	45
Piedmont	88	53	74	46
Coastal Plain	85	50	72	46
Tidewater	85	52	74	48
County				
Metropolitan	89	59	75	53
Nonmetropolitan	87	49	74	43
Size of Place				
Urban	89	51	73	45
Rural	84	55	76	49
Characteristics of Structures				
Year built				
After 1975	90	82	88	75
1970 to 1975	92	70	87	61
1960 to 1970	94	55	81	50
Before 1960	83	39	65	34
Characteristics of Residents				
Incomes under $15,000	81	47	66	40
Incomes over $15,000	94	58	84	53
High school education	84	47	70	39
Post-high school education	93	63	82	58
Household Type				
Single	85	51	71	46
Married, no children	93	58	83	53
Married, children	90	54	78	48
Single parents	76	52	62	38
Elderly	76	40	56	33
Race				
White	90	53	76	48
Nonwhite	70	46	61	33

Table 2-5. *Continued*

	Percent of Homes				
	With Storm Windows/ Double Panes[b]	*With Storm Doors*	*With Weather-Strip/ Caulking*	*With All Three*	*Thermally Efficient*[c]
Total	72	77	81	53	26
Locational Characteristics					
Region					
Mountain	70	76	81	51	26
Piedmont	75	78	84	59	28
Coastal Plain	66	78	75	44	22
Tidewater	67	74	76	50	26
County					
Metropolitan	73	74	83	55	26
Nonmetropolitan	71	79	80	53	26
Size of Place					
Urban	73	78	80	54	26
Rural	69	76	82	51	26
Characteristics of Structures					
Year built					
After 1975	78	70	88	50	40
1970 to 1975	70	70	84	53	34
1960 to 1970	74	76	85	54	30
Before 1960	71	82	79	55	20
Characteristics of Residents					
Incomes under $15,000	69	80	76	51	22
Incomes over $15,000	75	75	87	58	32
High school education	70	82	76	52	21
Post-high school education	75	69	90	56	35
Household Type					
Single	71	71	85	49	24
Married, no children	76	79	88	61	34
Married, children	70	77	84	55	27
Single parents	76	71	38	24	10
Elderly	67	81	71	48	18
Race					
White	73	78	85	57	28
Nonwhite	61	72	58	30	12

[a]Includes insulation when move into house and retrofit.

[b]Includes other improvements to windows, such as plastic films.

[c]Fully insulated, storm windows and doors, weatherstripping.

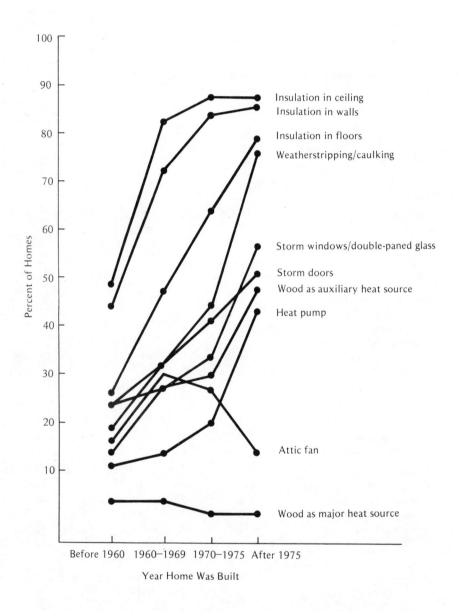

Figure 2-1. Age of structure and use of energy-efficient equipment. (figures in-clude only original equipment and exclude retrofitting by current owner).

percent have added it during the past year. Two-thirds have invested in either storm windows, storm doors, or weatherstripping, while almost one-half have added one of those.

As seen in Table 2-6, homeowners outside the Tidewater region, in nonmetropolitan and rural areas, older homes, those less affluent and less well educated, and the elderly are more likely than others to have retrofitted their homes. These changes to the structure appear to be in direct response to the deficiencies in thermal efficiency seen in Table 2-5. However, nonwhite households are less likely to have made improvements to their less thermally-efficient homes. In contrast to much previous research, these findings suggest that investments in energy-saving features are not made solely by a better informed, more affluent public. Rather the investments are made largely on the basis of a desire to increase the thermal efficiency of homes. However, as indicated in Table 2-5, even with these improvements the thermal efficiency of many homes can still be increased.

The Use of Tax Credits for Adding Insulation

One means of hastening improvements to the energy efficiency of homes is the enactment of economic incentive measures such as tax credits. An income tax credit for adding insulation or solar heating equipment to homes had been in effect in North Carolina for two years at the time the survey was conducted. However, only slightly more than one-half (58 percent) of owners of single-family dwellings who might have used the measure knew of the existence of the tax credit. Only 7 percent of eligible households (14 percent of those households which had added insulation during the past year) had taken advantage of the tax credit during that year.

Users of the tax credit tended to be younger, better educated, and higher-income individuals than those eligible homeowners who did not use the tax credit. (See Table 2-7.) In addition, users were slightly more likely to live in more expensive and somewhat newer homes. Overwhelmingly, users planned to stay in their current home in the near future, although nonusers were also planning to stay. In contrast to those who have retrofitted their homes who are less affluent and live in less thermally efficient homes, users of the tax credit are part of a more affluent and better informed public. The tax credit, then, now serves as an effective incentive to that segment of the population which has less need of improvement to the thermal efficiency of their homes. To increase effectiveness of the tax credit, broader educational efforts regarding its existence and the means of

Table 2-6. Retrofitting of Owner-occupied Homes (Selected Percentages)

	Insulation		Other Improvements to Structures			
	Ever Added	Added Past Year	Total[a]	Storm Windows[b]	Storm Doors	Weather-stripping/caulking
Total	44	17	67	46	47	46
Locational Characteristics						
Region						
Mountain	46	19	61	38	38	40
Piedmont	44	17	68	52	52	48
Coastal Plain	46	16	69	42	45	48
Tidewater	39	20	63	39	39	37
County						
Metropolitan	37	17	62	48	46	43
Nonmetropolitan	47	17	69	46	47	46
Size of Place						
Urban	42	17	65	47	45	44
Rural	49	18	72	45	51	50
Characteristics of Structure						
Year built						
After 1975	18	12	38	22	18	10
1970 to 1975	30	19	50	34	25	37
1960 to 1970	39	14	66	45	40	47
Before 1960	58	19	80	57	65	56
Characteristics of Residents						
Incomes under $15,000	47	17	67	48	52	44
Incomes over $15,000	40	18	68	46	42	48
High school education	45	18	68	48	51	45
Post-high school education	41	16	65	44	38	48
Household type						
Single	42	20	68	49	44	56
Married, no children	44	13	67	53	49	47
Married, children	44	19	65	40	41	46
Single parents	29	19	62	33	38	14
Elderly	48	15	73	58	63	46
Race						
White	44	18	67	48	47	48
Nonwhite	40	13	66	36	46	28

[a]Includes storm windows and doors, weatherstripping/caulking.
[b]Includes other improvements to windows, such as plastic films.

Table 2-7. Use of Tax Credit for Insulation, by Demographic Characteristics[a] (Selected Percentages)

Characteristic	User	Nonuser
Under age 40	46	34
College educated	61	35
Family income $15,000 or higher	76	45
Home worth $50,000 or more	54	47
Home built 1970 or later	32	28
Resided in home 10 years or more	50	54
Plan to stay in current home in near future	93	91

[a]Percentages are computed for a subsample of owners of single-family detached dwellings.

obtaining it should be addressed to those living in less thermally efficient homes who are likely to add insulation—the less affluent and the rural homeowner.

The next two chapters more closely examine conservation behavior and attitudes of residents. In particular, the focus is on changes in the level of heating and on the decision to invest in improving the thermal efficiency of homes.

SUMMARY

The energy efficiency of existing housing stock depends on such factors as size, age, degree of insulation and other weatherproofing improvements, and type of housing. The majority of people live in single-family detached dwellings, the most energy-consumptive type of residence. Single-family detached dwellings are especially common in nonmetropolitan and rural areas, which are also handicapped by the energy-intensive length of driving distances necessitated by a dispersed population. Single-family homes also tend to be larger, and over half were built before 1960. These characteristics of existing housing suggest the energy-intensive nature of current living patterns.

However, other findings presented in this chapter suggest significant attempts among homeowners to improve the thermal efficiency of their homes. Almost one-third have added insulation, while two-thirds have added either storm windows, storm doors, or weatherstripping. These improvements are apparently being made in the areas of greatest need—in those homes which are less thermally sound. However, over half of the existing homes are not fully insulated, and only one-fourth are fully thermally efficient as discussed in this chapter. Further, relatively few homeowners have taken advantage of tax credits for adding insulation.

The state is heavily dependent on fuel oil for heating and will be increasingly vulnerable to rises in energy prices. State policymakers could hasten the dissemination of information regarding alternative technologies as well as the benefits of increasing the thermal efficiency of homes.

NOTE

1. Due to the general lack of awareness among pretest respondents concerning R-values of insulation, a single question, that of the presence or absence of insulation, was asked. Thus, "fully insulated" does not refer to the degree of insulation but rather to the presence of insulation in the ceiling, floors, and walls.

REFERENCES

Burby, Raymond J. 1978. "Saving Energy in Urban Areas: Community Planning Perspectives." *University of North Carolina News Letter*, Vol. 63, No. 4 (October), p. 1-7.

Burby, Raymond J., and Mary Ellen Marsden. 1979. "Adoption of Energy Conservation Technologies in the Production and Use of Residential Environments." *Proceedings of the 1979 National Conference on Technology for Energy Conservation.* Silver Spring, Md.: Information Transfer Inc.

Cunningham, William H., and Sally Cook Lopreato. 1977. *Energy Use and Conservation Incentives: A Study of the Southwestern United States.* New York: Praeger Publishers.

Darmstadter, Joel, Joy Dunkerley, and Jack Alterman. 1978. *How Industrial Societies Use Energy: A Comparative Analysis.* Baltimore: The Johns Hopkins University Press.

Harrje, David T. 1978a. "Details of the First-Round Retrofits at Twin Rivers." *Energy and Buildings*, Vol. 1 (April), pp. 271-274.

Harrje, David T. 1978b. "The Twin Rivers Experiments in Home Energy Conservation." In Raymond J. Burby, III and A. Fleming Bell, eds., *Energy and the Community*. Cambridge, Mass.: Ballinger Publishing Company.

Hatch, John W. and Tony L. Whitehead. Forthcoming. "Increasing Energy Costs and the Poor: New Challenges for Community Organization." In Karen M. Gentemann, ed., *Social and Political Perspectives on Energy Policy*. Chapel Hill, N.C.: Institute for Research in Social Science.

Hoch, Irving. 1978. *Energy Use in the United States by State and Region.* Washington: Resources for the Future.

Klausner, Samuel Z. 1978. "Household Organization and Use of Electricity." In Seymour Warkov, ed., *Energy Policy in the United States: Social and Behavioral Dimensions.* New York: Praeger Publishers.

Newman, Dorothy Kog, and Dawn Day. 1975. *The American Energy Consumer.* Cambridge, Mass.: Ballinger Publishing Company.

Seligman, Clive, et al. 1978. "Behavioral Approaches to Residential Energy Conservation." *Energy and Buildings*, Vol. 1, pp. 325-337.

U.S. Bureau of the Census. 1970. *Census of Housing: 1970, Vol. 1*, Housing Characteristics for States, Cities, and Counties. Washington: U.S. Government Printing Office.

U.S. Bureau of the ·Census. 1970. *Census of Population and Housing, 1970*, Washington: U.S. Government Printing Office.

U.S. Bureau of the Census. 1978. *Residential Energy Uses.* Washington: U.S. Government Printing Office.

U.S. Department of Housing and Urban Development. 1977. *Residential Energy Consumption Detailed Geographic Analysis.* Summary Report. Office of the Assistant Secretary for Policy Development and Research. Washington: U.S. Government Printing Office.

Chapter 3

Household Energy
Conservation
Behavior

Mary Ellen Marsden and Michael W. McKinney

Although the structure of the housing unit accounts for the greater proportion of household energy consumption as delineated in the previous chapter, the behavior of household residents in the day-to-day operation of the home may account for a doubling of energy expenditures in structurally identical households (Seligman et al., 1978). Changes in the use of heating and cooling equipment and appliances, and in other operational procedures, can in fact result in an energy savings of 15 to 40 percent (Sizemore, 1978, p. 26; Thompson, no date). With increasingly curtailed energy supplies and rising energy costs, the investigation of factors influencing consumer conservation behavior in the operation of homes is of critical importance. Analyses presented in this chapter examine the conservation behavior of household residents, focusing on the most energy-intensive form of energy use in the household, space heating, which accounts for approximately two-thirds of household energy consumption (Cunningham and Lopreato, 1977, p. 10). In addition, consumer use of air conditioning and appliances is explored. The determinants of energy conservation behavior—economic disincentives, pro-conservation attitudes, energy conservation knowledge, and demographic correlates—are further investigated. A final section examines the degree of receptivity of household residents to current and potential energy policy alternatives. These analyses supplement the studies by Duncan MacRae, Jr. of the investment behavior of consumers in energy-saving features in households (presented in the supplementary analyses appended to this volume) as well as the analyses of the retrofitting of housing structures presented in the previous chapter.

DETERMINANTS OF ENERGY CONSERVATION

Numerous studies have found the most important predictor of household energy use to be family income (Newman and Day, 1975; Morrison and Gladhart, 1976; Cunningham and Lopreato, 1977), with energy consumption highest among upper-income households. However, household income may simply be viewed as an indicator of lifestyle, of the number of appliances and other energy-consuming goods, of the size and type of dwelling, of the level of information about energy conservation techniques, and of the belief in the need to conserve energy. More broadly then, energy conservation behavior may be defined as a function of conservation knowledge and attitudes and the economic disincentives associated with rising energy prices—factors all closely related to household income.

Energy Conservation Knowledge

The level of energy conservation knowledge has been relatively infrequently studied, but most researchers have found the public to be fairly ignorant of the nature of energy production and consumption or the most efficient conservation techniques. For instance, in a series of studies conducted by the Opinion Research Corporation in the 1970s, respondents were unaware of the sources of energy or the amount of energy required to carry out various functions in the home, such as space heating or water heating (Opinion Research Corporation, 1974, 1976). A study by Gottlieb and Matre (1976) similarly found that most respondents answered correctly only slightly more than five of ten energy knowledge questions. Further, Kilkeary (1975) found a relatively low level of energy knowledge, but knowledge was greater among high-income respondents and those families with children.

Energy conservation understanding was no greater among the households in this study, as judged by answers to a series of knowledge questions. Respondents were asked four questions as to which used more electricity: (a) a frost-free or a regular refrigerator; (b) an electric furnace or a heat pump; (c) a fluorescent or a regular light bulb; (d) a microwave or an electric oven. Correct answers to this "energy test" and the proportion of the sample that answered correctly are: frost-free refrigerator (67 percent), electric furnace (59 percent); regular light bulb (67 percent); and electric oven (64 percent). Thus for these items, energy knowledge was less than perfect. Two-thirds or less of the sample gave correct responses, an average only slightly better than chance. Overall, 6 percent of the sample gave no correct responses; 16 percent, one correct response; 23 percent, two correct; 30 percent, three correct; and 25 percent, all four correct.

Variation among household respondents in the level of energy knowledge was gauged by means of a simple additive index of the number of correct responses to the four energy knowledge items; results are presented in Table 3-1. Knowledge of energy-saving techniques is clearly higher among better-educated, higher-income, and younger respondents. Other figures not shown here reveal no significant differences in the level of energy knowledge between metropolitan and nonmetropolitan counties, by region of the state, or housing tenure. However, married respondents and those house-

Table 3-1. Level of Knowledge among Consumers

Respondent Characteristic	Percent of Respondents with High Energy Knowledge[a]
All respondents	25
Education	
High school or less	17
More than high school	40
Income	
Less than $15,000	20
$15,000 or more	36
Age	
Under 35	32
35-64	26
65 and over	10

[a]Knowledge index is a simple sum score of the number of correct responses to four knowledge items; "high" energy knowledge consists of those correctly answering all four items.

holds with children were slightly more likely to have high energy knowledge as measured here.

These figures suggest that state energy programs designed to increase the level of energy conservation knowledge of household residents can have substantial effect, particularly if addressed to the less affluent, less educated, and older segments of the population. A related item concerning the level of energy knowledge in the home revealed that two-thirds of homeowners (66 percent) were unaware of the temperature setting of their hot water heaters, while others gave meaningless responses beyond the normal range of temperature settings. The means of increasing energy knowledge to foster energy conservation are investigated below.

Sources of Energy Knowledge. Most respondents interviewed—over 80 percent—had been exposed to energy information on television, in newspapers or magazines, or with their utility bills, as shown in Table 3-2. Listening to the radio and talking with other people about how to save energy were on the other hand mentioned by only slightly over one-half of respondents. However, these sources varied in the level of credibility accredited to them. Utility companies were more frequently seen as the best source of information, followed by television; radio and talking with other people were viewed as less effective sources of information. These findings suggest that energy information programs would be most effective if addressed to the public through either utility companies or television—these sources are most frequently encountered and are viewed as more credible sources of information by household residents.

Energy Conservation Attitudes

Increasing public concern over the adequacy of energy supply and support for the need to conserve energy has been extensively

Table 3-2. Sources of Energy Information

Information Source	Percent Who Have Had Contact with Source	Percent Who See It as Best Source of Information
Television	88	29
Newspapers, magazines	83	19
Utility companies (bills)	82	36
Radio	59	1
Other people	56	2

documented in surveys of household residents (see discussion of this trend in McKinney, 1978; Murray, 1974). Results from a number of surveys examined by Olsen (1978, p. 94) show that by the middle of the 1970s, about one-half of the American people perceived that there was a serious long-term energy problem. Although research generally has found only a moderate link between energy conservation attitudes and behavior (Donnermeyer, 1977), increasing involvement in energy conservation practices is founded on awareness of the need to conserve in conjunction with rising energy prices.

Slightly over one-half of the respondents interviewed in this study and in previous studies view the need to conserve as "very serious," as shown in Table 3-3. In addition, people predict that shortages will increase in the future; 41 percent perceive that there are significant energy shortages now, while 51 percent foresee energy shortages in twenty years. However, perceptions of the existence of energy shortages appear to level off over time, in light of the responses for ten and twenty years from now. The perceived need to save is most prevalent among higher-income, younger or elderly respondents, although no differences are observed by the level of education. Current energy shortages are more readily seen by better educated and younger respondents as compared with their counterparts, but groups diverged more widely in their perception of the existence of an energy shortage over the next twenty years. Energy shortages

Table 3-3. Orientations Toward the Energy Situation

Respondent Characteristics	Percent Who See Need to Save "Very Serious"	Percent Who See Energy Shortages		
		Now	In 10 Yrs.	In 20 Yrs.
All Respondents	55	41	56	51
Education				
High school or less	54	38	51	45
More than high school	55	45	65	62
Income				
Less than $15,000	52	40	54	45
$15,000 or more	59	41	59	57
Age				
Under 35	57	47	66	69
35-64	52	36	53	61
65 and over	60	41	50	55

twenty years hence are predicted particularly by better educated, higher-income and younger respondents. Thus, while most respondents recognize the necessity of saving energy, they differ in the perceived magnitude and persistence of the problem.

Similarly, slightly over one-half of those interviewed feel that conservation will help the energy situation a great deal, as shown in Table 3-4. This view, however, is more prevalent among less well educated and older respondents. Although these orientations toward the need to conserve and the perceived value of conservation appear to differ among subgroups, the answer may be found in each group's perceptions of eventual solutions to the energy problem—whether new forms of energy or the conservation of existing supplies.

Research on energy and altruistic behavior and the problem of generating public support for conservation programs suggests that people will be more likely to conserve if they feel others are doing so (Martin, forthcoming). However, figures presented in Table 3-4 reveal that respondents do not perceive others to be making the same effort in conservation which they are making. Over one-half of the respondents feel they are making a great effort, compared to only 13 percent of others. Thus, one means of furthering widespread commitment to and involvement in energy conservation might center on increasing public awareness and discussion of current conservation patterns.

Table 3-4. Orientations Toward Energy Conservation

Respondent Characteristics	Percent Who Feel Conservation Will Help Great Deal	Percent Who Feel a Lot of Effort Made by:	
		Themselves	Others
All Respondents	56	54	13
Education			
High school or less	55	52	15
More than high school	49	57	11
Income			
Less than $15,000	52	56	15
$15,000 or more	54	51	13
Age			
Under 35	43	43	8
35-64	58	56	16
65 and over	59	70	13

Economic Factors

Rising energy prices over the past decade have increasingly received attention from researchers and policymakers, particularly from the standpoint of the impact of rising prices on lower-income households (Schwartz, 1978; Morrison, 1978; Welfare Research, 1978). Lower-income households spend a substantially larger part of the household budget on necessities such as fuel; when the price of those necessities increases, expenditures may even exceed income, and certainly decisions must be made between expenditures for necessities versus those for other household goods. Figures reported in Table 3-5 suggest that even though lower-income families were likely to have had problems paying fuel bills over the past year,

Table 3-5. Economic Factors in Energy Conservation

Respondent Characteristics	Percent with Major Problem Paying Fuel Bills	Percent Whose Heating Bills Went up a Great Deal
All Respondents	29	30
Education		
High school or less	23	29
More than high school	39	31
Income		
Less than $15,000	37	29
$15,000 or more	20	32
Age		
Under 35	24	28
35-64	32	31
65 and over	30	29
Household Type		
Singles	28	20
Married, children	24	29
Married, no children	28	33
Single parents	49	30
Elderly	30	29
Type of House		
Single-family detached	28	30
Multiple family	35	24
Mobile home	37	30

some higher-income families also expressed problems. Across all households, 53 percent had some trouble paying their bills, while 29 percent found these expenses to be a major problem. Similarly, 56 percent felt their heating bills had increased over the past year, and 30 percent felt they had increased a great deal. Problems in paying bills were particularly evident among households headed by single parents, and residents of multiple-family dwellings and mobile homes.

Further information on the cost of heating homes is provided in Table 3-6 in which respondents' estimates of the heating bills of last winter are presented. Although these figures must be interpreted with caution due to problems of respondent recall, they can be taken as broad range estimates of actual expenditures. A look at the percentage of households spending $300 or more for heating last winter makes apparent the fact that expenditures are comparatively higher among higher-income households, households other than those headed by singles, and residents of single-family detached dwellings and mobile homes. As discussed in Chapter 2, and in Klausner (1978), single-family detached dwellings are the most energy-consumptive, but household size and organization also influence the level of energy consumption.

Now the discussion turns to the investigation of factors influencing energy conservation in households—energy knowledge, attitudes, economic factors, characteristics of the respondent, housing structure, and household type. The analyses will examine household behavior in the use of heating and cooling equipment and appliances, and general conservation behavior across these areas. It must be remembered, however, that these analyses concern change in the level of energy consumption rather than current levels of energy consumption. For instance, lower-income households may have relatively low levels of energy consumption but may not participate widely in energy conservation practices; they have simply been conserving over a longer period of time, not just during the past year. These findings are informative, however, in that they are indicators of where major educational efforts may be addressed to promote energy conservation.

CONSERVING ENERGY IN HOMES

The public engaged in extensive attempts to save energy following the energy shortages of 1973-1974, although most actions taken involved relatively little effort or change in life-

Table 3-6. Estimates of Last Winter's Heating Bills (Percentage Distributions)

	Less than $100	$100-$200	$200-$300	$300-$400	$400-$500	$500-$750	Over $750	Total
Income								
Less than $15,000	6	22	33	22	11	4	1	100
$15,000 and over	4	13	28	22	13	16	3	100
Household Type								
Singles	6	34	24	18	12	6	—	100
Married, children	10	20	30	16	13	9	1	100
Married, no children	4	14	28	24	14	13	3	100
Single parents	—	11	46	14	14	11	4	100
Elderly	5	16	38	30	7	3	—	100
Type of House								
Single-family detached	4	16	30	24	13	10	2	100
Multiple family	16	34	28	12	6	3	—	100
Mobile home	—	23	46	20	6	6	—	100

style. Many households decreased their use of heating or lighting, while relatively few made structural changes in their homes (Olsen, 1978). Figures presented in Chapter 2 and Supplementary Analysis I of this study, however, suggest a broader and more intensive involvement in energy conservation. For instance, 17 percent of homeowners reported having added insulation during the past year, and substantial proportions of current and potential homeowners state intentions of further investing in energy-saving features for their homes (see also Chapter 4).

As seen in Table 3-7, half or more of households contacted in this study have engaged in energy conservation during the past year.

Table 3-7. Energy Conservation Behavior (Selected Percentages)

Respondent Characteristics	Turned Down Heat	Used Air Conditioning Less	Used Appliances Less	General Conservation High[a]
All Respondents	81	61	58	26
Education				
High school or less	79	61	59	21
More than high school	84	58	55	24
Income				
Less than $15,000	80	62	58	20
$15,000 or more	82	61	59	27
Age				
Under 35	79	58	54	19
35-64	81	59	61	26
65 and over	83	65	56	16
Household Type				
Single	82	62	51	23
Married with children	80	58	58	27
Married no children	79	58	60	21
Single parents	86	67	60	24
Elderly	83	65	56	16
Type of House				
Single-family detached	80	60	60	23
Multiple family	80	57	49	14
Mobile home	88	64	54	20

[a]Conservation index is a simple sum score of the number of conservation behaviors reported; "high" conservation consists of having decreased use of heating, air conditioning, and appliances.

Fully 81 percent decreased their use of heating, 61 percent of those with air conditioning decreased use, and 58 percent used appliances less. Overall, 26 percent reported a reduction in the use of heating, air conditioning, and appliances over the past year. Although the level of energy conservation among types of respondents differs somewhat by the type of conservation behavior, those groups most energy-conserving as judged by a general conservation index are the better educated, higher-income, young to middle-aged respondents, married couples with children, and residents of single-family detached dwellings. However, as previously noted, more affluent households and single-family homes are the most energy-consumptive and would be most likely to benefit from energy conservation.

Although these figures agree substantially with those of an earlier study (Bultena, 1976), they illustrate, in conjunction with information on investment behavior and structural changes to the house, that energy conservation can be increased substantially in the residential sector over current levels. Energy conservation behavior at present focuses on the more elastic and readily changeable forms of behavior which involve little discomfort, change in lifestyle, or investment of time or money. Greater commitment to energy conservation in the residential sector will be based on the availability of well-grounded knowledge about other means of conservation behavior and the energy-intensiveness of current living patterns, on public acceptance of the necessity of conserving, and on economic pressures generated by rising fuel costs. The impact of these factors on energy conservation behavior is investigated next, along with public acceptance of energy policy alternatives.

EXPLAINING CONSERVATION BEHAVIOR

Energy conservation behavior may be explained as the result of the interaction between rising fuel costs, perceptions of the necessity of saving, and knowledge of the means of effectively conserving energy. Using additive indices of conservation knowledge, attitudes, and behavior, as well as items concerning household income and the level of difficulty in paying fuel bills, the impact of these factors on conservation behavior is investigated in Table 3-8. Conservation behavior is related most closely to pro-conservation attitudes and knowledge and second is associated with higher levels of household income; it is least associated with perceived difficulty in paying fuel bills. While previous studies have found

Table 3-8. Determinants of Energy Conservation Behavior[a]

Predictors	Zero-order Correlation	Gamma
Conservation Knowledge[b]	.11**	.13
Conservation Attitudes[c]	.14**	.16
Economic Factors		
Income of household	.10*	.09
Difficulty paying fuel bills	.04	.06

**Significant at .01 level.
*Significant at .05 level.
[a]Index: decreased use of heat, air conditioning, appliances last year.
[b]Sum score of correct responses to four knowledge items.
[c]Sum score of two attitudinal items.

household income to be the central determinant of conservation behavior, these findings suggest that household attitudes and knowledge of the means of conserving may be as important. Although none of these factors explains a large part of the variance in conservation behavior, they are together important determinants.

These correlates of energy conservation behavior support the value of extensive federal and state involvement in energy conservation information programs designed to increase public awareness of and participation in energy conservation. Although rising fuel prices provide an impetus for saving energy, energy knowledge and pro-conservation attitudes generated by public information programs are basic factors influencing sustained and effective energy conservation behavior.

VIABILITY OF ENERGY POLICY ALTERNATIVES IN THE RESIDENTIAL SECTOR

As energy supplies tighten and prices rise, federal and state governments have become more active in instituting a residential sector energy policy designed to limit consumption or ease the financial burden on lower-income households. A survey of state energy offices presented in Supplementary Analysis III appended to this volume investigates the information, incentive, and regulatory programs prevalent in the fifty states. The final chapter examines policies needed to further encourage energy conservation.

The viability of these programs among household residents is explored here. Household residents were asked whether they favored government involvement in energy conservation education (information programs), programs to help the poor pay their heating bills if necessary (equity), policies setting insulation standards for new homes (regulatory), programs rationing heating fuel (supply), or policies involving raising the price of heating fuel (pricing) to increase energy conservation. Responses to each of these items, by selected respondent characteristics, are presented in Table 3-9.

Residents almost universally approve of state government involvement in information programs, and a majority approve of equity and regulatory types of programs. However, less than half favor supply strategies, and only 13 percent favor government involvement in pricing strategies to reduce demand. These findings strongly support those of previous studies which find the American public to be least amenable to policies involving rationing or increased prices (Gottlieb and Matre, 1976, p. 72; Bultena, 1976, p. 38). Voluntary programs of energy conservation based on the government's providing well grounded information to the public will meet with less resistance and may tend to be more effective—except in the event of a crisis situation which demands that stronger action be taken. Although there are few differences in the acceptance of information programs across groups of the public, equity and supply

Table 3-9. Consumers' Attitudes Toward Selected Energy Conservation Policies

Respondent Characteristics	Percent Favoring Type of Policy				
	Information	*Equity*	*Regulatory*	*Supply*	*Pricing*
All Respondents	94	77	73	46	13
Education					
High school or less	93	81	71	46	10
More than high school	96	70	77	45	18
Income					
Less than $15,000	93	84	69	49	12
$15,000 or more	96	68	80	44	16
Household Type					
Single	97	85	74	40	15
Married, no children	93	72	72	44	14
Married, children	96	75	78	44	13
Single parents	92	84	86	49	19
Elderly	90	81	56	55	10

programs are more favored by the less affluent, and regulatory and pricing programs by the more affluent. These orientations toward energy policy alternatives directly reflect the differential impact of the energy situation on socioeconomic groups and the need for varied approaches to energy conservation which guarantee equitable treatment of all segments of the population.

SUMMARY

Analyses presented in this chapter have delineated several determinants of energy conservation behavior, including energy conservation knowledge, pro-conservation attitudes, and economic factors, as well as demographic correlates. Conservation behavior is associated with pro-conservation attitudes and knowledge of con-servation techniques and is less closely related to economic factors. Although conservation behavior is more prevalent among the more affluent, the young, and residents of single-family dwellings, this behavior must be viewed apart from energy consumption levels, which may be higher among those groups. Further, much current conservation behavior involves little change in living patterns or in the structure of housing. Governmental policies providing energy information can have substantial effect and meet with public accep-tance, while pricing and supply strategies will meet with resistance. However, the equity of policies and programs across socioeconomic groups must receive continued attention due to the differential impact of energy prices on lower-income households.

REFERENCES

Bultena, Gordon. 1976. *Public Response to the Energy Crisis: A Study of Citizens' Attitudes and Adaptive Behaviors.* Ames, Iowa: Iowa State University, Department of Sociology.

Cunningham, William H., and Sally Cook Lopreato. 1977. *Energy Use and Conservation Incentives: A Study of the Southwestern United States.* New York: Praeger Publishers.

Donnermeyer, Joseph. 1977. "Social Status and Attitudinal Predictors of Residential Energy Consumption." Paper presented at annual meeting of the Rural Sociological Society, Madison, Wisconsin.

Gottlieb, David, and Marc Matre. 1976. *Sociological Dimensions of the Energy Crisis: A Follow-up Study.* Houston, Texas: University of Houston, The Energy Institute.

Klausner, Samuel Z. 1978. "Household Organization and the Use of Electricity."

In Seymour Warkov, ed., *Energy Policy in the United States: Social and Behavioral Dimensions*. New York: Praeger Publishers.

Kilkeary, Rovena. 1975. "The Energy Crisis and Decision-Making in the Family." Springfield, Va.: National Technical Information Service, U.S. Department of Commerce.

McKinney, Michael W. 1978. "Public Opinion and Energy Policy Alternatives." *University of North Carolina Newsletter*, Vol. LXIII (October), pp. 19-24.

Martin, Elizabeth. Forthcoming. "Altruism and Energy Conservation: Generating Public Support." In Karen M. Gentemann, ed., *Social and Political Perspectives on Energy Policy*. Chapel Hill, North Carolina: Institute for Research in Social Science.

Morrison, Bonnie Maas, and Peter M. Gladhart. 1976. "Energy and Families: The Crisis and the Response." *Journal of Home Economics* (January), pp. 15-18.

Morrison, Denton E. 1978. "Equity Impacts of Some Major Energy Alternatives." In Seymour Warkov, ed., *Energy Policy in the United States: Social and Behavioral Dimensions*. New York: Praeger Publishers.

Murray, James R., et al. 1974. "Evolution of the Public Response to the Energy Crisis." *Science*, Vol. 184, pp. 257-63.

Newman, Dorothy K., and Dawn Day. 1975. *The American Energy Consumer*. Cambridge, Mass: Ballinger Publishing Co.

Olsen, Marvin E. 1978. "Public Acceptance of Energy Conservation." In Seymour Warkov, ed., *Energy Policy in the United States: Social and Behavioral Dimensions*. New York: Praeger Publishers.

Opinion Research Corporation. 1974, 1976. *Public Attitudes and Behavior Regarding Energy Conservation: Detailed Tabulations by U.S. Population and Population Segments*. Princeton, New Jersey: Opinion Research Corporation.

Schwartz, T. P. 1978. "Short End of the Shortage? An Appraisal of the Purported Social Consequences of the 1973-74 Energy Shortage." In Seymour Warkov, ed., *Energy Policy in the United States: Social and Behavioral Dimensions*. New York: Praeger Publishers.

Seligman, Clive, et al. 1978. "Behavioral Approaches to Residential Energy Conservation." *Energy and Buildings*, Vol. 1, pp. 32-37.

Sizemore, Michael. 1978. "Saving Energy in Buildings." In Raymond J. Burby, III and A. Fleming Bell, eds., *Energy and the Community*. Cambridge, Mass: Ballinger Publishing Co.

Thompson, Grant P. no date. "The Role of the States in Energy Conservation in Buildings." *Energy Conservation Training Institute*. Washington: The Conservation Foundation.

Welfare Research, Inc. 1978. *The Impact of Rising Energy Costs on the Elderly Poor in New York State*. Albany, New York: Welfare Research, Inc.

PART II

Energy in New Housing

Chapter 4

Demand for Energy-efficient New Housing

Raymond J. Burby and Mary Ellen Marsden

Efforts to improve the energy efficiency of the residential sector may focus on both existing and new housing. With the nation's housing stock consisting of more than 75 million dwellings, retrofitting to make existing units more energy-efficient is an obvious and important target for energy policy and programs. The importance of new housing, which typically makes up between 2 and 3 percent of the housing stock each year, depends on the relative rates at which new and existing housing can be affected by a proposed policy or program (Socolow, 1977). For example, there has been considerable success in persuading households to improve the thermal efficiency of their homes by adding insulation, storm windows, and caulking and weatherstripping. On the other hand, programs which involve major capital investments, sophisticated technologies, or the design and orientation of the dwelling are usually more appropriately targeted at new housing (Division of Solar Energy, 1977). In addition, because housing has an extremely long life span, it is important that each dwelling added to our stock of housing be as energy-efficient as is economically feasible.

The housing industry is one of the most competitve in the nation. In addition to competing with each other, homebuilders must compete with the existing housing that comes on the market. As a result, homebuilders are very sensitive to cost and to consumer demand and preferences. However, as the President's Committee on Urban Housing (1969, p. 9) has observed, "When consumers create an effective demand, the U.S. homebuilding industry and housing market have proven their capabilities for producing a quality product and delivering it at reasonable prices." In this chapter, we examine current consumer demand for energy-efficient new housing. Information is provided on the types of households who are in the market to purchase a home, their preferences for housing prices and styles, and their interest in the energy-conserving features of their next house.

PROSPECTIVE HOMEBUYERS

The residential mobility intentions of North Carolina households are generally lower than those found for households in the United States as a whole. When asked whether they were likely to move in the next two or three years, 81 percent of the respondents reported that they planned to remain in their present dwellings, 5 percent thought they might move to a rental unit, and 13 percent expected to buy a home. In contrast, the U.S. Census has reported that 18 to 20 percent of Americans move annually (U.S. Bureau of the Census, 1977), or approximately 34 percent every three years (U.S. Bureau of the Census, 1978).

The characteristics of nonmarket households (those who plan to stay in their present houses) and households who are likely to be in the market for a rental or sale house are summarized in Table 4-1. Mobility rates and tenure (rental or ownership) intentions do not differ markedly across the major regions of North Carolina. However, people living in metropolitan areas were much more likely to be planning a move than those living in nonmetropolitan areas. In fact, the 28 percent two- to three-year prospective mobility rate for metropolitan households is similar to that found in previous national studies of residential mobility in metropolitan areas. It is bracketed by the 48 percent five-year prospective mobility rate found by Lansing, Mueller, and Barth (1964) and Lansing (1966) in two national metropolitan area samples, and the average of 24 percent in one-year rates found by Rossi (1955); Lansing (1966); Van Arsdol, Jr., Sabagh, and Butler (1968); Butler, Chapin, Hemmens, Kaiser, Stegman, and Weiss (1969); and Varady (1973). The characteristics of the individuals who expect to move are also

Table 4-1. Residential Mobility Intentions of North Carolina Households

Household Characteristics	Residential Mobility Intentions (%)[a]				
		Move and:		Not	
	Stay	Rent	Purchase	Ascertained	Total
Total Sample (N = 604)	81	5	13	1	100
Location					
Mountains (N = 84)	78	5	17	0	100
Piedmont (N = 320)	82	5	12	1	100
Coastal Plain/Tidewater (N = 200)	79	6	13	2	100
Metropolitan area (N = 219)	71	10	18	1	100
Nonmetropolitan area (N = 385)	86	2	10	2	100
Urban (N = 441)[b]	80	6	13	1	100
Rural (N = 163)	83	2	12	3	100
Current Residence					
Single-family detached (N = 487)	86	2	11	1	100
Multiple family (N = 70)	47	29	24	0	100
Mobile home (N = 46)	72	2	24	2	100
Household Type					
Singles (N = 78)	59	19	19	3	100
Single parents (N = 37)	81	5	14	0	100
Married with children (N = 268)	81	1	17	0	100
Married without children (N = 121)	84	5	8	3	100
Elderly (N = 100)	91	5	3	1	100
Age					
Under 35 (N = 194)	59	11	28	2	100
35-64 (N = 310)	91	2	7	0	100
65 or older (N = 100)	91	5	3	1	100
Income					
Less than $10,000 (N = 213)	84	7	9	0	100
$10,000-$14,999 (N = 100)	69	6	22	3	100
$15,000-$24,999 (N = 168)	83	4	12	1	100
$25,000 or more (N = 73)	78	1	21	0	100
Education					
High school or less (N = 391)	84	3	12	1	100
Some college or more (N = 212)	74	9	16	1	100
Race					
White (N = 509)	80	5	14	1	100
Nonwhite (N = 95)	86	3	10	1	100

[a]*Question:* How likely are you to move in the next two or three years? Are you certain to move, will you probably move, or do you plan to stay in your current house? (If certain or probable move, do you think you will rent or buy?)

[b]Urban residence included households living in cities with populations of 2500 or more.

consistent with the findings of previous research. Compared to residents in nonmarket households, prospective movers tend to live in multifamily housing, to be younger and/or single, and to have attended college.

Profiles of prospective renters and buyers are presented in Table 4-2. Housholds expecting to buy a home in the next two to three

Table 4-2. Prospective Renter and Buyer Profiles

| Characteristic | Percent of Prospective: | |
	Renters (N = 31)	Buyers (N = 79)
Current Residence		
Single-family detached	32	65
Multiple family	65	21
Mobile home	3	14
Total	100	100
Household Type		
Singles	48	19
Single parents	7	6
Married with children	10	58
Married without children	19	13
Elderly	16	4
Total	100	100
Age		
Under 35	68	70
35-64	16	26
65 or older	16	4
Total	100	100
Income		
Under $10,000	52	26
$10,000-$14,999	22	28
$15,000-$24,999	22	27
$25,000 or more	4	19
Total	100	100
Education		
High school or less	35	57
Some college or more	65	43
Total	100	100
Race		
White	90	89
Nonwhite	10	11
Total	100	100

years tend to be married couples with children (58 percent), but sizable numbers also are single persons (19 percent) and married couples without children (13 percent). They are likely to be living in a single-family detached house at the present time (65 percent) and to be young adults under thirty-five years old (70 percent). As shown in Table 4-2, the prospective buyer profile includes households in all income brackets. Obviously, part of this demand will have to be satisfied through the purchase of used housing and mobile homes. Households most likely to qualify for the purchase of a new home (those with incomes of $15,000 or more) comprise less than half of the households who expect to be in the market for an ownership unit.

Persons who expect to be in the market for a rental housing unit are strikingly different from those who expect to buy. Prospective renters are much more likely to be living currently in multifamily housing (65 percent vs. 21 percent), to be single (48 percent vs. 19 percent), to have incomes under $10,000 per year (52 percent vs. 26 percent), and to have had more formal education (65 percent vs. 43 percent with some college or more). On the other hand, there is little difference between persons who expect to buy or rent in terms of age or race.

The residential mobility data and buyer/renter profiles may be used by energy policy personnel and by homebuilders to identify the segments of the population to whom particular types of energy information may be addressed and for whom energy-related messages may be designed so that they are most effective. For example, since people living in metropolitan areas are more likely to be moving than persons in nonmetropolitan areas, energy messages telling households what type of energy conservation features to look for when shopping for a new home or apartment might be concentrated in metropolitan areas. Since movers to both rental and ownership housing tend to be younger adults (under age thirty-five), residential energy-related messages should be designed to appeal to and affect this age group. Since a majority of the persons who expect to buy a home in the next few years have a high school education or less, energy-related messages, to be most effective, should be designed and worded so that they can be understood easily by persons with this amount of schooling. A number of other uses of these data are possible, depending upon the particular needs of the policy analyst.

PROSPECTIVE BUYERS' PREFERENCES
FOR HOUSING PRICES AND STYLES

Data summarized in Table 4-3 further characterize the

Table 4-3. Price and Housing Style Preferences of Prospective Home Buyers

Preference	Percent of Prospective Home Buyers (N = 79)
Price of New Home[a]	
Under $30,000	35
$30,000-$39,999	26
$40,000-$49,999	20
$50,000-$59,999	9
$60,000 or more	10
Total	100
Maximum Monthly Payment[b]	
$200 or less	33
$201-$249	14
$250-$299	21
$300 or more	32
Total	100
Housing Style[c]	
One story (ranch)	57
Split level	17
Two story	17
Townhouse	1
Condominium apartment	3
Mobile home	5
Total	100
Willing to Move to Townhouse/Condominium if Rising Costs Make Purchase of House on Its Own Lot Very Expensive[d]	
Yes	47
No	53
Total	100

[a]Question: How much would you be willing to pay for a house?

[b]Question: What is the largest amount you think you will be able to afford in monthly payments? $200 a month, between $200 and $250, $250 to $300, $300 to $400, over $400 a month?

[c]Question: What kind of house would you most likely be looking for? A one-story house, split level, two-story house, townhouse, apartment, or mobile home?

[d]Question: If rising housing costs made it very expensive for you to move to a house on its own lot, would you be willing to move to a townhouse or apartment?

market for ownership housing by summarizing prospective buyers' preferences for housing prices and styles. The price expectations of persons who think they will be in the market for a home are strongly skewed toward the lower end of the housing price spectrum.

For the country as a while, the National Association of Home Builders has projected that during 1979 the price of new homes ". . . will shoot up another 10 percent to $69,000 (average) and $63,000 (median)" (Mulligan, 1978). Although the median-priced new home being built in North Carolina is lower (just over $55,000 in 1978), it is well beyond the affordability of most persons who are likely to be in the market for a home.

The increasing disparity between the price structure of new housing (see Table 5-8 in Chapter 5) and the housing prices desired by persons in the market (Table 4-3) has some negative implications for the adoption of energy conservation features. Even though energy conservation features reduce operating costs, if they add to the first costs of housing, they are likely to further exclude households from effective participation in the market. This may result in builder resistance to the installation of any energy conservation features beyond those required by the state building code.

Builders may be squeezed from several directions. Consumers and public officials may demand the construction of the most energy-efficient homes possible, while at the same time they look for new houses that are affordable by a large segment of the market. In order to meet both demands simultaneously, builders may have to make tradeoffs with other characteristics of their housing products—possibly by building smaller houses than before or by cutting back on other features. This strategy would probably be successful if builders were competing only among themselves. However, they are also competing with the existing stock of housing, some proportion of which comes on the market each year. If the existing stock becomes more attractive to consumers because it offers more space and other features per unit of the consumers' housing dollar, then the demand for used housing relative to new housing will increase. Although the price of used housing will rise so that over time it becomes a somewhat less attractive alternative to new housing, in the short run the net effect of builders' attempts simultaneously to build energy-efficient houses and to maintain affordable prices by cutting back on space and other features desired by consumers will be the loss of some proportion of the potential market. Of course, if consumers value energy efficiency more than housing space, this effect will be minimized.

One way of cutting back on the costs of building housing is through the construction of townhouses and condominium apartments rather than single-family detached homes on their own lots (Real Estate Research Corporation, 1974). In addition, studies have shown that, on average, townhouses and garden apartments require less energy for heating and cooling than single-family detached homes with comparable floor space (Hittman Associates, 1978). Although the higher-density housing is less expensive per square foot to construct and is more energy-efficient, the data summarized in Table 4-3 indicate that most persons still prefer a house on its own lot. When asked what kind of house they would be looking for, 57 percent of prospective homebuyers cited a one-story ranch house. Seventeen percent reported they would be looking for a split-level house and another 17 percent would be in the market for a two-story house. A mere 1 percent reported they would be in the market for a townhouse, and only 3 percent were interested in purchasing a condominium apartment. The remaining 5 percent of the persons who expected to buy a home when they moved thought they would purchase a mobile home.

Buyers' resistance to higher-density housing is not unique to North Carolina. A recent national market survey of prospective home purchases found that 97 percent would first attempt to purchase a single-family detached home rather than a townhouse or condominium apartment (Consumer/Builder Survey on Housing, 1977). Buyer resistance is further underscored by a question concerning whether they would be willing to move to a townhouse or apartment if rising housing costs made it "very expensive" to have a house on its own lot. Less than a majority—only 47 percent—of the prospective homebuyers reported that they would be willing to move to a townhouse or an apartment under these circumstances. The proportions of prospective homebuyers who said that they would be willing to move to the more energy-efficient housing were higher in nonmetropolitan than in metropolitan areas (57 percent vs. 35 percent); among persons currently living in multifamily housing verus those dwelling in single-family detached units (61 percent versus 40 percent); and among persons with moderate incomes between $10,000 and $14,999 per year (71 percent). Persons with low incomes of below $10,000 (44 percent), middle incomes of $15,000 to $24,999 (45 percent), and high incomes of $25,000 or more (35 percent) were less willing to consider townhouse or apartment living. The amount of formal education persons had received and whether they lived in the mountains, Piedmont, or coastal region, or in an urban or rural area, made little difference in terms of their willingness to live in higher-density housing.

The fact that 71 percent of the moderate-income households would consider townhouse or apartment living is encouraging, particularly since they represent the segment of the market that is most likely to be hard hit by rising housing costs. Lower-income households are probably not an effective market segment, while middle- and upper-income households have considerably more options for housing types and prices. Helping the homebuilding industry recognize and meet the potential demand for energy-efficient housing types by this moderate-income market segment would seem to be a worthwhile project for energy conservation personnel.

ENERGY EFFICIENCY AND THE CHOICE OF HOUSING

Although large numbers of families are not yet willing to move to higher-density housing in an effort to save energy and reduce housing and fuel costs, households are becoming increasingly sensitive to the energy-consuming and conserving features of their housing. This trend is evident in the concern of consumers for energy costs in the choice of their current homes and also in their reported interests in the energy conservation features of homes they expect to acquire in the future.

The Role of Energy Costs in the Choice of the Current Home

Overall, 45 percent of the homeowners we interviewed considered the probable cost of heating and cooling to be an important factor in the decision to purchase their current homes. As shown in Table 4-4, 22 percent considered such costs to be "very important." Concern for energy efficiency has increased through time. Thirty-five percent of the homeowners of less than five years viewed energy efficiency as very important in the choice of their homes, compared to only 13 percent of those who acquired their home twenty or more years ago.

Although concern for energy efficiency is spread across all segments of the homeowning public, those for whom it was most critical in their choice of housing were buyers of the newest and the lowest-priced homes.[1] In addition, there is evidence of a curvilinear relationship between socioeconomic status and concern for energy efficiency in the choice of the existing home, with such considerations most prevalent among both lower- and upper-middle-income families. The concern for energy efficiency was lowest among moderate- and upper-income families (see related discussion in

Table 4-4. Importance of Energy Efficiency in the Choice of Current Home

Household and Housing Characteristics	Percent of Homeowners Who Viewed Energy Efficiency as Very Important in Choice of Current Home[a]
All Homeowners	22
Length of Residence in Home	
Less than 5 years	35
5-9 years	23
10-14 years	14
15-19 years	21
20 or more years	13
Income	
Less than $5,000	28
$5,000-$9,999	20
$10,000-$14,999	16
$15,000-$19,999	24
$20,000-$24,999	31
$25,000-$29,999	14
$30,000 or more	22
Education	
Less than high school education	27
High school education	15
Some college	27
College graduate	25
Postgraduate training	14
Age	
Under 30 years old	20
30-39	29
40-49	24
50-64	20
65 and older	16
Year Home Built	
Before 1960	17
1960-1969	20
1970-1975	30
1976 or later	40
Value of Home	
Under $20,000	30
$20,000-$29,999	22
$30,000-$39,999	17
$40,000-$49,999	22
$50,000 or more	22

[a]*Question:* At the time you chose your present home, how important was the probable cost of heating and cooling in your decision to move there? Was it very important, somewhat important, not very important, or not even a factor?

Cunningham and Lopreato, 1975). The fact that concern for energy efficiency is not solely the province of lower-class homeowners suggests that the demand for energy efficiency is generated not only by economic pressures but also by familiarity with energy conservation alternatives.

Another indicator of homeowners' increasing concern for energy-related aspects of housing is the trend through time in the use of energy conservation features. As seen in Figure 2-1 (p. 34), the use of almost all energy-saving features is much higher in newer homes. In homes built after 1975, over 80 percent are fully insulated, 76 percent have weatherstripping, 60 percent have storm windows or double-paned glass, and 52 percent have storm doors.[2] Forty-seven percent of homes use wood as an auxiliary heat source, and 43 percent of newer homes have heat pumps. The only mechanism to decrease in use in recent years, attic fans, reflects the almost universal use of central air conditioning in new homes (Table 5-8, p. 92).

These data demonstrate increasing demand by the consumer for energy-efficient housing features and the characteristic responses of builders to that demand. To date the greatest advances have occurred in improving the thermal efficiency of structures rather than in installing more innovative equipment. Notably absent in the existing housing stock is the use of highly innovative energy-saving technologies such as active solar space heating and solar hot water heating. However, concerns for energy efficiency are even more apparent among prospective homebuyers.

Energy Efficiency in the Next House

Compared to the 45 percent of homeowners who considered energy efficiency in selecting their current homes (and the 22 percent who rated energy efficiency as a very important factor in their choice), 87 percent of the prospective homebuyers we interviewed said that they would think about having more energy-saving features in their next house. See Table 4-5. The energy conservation features prospective buyers said they would be looking for most were devices to improve the thermal efficiency of the house, including insulation, storm windows and storm doors. Next most frequently mentioned were various energy-saving appliances. Finally, a few prospective buyers (less than 10 percent for each feature) mentioned heat pumps, woodstoves or fireplaces, solar heating or hot water, and the general design of the house. When asked whether they had thought about having solar hot water heat in their next house, a remarkably

Table 4-5. Prospective Home Buyers' Interest in Energy-efficient Housing

Indicator	Percent of Prospective Buyers (N = 79)
Thought about Energy Saving Features of Next Home[a]	
Yes	87
No	13
Total	100
Energy Saving Features Would Most Likely Look for in Next Home[b]	
Insulation, storm windows, storm doors	51
Energy-saving appliances	19
Wood stove/fireplace	7
Heat pump	6
Solar space or hot water heating	6
Design of house	3
Don't know	8
Total	100
Thought about Adding Solar Hot Water Heating[c]	
Yes	25
No	75
Total	100
Willingness to Spend More to Save on Heating Bills	
Spend $200 more to save $50 per year[d]	
Yes	90
No	10
Total	100
Spend $600 More to Save $100 per Year[e]	
Yes	85
No	15
Total	100
Spend $1200 More for Heat Pump to Save One-third on Heating Bills[f]	
Yes	80
No	20
Total	100

[a] *Question:* Has the cost of energy made you think about having more energy-saving features in your new home?

[b] *Question:* (If yes) What would you most likely be looking for?

[c] *Question:* Have you thought about adding a solar hot water heater?

[d] *Question:* If you were able to save $50 per year on heating bills, would you be willing to spend $200 more for your new home?

[e] *Question:* If you were able to save $100 per year on heating bills, would you be willing to spend $600 on additional construction costs for energy-saving devices in your next home?

[f] *Question:* Would you consider buying a new home with an electric heat pump which would cost $1200 more to purchase, but would save you one-third on your heating bills?

high proportion—25 percent—said that they had considered this energy-saving feature.

In addition to reporting that they would think about having various energy conservation features when they selected their next home, very high proportions of the prospective homebuyers indicated a willingness to spend more on the house in order to achieve savings in their heating bills. Ninety percent said they would spend $200 more to save $50 per year; 85 percent would spend $600 more to save $100 per year; and fully 80 percent indicated that they would spend $1200 more for a heat pump if they could save one-third on their heating bills.

Table 4-6 illustrates by selected household characteristics the percentages of households which said they would consider the energy-saving features of their next house, would pay $600 more to save $100 in heating bills, and would consider solar hot water heating. In general, it can be seen that concern for energy conservation among prospective homebuyers is not limited to any particular type of buyer. Over 80 percent of those living in each region in North Carolina—in metropolitan and nonmetropolitan areas, and in urban and rural areas—report that they will be thinking about energy-saving features when they select their next home. Although moderate- and middle-income households were more likely to say that they would consider energy-saving features than lower- or upper-income families, over three-quarters of each group said they would be concerned about energy in choosing their housing. Similarly, homeowners of every age group, race, and level of education say they will give attention to energy when they buy their next home. Every type of household will be thinking about energy. Furthermore, every type indicated that it was willing to pay more for the next house if the additional energy conservation features would result in savings on the annual heating bill.

In the case of solar hot water heating, prospective demand was somewhat higher in nonmetropolitan areas than in metropolitan areas—32 percent vs. 18 percent of the households in these areas said they would consider it when they acquire a new home. With the exception of persons expecting to buy a mobile home, and lower-income households, which were much less likely than average to be interested in solar hot water heating, there were few striking differences in concern for solar hot water heating across various population groups.

SUMMARY

The intentions of North Carolina households to move, taken

Table 4-6. Types of Households Most Likely to Demand Energy-efficient New Homes

Type of Household	Percent of Prospective Buyers Who Would:		
	Think about Energy Saving Features of Next Home	*Pay $600 More to Save $100 Annually*	*Think about Adding Solar Hot Water Heating*
Total Sample (N = 79)	87	85	25
Location			
Mountains	79	86	29
Piedmont	85	85	23
Coastal Plain/Tidewater	92	81	27
Metropolitan area	87	87	18
Nonmetropolitan area	85	81	32
Urban	83	83	27
Rural	95	85	20
Current Residence			
Single-family detached	86	75	27
Multiple family	89	100	28
Mobile home	82	100	9
Income			
Less than $10,000	76	76	14
$10,000-14,999	95	86	23
$15,000-$24,999	91	95	33
$25,000 or more	80	73	27
Age			
Under 35	87	87	22
35-64	82	77	32
65 or older	100	67	33
Education			
High school or less	83	85	20
Some college or more	91	82	32
Race			
White	86	83	24
Nonwhite	89	89	33

as a whole, are somewhat lower than national averages. However, within metropolitan areas North Carolinians are about as likely to move as other metropolitan households in the nation. Between 10 and 15 percent of the households interviewed can be expected to be in the market to purchase a home during the coming three years.

Prospective homebuyers are likely to be married couples with children, younger individuals, and those who are currently living in single-family detached housing. In comparison, prospective renters are more likely to be currently living in multifamily housing, to be single, and to have annual family incomes of less than $10,000.

Comparing prospective homebuyers' expectations of housing prices and the actual price structure of homes being built reveals an increasing gap in people's ability to afford new housing. This may create pressure on builders to eliminate various housing features, including some which contribute to energy conservation. In addition, there is little consumer interest in moving to more energy-efficient housing types such as townhouses and condominium apartments. Even when asked whether they would be willing to live in higher-density housing if a house on its own lot became very expensive, a majority of prospective buyers said they would be unwilling to live in a townhouse or condominium apartment. The only major market for this type of housing appears to be among people with incomes between $10,000 and $14,999 per year—in this group 71 percent indicated a willingness to live in such dwellings.

Although most persons are dissatisfied with the idea of living in higher-density housing, they are becoming increasingly concerned with the energy efficiency of their homes. While only 45 percent of current homeowners said they had considered the cost of heating and cooling in selecting their current house, 87 percent of those who expect to buy a home in the next three years said they would pay heed to the energy-saving features of that home. Prospective buyers were particularly interested in features contributing to thermal efficiency, including insulation, storm windows and storm doors. In addition to expressing a strong interest in energy conservation features, a very high proportion of the individuals who will be in the market for a new home said they would be willing to pay extra for their next home in order to save on heating bills.

In sum, the demand for energy-efficient new housing is very strong. In the following chapter, we examine institutional characteristics of the housing industry that may affect the industry's ability to meet this demand. Chapter 6 then focuses on the energy-related decisions of individual homebuilders.

NOTES

1. Because households are reporting on past decisions, associations between their present characteristics (such as income, age and education) and purchase

decision factors must be viewed as suggestive only, since household characteristics may have changed markedly in the years intervening between when
their home was acquired and when they were interviewed for this study.
2. These figures are approximations of original equipment and features supplied
with the house. They were calculated by subtracting from the proportion
of current owners who said their house had a feature, the proportion who
also reported they had added the feature since they moved to the house
(retrofitting). Since previous owners also may have added a feature, the
proportion of housing units estimated to have had various energy conservation features as original equipment may be overstated slightly.

REFERENCES

Butler, Edgar W., F. Stuart Chapin, Jr., George C. Hemmens, Edward J. Kaiser,
Michael A. Stegman, and Shirley F. Weiss. 1969. *Moving Behavior and Resi-
dential Choice: A National Survey*. National Cooperative Highway Research
Board, Research Program Report 81. Washington: Highway Research Board,
National Academy of Sciences-National Academy of Engineering.

"Consumer/Builder Survey on Housing." 1977. *Professional Builder* (December),
p. 58.

Cunningham, William H., and Sally Cook Lopreato. 1977. *Energy Use and Conservation Incentives: A Study of the Southwestern United States*. New York:
Praeger Publishers.

Division of Solar Energy, U.S. Energy Research and Development Administration. 1977. *Solar Energy in America's Future: A Preliminary Assessment*.
Washington: U.S. Government Printing Office, March.

Hittman Associates, Inc. 1977. *Residential Energy Consumption Detailed
Geographic Analysis*. Summary Report. Office of the Assistant Secretary
for Policy Development and Research, Department of Housing and Urban
Development. Washington: U.S. Government Printing Office.

Lansing, John B. 1966. *Residential Location and Urban Mobility: The Second
Wave of Interviews*. Ann Arbor, Michigan: Survey Research Center, Institute
for Social Research, The University of Michigan.

Lansing, John B., Eva Mueller and Nancy Barth. 1964. *Residential Location
and Urban Mobility*. Ann Arbor, Michigan: Survey Research Center, Institute
for Social Research, The University of Michigan.

Mulligan, Bill. 1978. "Housing in 1979: A Slide But Not a Slump." *Housing*
(December), p. 45.

President's Committee on Urban Housing. 1969. *A Decent Home. The Report
of the President's Committee on Urban Housing*. Washington: U.S. Government Printing Office.

Real Estate Research Corporation. 1974. *The Costs of Sprawl: Environmental
and Economic Costs of Alternative Residential Development Patterns at the
Urban Fringe: Detailed Cost Analysis*. Washington: U.S. Government Printing
Office, April.

Rossi, Peter H. 1955. *Why Families Move*. Glencoe, Ill.: The Free Press.

Socolow, Robert, H. 1977. "The Coming Age of Conservation," In Jack M.

Hollander, Melvin K. Simmons, and David O. Wood, editors, *Annual Review of Energy, Volume 2, 1977.* Palo Alto, Calif.: Annual Reviews, Inc., pp. 239-289.

U.S. Bureau of the Census. Various dates. *Construction Reports,* Series C40: "Housing Authorized by Building Permits and Public Contracts." Washington: U.S. Government Printing Office.

U.S. Bureau of the Census. 1977. *Current Population Reports,* Series P-20, No. 305, "Geographic Mobility: March 1975 to March 1976." Washington: U.S. Government Printing Office.

U.S. Bureau of the Census. 1978. *Current Population Reports,* Series P-20, No. 331, "Geographic Mobility: March 1975 to March 1978." Washington: U.S. Government Printing Office.

Van Arsdol, Maurice, Jr., Georges Sabagh, and Edgar W. Butler. 1968. "Retrospective and Subsequent Residential Mobility." *Demography,* Vol. 5, pp. 249-67.

Varady, David P. 1973. "Moving Intentions and Behavior in the Cincinnati Model Neighborhood: The Utility of the Survey Approach in Forecasting Residential Mobility." Paper presented at the Association of Collegiate Schools of Planning, American Institute of Planners Annual Conference, Atlanta, Georgia, October 22.

Chapter 5

The Homebuilding Industry
and Energy Conservation

Raymond J. Burby

In order that consumer demand for energy-efficient new housing be realized, homebuilders must correctly read the market and produce houses which minimize unwanted heat gain and loss and which incorporate energy-saving appliances and heating and cooling equipment. Pointing in particular to a number of characteristics of the homebuilding industry which act as institutional constraints to the construction of energy-efficient homes (Council of State Governments, 1976), some have questioned the ability of the industry to perform this vital function. In this chapter, we examine the characteristics of the homebuilding industry in one state—North Carolina—in order to shed light on unique characteristics of this industry which shape its ability to help the nation meet its energy conservation goals for the residential sector.

SIZE OF THE INDUSTRY

Construction is the largest industry in the United States. Every year it accounts for about 10 percent of the nation's gross national product. Housing construction represents annually about one-third of new private construction and about one-quarter of all new construction (Marketing Research Committee, 1975). Beyond its sheer magnitude, the housing industry is one of the most complex in the United States. Including all firms which share in receipts for housing, it involves millions of establishments.

At the heart of the industry are the homebuilders. They are the focus of this chapter—the firms actually producing finished housing for sale to households. However, broadly defined, the industry includes a number of other groups. The acquisition and development of land upon which housing is erected involves realtors, lawyers, civil engineers, land planners, landscape architects, specialized land development companies, merchant builders and others. Builders usually procure construction materials from specialized wholesalers and retailers, including lumberyards and hardware stores. Designs for houses may be obtained from architects, from builders' own inhouse designers, and from companies selling "stock" plans. On-site construction activities are usually subcontracted to a myriad of specialized craftsmen—according to one estimate, an average of fourteen subcontractors are involved in the construction of a single-family house (Pynoos, Schafer, and Hartman, 1973). Financing of construction and the home mortgage for the final buyer may involve another array of firms, ranging from commercial banks and savings and loan associations to insurance companies. Sale of the finished product may be the responsibility of the homebuilder's own staff, but often this activity is undertaken by other companies operating on a commission basis. Finally, public agencies are often involved in every stage of the building process, from the establishment of rules governing the subdivision of property to the enforcement of warranties through the court system.

The homebuilding industry in North Carolina appears to be a microcosm of the industry nationally. Although easy entry and exit (the failure rate in homebuilding is one of the highest of any industry) make precise estimates difficult, it appears that over 3,000 homebuilding firms are active in the state at any given time.[1] This finding is based on records of the North Carolina Home Builders Association, North Carolina Licensing Board for Contractors, and our own screening of building and contracting firms.

The size and complexity of the homebuilding industry have two major implications for energy conservation policy. First, energy policy must be designed to affect the full range of individuals involved in the industry. Unlike the automobile industry, the promotion of energy-efficient products cannot be achieved by changing the behavior of one or two or three major companies. For change to occur, a large number of firms must modify their modes of operation. Second, the complex nature of the homebuilding industry means that no one group is totally responsible for the adoption of energy conservation practices and features. In fact, in comparison with other major industries, homebuilding entrepreneurs are notably dependent on outsiders. As a result, it has been said, "Builders have little influence over the rate of technological development in the industry . . ." (President's Committee on Urban Housing, 1968, p. 117).

HOMEBUILDING FIRMS

There are a number of characteristics of homebuilding firms that have implications for residential energy conservation policy: (1) types of homebuilding firms; (2) their size and organization; (3) characteristic modes of operation; (4) location of production; and (5) the diversity of functions that building firms perform. Each of these is considered in turn.

Type of Firm

The President's Committee on Urban Housing (Kaiser Committee) identified five types of housing producers in the United States: (1) merchant builders; (2) general contractors; (3) home manufacturers; (4) mobile home manufacturers; and (5) owner-builders. Home manufacturers and mobile home manufacturers, although increasing in importance as suppliers of housing, were not included in the scope of this research. Owner-builders—persons who act as general contractors for the construction of their own dwelling units— also were not included in the study, as their numbers have been shrinking steadily and they are no longer considered to be an important segment of the industry. Thus, the focus of our research is on merchant builders and general contractors.

Merchant builders (often referred to as operative or speculative builders) build houses to their own designs, on their own land, for sale or rental to others. In contrast, general contractors (sometimes called custom builders) build on land owned by others, usually according to plans supplied by the landowner. While merchant builders' decisions have an obvious and direct influence on the energy efficiency of the houses they build, general contractors are much less able to influence the characteristics of housing. The distribution of building firms between these two types indicates the extent to which residential energy policy can affect the energy efficiency characteristics of new housing by affecting builder decisions. The higher the proportion of merchant builders, the more important are builders (as opposed to consumers, for example) as targets for residential energy policy.

As shown in Table 5-1, relatively few homebuilding firms in North Carolina can be classified as either pure merchant builders (16 percent) or pure general contractors (25 percent). Most firms (59 percent) engage in both speculative construction for their own account (merchant building) and in general construction, building custom homes to buyers' and architects' specifications. Therefore, it appears that the vast majority of homebuilding firms play an independent role in decisions about at least some of the houses they construct and are a valid and significant target for energy conservation policy efforts.

Whether a firm acted solely as a general contractor or a merchant builder or mixed the two activities was related to a number of other characteristics of the company and its operations. General contractors tended to have the most experience in homebuilding, and their firms, on the average, had been engaged in building homes for a longer period of time than had either merchant builders or mixed merchant builder/general contractors. Firms that engaged solely in merchant building were most likely to be involved also in property management and to be headed by enterpreneurs with more formal education. Firms that mixed merchant and custom building tended to have the highest annual volume of construction (number of homes built) and the greatest geographic scope of operation; furthermore, they were most likely to engage in residential land development and real estate in addition to homebuilding.

Table 5-1. Distribution of Homebuilders, by Type of Builder

Type of Builder	Percent of Builders (N = 100)
General contractors (total volume consists of homes built to owners' and architects' specifications)	25
Merchant builder/contractor (built both speculative homes on own land and homes built to owners' and architects' specifications)	59
Merchant builders (total volume consists of speculative homes built on own land)	16
Total	100

Size and Organization of Firms

The homebuilding industry is noteworthy for the small size of the firms engaged in the production of housing (Beyer, 1965). As shown in Table 5-2, the industry in North Carolina follows this national pattern. Of a random sample of 100 homebuilders interviewed for this study, 29 percent had constructed fewer than 5 houses during 1978. The median homebuilder in North Carolina constructed only ten homes during that year.

Several factors contribute to the survival of small firms in the industry. One is the size and location of the market. The absence of a large metropolitan area in North Carolina and the dispersed character of the population inhibits the development of large firms catering to a mass housing market. Second, the dispersed character of the market and diversity in local conditions promotes the success of small firms that are familiar with highly localized housing preferences and other market conditions. Third, the unstable character of the housing industry, with sharp changes in demand, encourages firms to avoid large fixed overhead costs (Pynoos, Schafer, and Hartman, 1973).

The small size of the homebuilding companies is related to the characteristic form of organization of the firms in the industry. Of the homebuilding businesses interviewed for this study, 30 percent were single proprietorships, 11 percent were partnerships, 37 percent were family-held corporations, and 19 percent were nonfamily closely-held corporations. Only 3 percent of the firms were organized as public corporations or used other organizational forms that allowed them to tap broad sources of equity capital.

The size and organization of homebuilding firms have implications

Table 5-2. Size of Homebuilding Firms (Construction Volume)

Number of Housing Units Constructed, 1978	Percent of Home Builders (N = 100)	Percent of Homes Built by Sample (N = 2260)
1-4	29	3
5-9	16	4
10-14	17	8
15-24	17	13
25-49	10	13
50-99	6	18
100 or more	5	41
Total	100	100

for residential energy conservation policy. A number of observers, noting the small size of the firms engaged in homebuilding, have come to negative conclusions about the efficiency of the industry and its ability to adopt new ideas. According to Beyer (1965, p. 214), for example,

> It is evident that when builders construct less than five or ten units a year, they operate on a handicraft basis . . . do not use modern tools and mechanical processes. Little, if any, advantage is taken of the availability of standardized parts and modern technology. This causes excessive wastes of both materials and labor.

If small firms are more likely than others to benefit from programs designed to increase the efficiency of their operations and the adoption of energy-efficient building techniques and features, then they are a natural target for energy conservation programs.

An argument against a focus on small firms is the fact that, as shown in Table 5-2, the inefficiencies of very small building firms may have little actual impact, since they account for a very small proportion of the new homes built. Firms that built less than ten houses in 1978 accounted for less than 10 percent of the total volume of new housing. In comparison, the largest builders (those who built 100 or more houses in 1978) produced 41 percent of the new housing. Thus, to have the most impact on the energy efficiency of new housing, energy programs might best be directed toward medium- to large-scale homebuilding firms. For example, if programs are directed at firms constructing twenty-five or more houses per year, the data in Table 5-2 indicate that 72 percent of the new housing constructed in North Carolina could be affected. Since only 21 percent of the homebuilding firms in North Carolina could be classified as medium-scale (twenty-five to ninety-nine homes per year) or large-scale (100 or more homes per year), the target group for energy policy in this particular state could be reduced from the 3,000+ firms that comprise the homebuilding industry to about 630 firms.

Homebuilding Firms' Modes of Operation

In addition to the characteristic small scale of the operations of homebuilding firms, the industry is noteworthy for fragmentation of the production process. Typically, homes are built through ad hoc arrangements in which ". . . production organizations are assembled, dispersed, and reassembled for each construction job. . . ." (Grebler,

1950, p. 55). As a result, most homebuilders do not have a large number of in-house employees. As shown in Table 5-3, 69 percent of the firms interviewed employed less than ten persons full- and part-time during September 1978. Only 11 percent of the firms employed twenty or more persons. Rather than assigning production functions to their own employees, homebuilding firms typically subcontract a number of building operations to special trade contractors or to subcontractors.

Table 5-4 summarizes the proportion of homebuilding firms reporting that they typically subcontracted, used their own employees, or mobilized a combination of subcontractors and their own employees to complete each of eight key building and marketing tasks. A majority of homebuilders used their own employees for only two of the eight tasks—framing the house, and marketing and sales. In contrast, over 90 percent of the builders subcontracted heating, ventilating and air conditioning (HVAC), plumbing, and electrical work. Two-thirds or more subcontracted landscaping and the installation of insulation.

The practice of subcontracting many of the operations involved in the production of housing has important implications for energy conservation policy. Almost thirty years ago, Grebler (1950, p. 55) noted that subcontracting in the homebuilding industry seriously weakened the managerial influence of the builder. In addition, Grebler noted that managers' ability to direct and influence their own labor was weakened by the "temporary and casual" relationships between employers and employees in the homebuilding industry and by the employees' tendency to change frequently from employee to employer to self-employed status. Thus, even if energy policy was effective in motivating builders to improve the energy efficiency of the homes they produce, there is some question as to

Table 5-3. Number of Employees

Number of Persons Employed Full and Part Time, September 1978	Percent of Homebuilders (N = 100)
3 or less	28
4-6	21
7-9	20
10-19	20
20 or more	11
Total	100

Table 5-4. Use of Subcontractors to Perform Selected Homebuilding Operations[a]

| | Percent of Home Builders (N = 99) | | |
Homebuilding Operation	Task Performed by Own Employees	Task Performed by Own Employees and Subcontractors	Task Performed by Sub-contractors
Electrical work	1	2	97
Framing	58	4	38
Grading the lot	20	3	77
Heating, ventilating, and air conditioning (HVAC)	1	1	98
Insulation	23	10	67
Landscaping the lot	27	5	68
Marketing and sales	62	16	22
Plumbing	6	1	93

[a]Question: Now, getting back to your company. In building (single-family detached) homes, which of the following activities do you usually do within your firm with your own employees and which are usually subcontracted or otherwise done outside of your firm? [HAND CARD C.] First, what about . . . .

whether builders have enough control over the production process to see that their housing products live up to their good intentions.

Fragmentation of the housing production process has also been held responsible for difficulties encountered in the introduction of new products and innovative technologies into the homebuilding industry. For example, Hirschberg and Schoen (1974, p. 459) have written

Two distinctly cultural aspects of institutional characteristics also shape the industry and must be accounted for in efforts to introduce changes. The industry is *craft-based* and operates through a series of individual craft unions that contribute separate skills and functions to the construction process. These unions have a great deal of control over acceptance of individual technological innovations. For this reason and because there is a relative absence of "performance specification" there tends instead to be a heavy reliance on previous "ways of doing things," and a general resistance to change of any sort. The result is a conservative social system, likewise, generally resistant to change.

In order to overcome this built-in bias toward maintaining the status quo, builders must share with their subcontractors important energy-related decisions about their housing products rather than leaving the decisions entirely to the subcontractor.

To determine the extent to which builders currently have the potential to shape energy-related decisions about their housing products, we asked those who subcontracted heating, ventilating, and air conditioning work (98 percent of the builders) and those who farmed out the installation of insulation (67 percent of the builders) to indicate who was responsible for decisions about key aspects of these two operations. In the case of HVAC systems, two energy-related decisions seem to be particularly important: (1) specification of the type of heating/air conditioning system (for example, whether an electric heat pump or resistance heating is to be used); and (2) specification of the capacity of the system (for example, whether it will meet or, as is often the case, exceed design requirements). The results are summarized in Table 5-5.

Homebuilders are much more likely to play a role in decisions about the type of heating system installed than they are in specifying the size of the system. In almost half of the cases (45 percent), builders left decisions about the capacity of the heating system entirely up to a HVAC contractor. In the case of insulation, builders tended to have a greater role in product decisions. Two-thirds indicated that they were responsible for decisions about the type of insulation used, and 87 percent reported that they determined the

Table 5-5. Locus of Responsibility for Decisions about HVAC Systems and Installation of Insulation

| | Percent of Builders | | |
Decision	Builder Specifies[a]	Joint Decision	Subcontractor Specifies
HVAC Systems			
1. Type of heating equipment used	55	38	7
2. Capacity of heating equipment	14	41	45
Insulation			
1. Type of insulation	66	16	18
2. Amount of insulation	87	10	3

[a]Includes builders who performed function within the firm and builders who subcontracted the function, but made decisions regarding heating and insulation.

amount of insulation to be installed. Thus, policies and programs designed to promote the use of adequate amounts of insulation should be directed, for the most part, at the homebuilding firm. Efforts to promote the use of energy-efficient HVAC equipment, and to insure that systems are installed to match, not exceed, design requirements, must be directed at both homebuilding firms and HVAC contractors if they are to result in marked changes in the energy efficiency of new housing.

Location of Production

In addition to the small scale of homebuilding firms and the fragmentation of the production process, a third noteworthy characteristic of the homebuilding industry, both nationally and in North Carolina, is localization of production (The President's Committee on Urban Housing, 1968, p. 117). When builders were asked in how many counties their firms had produced homes during 1977 and 1978, a majority (55 percent) reported that they limited their operations to one county. Another 27 percent said they had operated in only two counties. Such localization of production has implications for the adoption of new energy conservation technologies. If consumer demand for new technologies, such as solar hot water heating, is spread thinly across a state or region, homebuilding firms operating in only one or two small geographic areas are unlikely to recognize the market for homes incorporating the new features. As a result, builder use of new technologies will lag behind consumer demand, even though builders, as a rule, are very sensitive to the marketplace. For energy policymakers, this phenomenon suggests that the diffusion of new energy-conserving technologies could be speeded up if builders were given assistance in accurately identifying the market for such technologies. For example, if there existed credible market projections indicating the demand, by county, for homes with solar hot water heating, it seems likely that more builders would attempt to satisfy this market segment. Without accurate market demand information, the extreme localization of building operations suggests that builders will not respond to very specialized markets that are spread thinly rather than concentrated in the locales where they are used to doing business.

Diversity of Functions

A final policy-relevant characteristic of homebuilding firms is the diversity of functions which they perform. Because of the highly cyclical demand for new housing, firms engaged in homebuilding often perform other functions so that they have a cushion to fall back upon when there is a downturn in the market. For example, among North Carolina homebuilders, 56 percent were involved with nonresidential construction and 36 percent with multifamily construction in addition to building single-family detached homes. Also, some firms have moved toward vertical integration of functions in the homebuilding process. Almost half (47 percent) of the homebuilders interviewed were engaged in residential land development at the start of the process, and 47 percent operated as real estate brokers at the end of the process. Finally, 32 percent of the firms reported that they provided property management services.

For energy policymakers, the diversity of functions that characterizes homebuilding firms indicates that they are likely targets for energy conservation information that spans a broader focus than housing construction. For example, as states develop residential energy conservation information programs, homebuilding firms would seem to benefit from educational materials covering energy-efficient subdivision design, light residential building, and even retrofitting, inasmuch as almost a third of the state's homebuilding firms also act as property managers.

THE ENTREPRENEUR

The homebuilding industry is not characterized by firms that employ large bureaucracies. Instead, most firms are small and organized in such a way that decision-making authority is highly centralized. This facet of the industry simplifies the problem of delivering energy conservation messages and incentives. As an aid to the development of energy conservation programs for the homebuilding industry, this section describes selected characteristics of the executives who have authority for the energy-related aspects of their housing products.

The age, education, and experience in homebuilding of such executives are summarized in Table 5-6. The median age of building executives was forty-two. They did not concentrate in any one age bracket: 22 percent were under age thirty-five; 30 percent were between thirty-five and forty-four years old; 22 percent between forty-five and fifty-four; and 26 percent were fifty-five or older. Executives with general contractors tended to be somewhat older than average; those with merchant builder/contractors, somewhat younger than average.

Table 5-6. Selected Characteristics of Homebuilding Executives

	Percent of Executives, by Type of Firm[a]			
Characteristic	Total	General Contractor	Merchant Builder/ Contractor	Merchant Builder
Age				
Under age 35	22	8	32	6
35-44	30	28	30	31
45-54	22	32	19	19
55 or older	26	32	19	44
Total	100	100	100	100
Education				
Less than high school	8	8	8	6
High school graduate	34	56	29	19
Some college	26	16	29	31
College graduate	32	20	34	44
Total	100	100	100	100
Experience in Homebuilding				
Less than 10 years	31	20	39	19
10-19 years	30	20	32	37
20 or more years	39	60	29	44
Total	100	100	100	100
Counties of Residence in North Carolina				
One	48	52	44	56
Two	33	32	34	31
Three or more	19	16	22	13
Total	100	100	100	100

[a]See Table 5-1 for a definition of types of homebuilders. The number of respondents of each type is: general contractors, $N = 25$; merchant builder/contractor, $N = 59$; merchant builders, $N = 16$.

The median homebuilding executive was a high school graduate with some college education. Only 8 percent of the executives had not graduated from high school, while about a third (32 percent) were college graduates. Executives with merchant builders/contractors and merchant builders tended to have more formal education than executives with general contracting firms; over 70 percent had at least some college education versus 36 percent of the general contractors' executives.

The median homebuilding executive had over fourteen years of experience in building homes. While general contracting executives had the least formal education, they had the most experience. Sixty percent of the executives with general contracting firms had twenty or more years of experience. Reflecting the localized character of the homebuilding industry, however, builders often did not have much experience with different communities in North Carolina. Almost half of the executives (48 percent) had lived in only one North Carolina county. Only 19 percent had lived in three or more counties. Thus, a builder's expertise tends to come from living and working in one market area.

Attitudes Toward the Energy Problem

The attitudes of homebuilding executives toward the energy problem in the United States were similar to those of households generally (see Chapter 3). Sixty-one percent rated the need to save energy as "very serious." Fifty-five percent of the respondents to the statewide household survey gave the same answer. Homebuilders and households were not particularly sanguine about the results of others' efforts to save, however. Less than half of the homebuilders (48 percent) and only 52 percent of the households felt "people's efforts to save energy in homes and personal driving can help reduce our total energy use a great deal." Nevertheless, most builders (68 percent) and households (73 percent) did not believe that people have the right to use as much energy as they can pay for. In sum, homebuilding executives are concerned about the energy problem in the United States; while they are somewhat leery of our ability to save large amounts of energy, they believe that we have an obligation to try.

Attitudes Toward Proposed Energy Policies

As outlined in the introduction to this study, a number of policies have been proposed as means of promoting energy conservation in the residential sector. Homebuilding executives were asked if in the event of another energy shortage, they felt the government should pursue each of nine policies. Their answers are summarized in Table 5-7. Builders strongly favored policies that provided incentives for energy conservation. Seventy-two percent of the executives favored increased tax rebates for households who added insulation or solar equipment; 81 percent favored the provision of low-interest loans for people to insulate their homes. However, the executives were less enthusiastic about other types of policies that have been proposed

Table 5-7. Homebuilding Executives' Attitudes Toward Selected Energy
Conservation Policies

Policy	*Percent Favoring Policy, by Type of Firm[a]*			
	Total	*General Contractor*	*Merchant Builder/ Contractor*	*Merchant Builder*
Equity Policies				
1. Help families pay for heating bills	17	24	17	6
Incentive Policies				
1. Increase the amount of tax rebates available to households to add insulation and solar equipment	72	68	74	69
2. Provide low-interest loans for people to insulate their homes	81	96	75	81
Pricing Policies				
1. Increase the tax on gasoline	22	12	29	13
2. Raise the price of heating fuels	18	0	25	19
Regulatory Policies				
1. Require that only energy-efficient new homes be built, even though those homes would cost more	48	44	51	44
2. Require disclosure of estimated annual heating and cooling costs of new homes	50	52	47	56
3. Discourage development of outlying land until land closer to existing development is used	15	20	14	13

[a]See Table 5-1 for a definition of types of homebuilders. The number of respondents of each type is: general contractors, $N = 25$; merchant builder/contractors, $N = 59$; merchant builders, $N = 16$.

as means of promoting greater energy conservation. About half
would favor government regulations requiring disclosure of estimated
annual heating and cooling costs for new housing (50 percent). Far
fewer—only 15 percent—thought that governments should promote
energy-efficient land development patterns by discouraging the
development of outlying areas until land closer to existing development is used.

Both homebuilders and residents were opposed to the use of pricing policies to discourage energy use. Only 22 percent of the homebuilding executives (and 9 percent of the residents) interviewed favored increases in the tax on gasoline; only 18 percent of the builders (and 13 percent of the residents) favored government policies that would raise the price of heating fuels. While builders and households were opposed to the use of pricing policies to save energy, they differed strongly on the merits of policies designed to distribute more equitably the hardships produced by energy shortages and rising fuel prices. Only 17 percent of the executives, in contrast with 77 percent of the consumers, felt that the government should help families pay for heating bills.

HOUSING PRODUCT MIX

To this point, our overview of the homebuilding industry has examined the characteristics of building firms and of the executives who direct the operations. To conclude our review of the industry, in this section we briefly describe the mix of housing products that the homebuilding industry is currently producing. Because of our interest in decisionmaking by building firms, the product mix data presented refer only to speculative housing. Data related to custom homes were not collected, since in most instances the owner of the custom home rather than its builder is responsible for the characteristics of such housing. The housing product data were assembled by our asking builders about the characteristics of the most recent speculative home their firm had constructed. Thus, the data provide information on a cross-section of new housing, including its price, type, and selected features. This information is summarized in Table 5-8. Additional energy-related characteristics of new housing are presented in the following chapter.

Although multiple-story housing is considered to be more energy-efficient since less roof surface area is exposed to the elements per square foot of floor area, about two-thirds of the builders were using the one-story ranch style for their most recent speculative house. In this respect, builders are closely matching consumer preferences for housing types (Chapter 4). The median size of new houses being built was about 1,600 square feet. As shown in Table 5-8, relatively little "budget housing" with less than 1,250 square feet was being built—only 21 percent. On the other hand, a mere one-third of these speculative houses contained 2,000 or more square feet. The median price of new speculative homes was just over $55,000.

Table 5-8. Selected Characteristics of New Speculative Housing in North Carolina

Characteristic	Percent of Speculative Houses (N = 80)[a]
Housing Style	
One story (ranch)	66
Split level	7
Two story	20
Three story	3
Other	4
Total	100
Size of Houses	
Under 1250 sq. ft.	21
1250-1499 sq. ft.	19
1500-1749 sq. ft.	20
1750-1999 sq. ft.	7
2000 or more sq. ft.	33
Total	100
Price of Houses	
Under $35,000	9
$35,000-$44,999	23
$45,000-$54,999	17
$55,000-$64,999	13
$65,000-$79,999	21
$80,000 or more	17
Total	100
Features Utilized	
Rangehood with fan	100
Two or more bathrooms	91
Central air conditioning	89
Fireplace	85
Dishwasher	85
Separate family room	73
Separate dining room	69
Patio or deck	69
Garage	64
Garbage disposal	53
Bathroom heater	23
Trash compactor	11
Enclosed/screened porch	10
Microwave oven	10
Central vacuum system	5

[a]Data refer to "most recent speculative house" built by random sample of homebuilders. Five builders, who did not build a speculative house in 1978, reported on houses they had constructed in prior years.

A number of the features which builders include in the houses they construct have energy use implications. For example, 85 percent of the homes included fireplaces. As noted in the following chapter, less than a fifth of the fireplaces installed were energy-efficient units that drew directly on outside air for combustion; the remainder—80 percent of the fireplace installations, representing over half of the new speculative housing being built—have fireplace units that have the potential to increase, rather than decrease, winter heating fuel requirements. Homebuilders were installing a number of energy-consuming appliances. Eighty-nine percent of the speculatively-built houses contained central air conditioning; 85 percent had automatic dishwashers; and 53 percent had garbage disposal units. Relatively few—10 percent—were being equipped with energy-efficient microwave ovens. Thus, in responding to consumer demand, builders were producing homes which contained built-in energy-consuming features. Of course, they were also taking a number of steps to improve the energy efficiency of their housing products. These steps and factors that were associated with energy-conscious home building are discussed in the next chapter.

SUMMARY

In this chapter we have examined a number of institutional characteristics of the homebuilding industry that have implications for energy policy and programs. Unlike most other major industries, homebuilding consists of an extremely large number of producing units. In North Carolina, we estimated that over 3,000 general contracting and merchant building firms are producing housing. Other important characteristics of the homebuilding industry include:

1. the small size of most firms—the average builder produces only about ten houses per year;
2. fragmentation of the production process—many operations which affect the energy efficiency of the housing which firms produce are subcontracted to other firms;
3. localization of production—most firms operate in only one or two counties;
4. diversity of functions—many homebuilders engage in other activities besides producing housing units.

In combination, these institutional characteristics of the industry have the potential to inhibit the adoption of new ideas for saving energy in housing.

Although institutional constraints may limit the diffusion of energy conservation ideas and new technologies, the characteristics of homebuilding executives are such that institutional handicaps may be overcome. Key executives in building firms tend to be young or middle-aged (almost three-quarters are under fifty-five years old), generally well-educated (over half have attended college), and widely experienced in their industry (almost 40 percent have twenty or more years of experience). Finally, builders reflect the average citizen's deep concern for the energy problems facing our state and nation. They believe that the need to save energy is very serious, and they favor policies that provide households with incentives to conserve.

NOTE

1. This estimate is in general agreement with figures developed by the U.S. Census Bureau's latest Census of Construction Industries. In 1972, the Census estimated that 3,120 establishments were engaged as "general contractors—single-family houses" and as "operative builders" in North Carolina. (U.S. Bureau of the Census, 1974.)

REFERENCES

Beyer, Glen H. 1965. *Housing and Society*. New York: The Macmillan Company.

Council of State Governments. 1976. *Energy Conservation: Policy Considerations for the States*. Lexington, Ky.: The Council.

Grebler, Leo. 1950. *Production of New Housing: A Research Monograph on Efficiency in Production*. New York: Social Science Research Council.

Hirschberg, Alan, and Richard Schoen. 1974. "Barriers to the Widespread Utilization of Residential Solar Energy: The Prospects for Solar Energy in the U.S. Housing Industry." *Policy Sciences*, Vol. 5, pp. 453-468.

Marketing Research Committee, Producers' Council, Inc. 1975. *Guide to Construction Marketing Research*. Washington: Producers' Council, Inc.

President's Committee on Urban Housing. 1968. *A Decent Home: The Report of the President's Committee on Urban Housing*. Washington: U.S. Government Printing Office.

Pynoos, Jon, Robert Schafer, and Chester W. Hartman, eds. 1973. "Production." In *Housing Urban America*. Chicago: Aldine Publishing Company, pp. 299-305.

Rogers, Everett M. 1962. *Diffusion of Innovation*. New York: The Free Press.

U.S. Bureau of the Census. 1974. *1972 Census of Construction Industries. Vol. II. North Carolina*. Washington: U.S. Government Printing Office.

Chapter 6

Energy Conservation Decisions
for New Housing

Edward J. Kaiser, with Raymond J. Burby

The previous chapter describes the structure of the home-building industry in North Carolina. In this chapter, we explore the industry's energy conservation practices and inclinations. This is done in two ways: (1) by describing the current and emerging status of energy conservation practices in homebuilding; and (2) by exploring various explanations for energy-conserving practices among builders across locations in the state.

The chapter is organized into four main sections. The first is a status report on current and emerging energy-conserving practices in homebuilding. The second and largest section focuses on reasons for the use or nonuse of energy conservation features in new homes by ₁individual builders and by the industry as a whole. The third section discusses builders' satisfactions and problems with energy conservation features, and the obstacles to producing more energy-efficient dwellings. The last section summarizes major findings and suggests policy implications of the empirical analyses.

ENERGY-EFFICIENT FEATURES
IN NEW HOMES: THE STATUS
IN 1978

Information about the status of energy-efficient construction in the fall of 1978 is useful in two ways. First, it has current application as an up-to-date empirical estimate for scholars and policymakers. Second, it can serve ultimately as a bench mark against which future builder surveys can be compared to measure changes in the use of energy efficiency features in residential construction.

There are dozens of design and construction features which can be incorporated into new homes to reduce energy consumption. Many are aimed at improving the thermal performance of the house— that is, they reduce unwanted heat loss in the winter and unwanted heat gain in the summer. These generally focus on reducing heat transfers through the shell of the house—through walls, ceilings and floors, and through and around windows, doors and other openings. Thermal performance also applies to heat loss through ducts and pipes, however, and even heat loss due to the shape of the house and its orientation with respect to sun and wind. Proper orientation of a house can reduce unwanted heat gain and loss and help to capture passively solar heat gains in the winter and cool air in the summer.

Other features are aimed at improving the efficiency of the heating and cooling system. These include the type of equipment and energy used, the controls on the system (such as thermostats), and the supplementary heating and cooling equipment (such as fans, stoves and fireplaces). Care must be taken that the system is designed to match more exactly the heating and cooling needs of the particular dwelling in its particular microlocation.

Much of the examination of energy-conserving practices in this chapter divides the features into these two major groups—those that improve the thermal performance of the dwelling, and aspects of the heating and cooling system.

Features Currently Employed

The use of energy conservation features in new homes by North Carolina homebuilders is summarized in Table 6-1. The twenty features itemized are divided into the two groups mentioned above: (1) types of heating and cooling equipment; and (2) construction features to improve thermal performance with respect to heat gain and loss. The left-hand column of numbers refers to the percent of

Table 6-1. Energy Conservation Features Used by the Homebuilding
Industry, 1978

Energy Conserving Feature	*Estimated Percent*	
	Builders[a]	*Houses[b]*
Heating/Cooling Equipment Features		
1. Heating/cooling system closely sized to match design loads	88	96
2. Heat pump heating/cooling system	82	85
3. Attic fan to draw in cool night air	25	11
4. Clock thermostat on heating/cooling system	14	29
5. Wood stove	5	2
6. Solar hot water heating	4	1
7. Active solar space heating	0	0
Construction Features Affecting the House's Heat Loss/Gain		
1. Storm windows/double glazed windows	93	90
2. Square- or rectangular-shaped house	82	81
3. Insulated ceiling access panel	67	66
4. Insulation exceeding building code standards	64	58
5. Glass area 10% or less of floor area	65	75
6. Landscaped lot with deciduous trees for summer shade	51	49
7. Fireplace which uses outside air for combustion	28	15
8. Insulated hot water pipes	23	34
9. Thirty-inch roof overhang to let in winter sun while providing summer shade	20	8
10. Passive solar heating using a maximum of south-facing glass	10	7
11. 2 x 6 framing for extra insulation	8	5
12. Reflective glass	4	0
13. Insulated shutters	1	0

[a]Percent of builders who used conservation feature on latest speculative house built by firm. ($N = 80$).

[b]This estimate is obtained by weighting the builder's use of the feature by the number of houses he built in 1978. Hence, larger builders received more weight in this "weighted average" approach.

builders in the sample who used the particular feature in their most recent speculatively-built houses. The right-hand column weights the use of the particular feature by the number of houses constructed by the builder in 1978. Thus, use by larger builders received more weight, and the result is an estimate of the percent of new speculative houses that are incorporating a particular feature instead of the percent of builders who are using the feature.

First, with regard to equipment features, it can be seen that two features have been especially widely adopted—the selection of (1) heating/cooling systems to match closely but not exceed design loads (used by 88 percent of the builders and 96 percent of houses), and (2) energy-efficient heat pumps (82 percent and 85 percent, respectively). To improve the thermal performance of the house

> over 90 percent of the builders were incorporating storm or double-glazed windows
>
> over 80 percent were utilizing a square or rectangular shape
>
> about two-thirds had adopted insulated ceiling access panels, insulation exceeding the requirements (R-19 in ceilings, R-11 in walls and floors) of the North Carolina Uniform Residential Building Code, and had limited the glass area to 10 percent or less of the floor area.[1]

The data show that builders are definitely taking steps to produce more energy-efficient homes. However, almost no builders are employing solar features or using reflective glass or insulated shutters.

Emerging Practice: Energy Conservation Features Most Likely to be Employed Next

For a reading on emerging as well as current practice, the study asked builders what feature they would be most likely to add if conditions warranted production of a more energy-efficient dwelling. Table 6-2 shows the responses. The next level of energy-efficient features is most likely to include more insulation (17 percent) and an energy-efficient fireplace (15 percent). In examining relative increases (the proportion of those not already using a feature, but who would go to that feature next), one finds that builders will continue to turn first, to storm windows and increased insulation to improve thermal efficiency, then to heat pumps and working fireplace heating systems. In spite of these observations, the predominant impression is that builders will not adopt any one energy conservation feature. In addition, few are willing to consider solar heating principles yet.

Emerging Practice: Energy Conservation in Subdivision Design

Although most attention to energy conservation in the residential sector has focused on individual homes, additional opportunities

Table 6-2. Energy Conservation Features Most Likely to be Added in the Next House if Conditions Warranted a More Energy-efficient Dwelling[a]

	Percent of Builders Who Would Use the Feature Next (N varies)	
Energy Conservation Feature	*As Percent of the Total Sample (N = 80)*	*As Percent of Those Not Yet Using the Feature*
Insulation exceeding building code standards	17	47
Fireplace which uses outside air for combustion	15	21
Attic fan to draw in cool night air	10	13
2 X 6 framing for extra insulation	8	9
Solar hot water heating	8	8
Glass area 10% or less of floor area	7	20
Insulated hot water pipes	6	8
Storm windows/double glazed windows	4	57
Thirty-inch roof overhang to let in winter sun while providing summer shade	4	5
Heat pump heating/cooling system	3	16
Landscaped lot with deciduous trees for summer shade	3	6
Clock thermostat on heating/cooling system	3	3
Active solar space heating	3	3
Insulated ceiling access panel	1	3
Wood stove	1	1
Insulated shutters	1	1
Passive solar heating using a maximum of south-facing glass	0	0
Square- or rectangular-shaped house	0	0
Heating/cooling system closely sized to match design loads	0	0
Reflective glass	0	0

[a]*Question:* Now, thinking about the energy conservation features that you did not use in that house, which *one* would you most likely use if conditions prompted you to build a more energy-efficient house? (Referring to list of features on the card considered in the previous question)

to conserve are present in the location and design of subdivisions. According to an official of the U.S. Department of Energy, savings through the energy-conscious design of new neighborhoods could result in a 5-percent reduction in national energy consumption by the year 2000 (Leighton 1977).

A number of ideas for saving energy through modifications in neighborhood design and development have been suggested. For example, townhouses, low-rise apartments, and high-rise apartments require about half (or less) the energy for heating that is required by single-family detached homes (Hittman Associates, 1978). Research by the Real Estate Research Corporation (1974) suggests that electricity requirements can be cut by about 25 percent by designing subdivisions with clustered housing and a mixture of dwelling types.

In addition to the clustering of housing, there are a number of other ways to save energy through neighborhood design. For example, one can provide for neighborhood commercial land uses. In Portland, Oregon, it was estimated that if neighborhood grocery stores were available, the number of automobile shopping trips could be reduced by about 15 percent, and the average length of the trips could be reduced 25 percent (Hemphill, 1977). In Davis, California, it has been estimated that by reducing the required width of residential streets and increasing street landscaping, outside temperatures can be reduced by 10° F in the summer, with a consequent 50-percent reduction in the amount of electricity required for air conditioning. Air conditioning loads can also be reduced by orienting subdivision lots properly, preserving deciduous landscaping which screens south-facing windows, and orienting units to capture cooling summer breezes. Additional energy can be saved through the provision of neighborhood walking and bicycling paths. In Portland, Oregon, it was estimated that if paths were available, a 2-percent reduction in shopping, recreation, and school vehicular trips could be achieved (Hemphill, 1977). Also, by designing neighborhoods to preserve "access to the sun" (solar access), options for the future use of solar energy can be preserved (Jaffe, 1978).

Realizing energy savings through neighborhood design will require major changes in the usual ways of subdividing land and adjustments to local land development codes to allow for clustering, energy-efficient streets and lot orientations. In order to evaluate the interest of developers in these new ideas, we first asked the sample of home-builders whether their firms engaged in residential land development. The forty-three firms which were also land developers were then questioned as to how probable it was that their firm would adopt each of a series of nine energy-saving ideas for subdivision design and development. Their responses are summarized in Table 6-3.

A majority of the builder/developers indicated that it was either very probable or somewhat probable that their firms would use four of the ideas during the next five years. These were:

1. location of the subdivision near existing community facilities
2. landscaping with deciduous trees to shade streets in summer

Table 6-3. Probable Use of Energy Conservation Ideas for Subdivision Design[a]

	Percent of Builder/Developers Who Rate Probability of Use During Next Five Years: (N = 43)		
Energy Conservation Idea	*Very Probable*	*Somewhat Probable*	*Not Probable*
1. Location near existing community facilities, such as shopping, schools, employment	59	25	16
2. Landscaping with deciduous trees to shade streets in summer	49	26	25
3. Two or more land uses included in project, such as residential and retail, residential and recreation, residential and employment	30	28	42
4. Cluster design with community open space	19	32	49
5. Bicycle/walking paths	14	33	53
6. Orienting all or most lots in a north-south direction	16	19	65
7. Solar access covenants	9	14	77
8. Narrow street paving to reduce solar absorption	14	7	79
9. Installing one central heating and electric generating system for the entire development	0	2	98

[a]*Question:* In addition to residential building, does your firm also subdivide and develop residential land? If yes, Here is a list of energy conservation features that have been suggested for use in subdivision design and development. [HAND CARD G.] For each, please tell me whether it is very probable, somewhat probable, or not probable that you will use it during the next five years. First, what about . . . .

3. application of two more land uses to reduce travel needs of the residents
4. use of a cluster lot design with community open space.

These practices, of course, will require the least amount of change in the current modes of operation of developers. More radical ideas were much less likely to be viewed as probable candidates for adoption. Only 35 percent thought it was very or somewhat probable that they would attempt to orient lots in a north-south direction; 23 percent indicated some likelihood of using solar access covenants; 21 percent thought they might use narrower streets than usual; only 2 percent thought there was any chance of their using a central heating and generating system (ICES) for a subdivision they might develop. In sum, it appears that while a number of potentially good ideas for saving energy through subdivision design are available, developers must be given more information about their usefulness in saving energy and their market acceptance if they are to be adopted more rapidly. If the facts are not presented in detail, most developers will not make the difficult transition from concept to reality.

FACTORS INFLUENCING THE ADOPTION OF ENERGY EFFICIENCY FEATURES IN THE CONSTRUCTION OF NEW HOUSES

A simple conceptual framework to explain the adoption of energy conservation features by residential builders was used to structure the questionnaire and guide the analysis.[2] As shown in Figure 6-1, we have found it useful to view the adoption of these features as a function of three sets of variables: (1) predisposing factors; (2) an adoption/nonadoption process; and (3) public policy. The focus in this research is the decisions by builders whether or not to adopt energy features in the speculative houses they build.

Literature indicates that two types of predisposing factors should be analyzed: (1) builder characteristics, including both personality traits and the makeup of the firm; and (2) contextual factors, such as climate and housing-market conditions. These predisposing factors supposedly tilt one way or the other the probability of a builder's using energy efficiency features, can influence various aspects of the adoption/nonadoption process, and can possibly modify the effects of public policy on various aspects of energy-efficient construction.

To explain the decisions of builders regarding the incorporation of energy features in speculatively built homes, three sets of variables related to the adoption/nonadoption decision should be measured and evaluated:

1. primary motivation to consider energy-efficiency features
2. criteria used in making final decisions
3. sources used in the development of awareness of initial stimuli and in final decisions.

Builder interest in incorporating energy conservation features into new houses is triggered by some stimulus. It may be market demand, it may be the actions of competitors, or it is possibly an awareness of opportunities, perhaps stimulated by educational or incentive programs of professional associations, public interest groups or government. As builders learn more, they may begin to consider

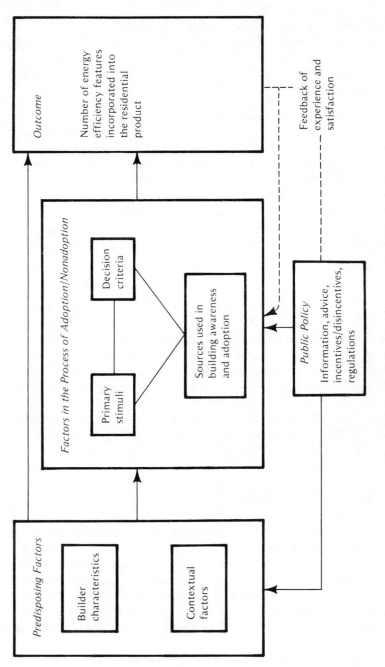

Figure 6-1. Energy feature adoption paradigm.

seriously the adoption of specific energy conservation features in certain houses. The final decision of whether or not to adopt energy conservation technologies and devices depends on the decision criteria that are used, and on how builders assess particular energy conservation features in terms of these criteria. Decision criteria may include market demand, cost, ease of installation, product reliability, and profit margin. Both awareness and decision criteria are thought to depend on the sources of information that builders use, as well as the predisposing factors discussed above.

Public policies may influence decisionmaking directly, such as through building regulations, or indirectly, by affecting predisposing factors, information sources, decision criteria, which then influence energy conservation decisions. In addition, a builder's future use of energy-saving features will be modified by his experience with specific features; hence, feedback operates on the system.

The analysis below will explore the role of the factors outlined in the energy adoption paradigm. Each set of factors is examined primarily in terms of the strength and direction of its relationship to the use of energy efficiency features in the builder's most recently built speculative houses.

The dependent variable, the adoption of energy-saving features, is measured in terms of the number of energy conservation devices (of the twenty listed above in Table 6-1) that the builders used in their most recent speculatively built houses. Three indices of the extent of use of conservation features were created as indicators of the range of energy-saving practice, i.e., the dependent variables: (1) the number of energy-efficient heating/cooling devices used (ranging from none to seven); (2) the number of construction features affecting unwanted heat gain/loss (ranging from none to thirteen); and (3) the total number of either type of feature (ranging from none to a possible twenty).

The Role of Predisposing Factors

Table 6-4 shows the statistically significant relationships between predisposing factors and the number of energy conservation features used in builders' most recently built speculative houses. Builder characteristics are shown in the top part of the table, and contextual factors appear in the bottom part. These variables and others which were ultimately insignificant were selected on the basis of the literature on innovation adoption, the behavior of the firm, and the urban development process.

With regard to personality characteristics and characteristics of the

Table 6-4. Predisposing Factors: The Influence of Builder Characteristics and Contextual Factors on the Use of Energy Conservation Features in New Houses

	Dependent Variables: Number of Features Used^a (N = 80)		
Independent Variables: *Predisposing Factors*	*Energy- efficient Equipment*	*Thermal Efficiency Features*	*Total Number of Features*
Builder Characteristics			
Active involvement in determination of heating system characteristics vs. reliance on sub-contractors	.21	.33	.36
Attitude toward trying new products	NS	.30	.20
Price range of most firms' speculatively built houses	.16	.18	.22
Education	NS	.17	.18
Age	NS	−.18	NS
Number of houses built per year	NS	−.19	−.18
Number of building operations done within firm vs. number subcontracted	.16	.18	.16
Number of years company in business	NS	NS	−.17
Self-concept: more leader than follower	.22	NS	NS
Active involvement in determinations of insulation characteristics vs. reliance on subcontractors	.18	NS	NS
Contextual Factors			
Net migration in county, 1970-1975	−.21	NS	NS
City population growth, 1970-1977	−.23	NS	NS
Percent owner-occupied units in county	NS	.17	NS

^{a}The statistic shown is Kendall's Tau$_c$.
NS = Not statistically significant at the .05 level.

firm, builders who used energy-efficient equipment in their most recently constructed speculative house tended to be more actively involved in determining the heating system and insulation specifications, to think of themselves as leaders rather than followers, and to build more expensive houses on the average. Builders who tended to use more thermal efficiency features were inclined to try new products on their own and to become actively involved in deciding on the heating system. They were also younger and better educated, built fewer and more expensive houses, and integrated a broad range of building operations within the firm. Overall, the evidence suggests that more innovative builders and the ones more involved in the planning and the building processes are those more likely to build more energy-efficient houses. Many other indicators of the builders' social or business ties and the ways in which their firms are organized seem to be entirely unrelated to the use of energy conservation features.[3]

Only three contextual factors (out of thirteen tested) have statistically significant relationships with the number of energy conservation features used in the builders' most recently constructed speculative houses: net migration, population growth and percent of owner-occupied units (vs. rental units) in the housing stock of a particular county. Houses built in slower-growing but wealthier housing markets seem more likely to include energy conservation features than those being built in more dynamic markets. At the same time, other measures of building activity, urbanization, and wealth, such as the rate of building, level of urbanization, median home value and median education, exhibit no relation to the use of energy conservation features. Furthermore, climatic variation, at least within the single state of North Carolina did not play a part.[4] Thus, we conclude that the contextual factors of climate and population dynamics have less effect on the use of energy conservation features in new homes than do builder characteristics.

The Adoption Process: Primary Stimuli

Marketing and Cost Factors. When asked open-ended questions about what caused them to consider a conservation feature in their most recent house and what factors affect the use of energy conservation features in general in their market area, builders emphasized market demand and cost factors above all others (Table 6-5). One-third of the respondents chose either marketing or cost factors as original stimuli in their most recent house, while over 40 percent chose these factors as the best explanation for the overall use of energy conservation features in their market area.

Though market-oriented, most builders do not consider the adoption of energy conservation features as an innovation in the sense of their creating a substantially different housing product to expand beyond their previous markets. Rather, their motivation is "to maintain adequate sales and marketability of . . . houses" of the type they already build for whatever market they are already serving.[5] Thus, the incorporation of energy-conserving features is part of the pattern of conservative, adaptive economic behavior.

Cost and marketability appear to be closely linked. Monetary considerations, both from the standpoint of initial costs (which

Table 6-5. Stimuli to Consider Putting Energy Features into New Houses

Stimulus Category	*Percent of Builders Who Cited Stimulus*	
	With Respect to Their Own Most Recent Speculative House[a] (N = 76)	*With Respect to Builders in General in This Market Area[b] (N = 100)*
Marketing ("sales," "customer demand," "consumer desires")	36	41
Cost factors (mostly cost of energy)	32	43
Awareness/knowledge of energy conservation features	21	25
Technical efficiency	17	NA
Government regulations	5	15
Builder ethics, pride	7	6
Other miscellaneous stimuli (none more than 4 percent)	26	16

[a]*Question:* What was it that caused you originally to consider using (energy feature being probed about most recent speculative house)? (Feature is: extra insulation, 42 percent; heat pump, 39 percent; passive solar heating, 7 percent; 2 X 6 framing, 7 percent; solar hot water, 3 percent; fireplace with outside air, 3 percent.)

[b]*Question:* What do you think are the major factors that affect the use of energy conservation features by builders? (An open-ended question, coded later in the office; not limited to one factor if several mentioned.)

the market must be willing to pay) and operating expenses (which consumers hope to reduce by installing energy-conserving features) are key factors in determining whether energy conservation features are marketable and therefore whether they are included in new homes.

The importance of the marketability/cost relationship is demonstrated further in Table 6-6. Builders were asked what they thought was the best explanation of why consumers hesitate to invest in energy conservation features. As shown in the table, one-third of the builders thought that consumer uncertainty about savings in operating costs was the best explanation. Another quarter of the sample thought that buyers were unwilling (or perhaps often unable) to pay the extra initial cost of added conservation features even if they would save money in the long run. Still another fourth thought that the logical interpretation was that buyers think it takes too long to get back the initial costs. Thus, 80 percent cited one of these three economic reasons.

Table 6-6. Builders' Estimates of the Most Important Reason for Consumer Resistance to Energy Conservation Features[a]

Reason	Percent of Builders Who Cited Reason
Buyers are uncertain about the amount of savings in operating costs	33
Buyers are not willing to pay for extras even if they will save money in the long run	24
Buyers think it takes too long to get back the initial cost of most energy conservation features	23
Buyers are just not that concerned about energy conservation	6
Buyers doubt resale value of energy conservation features	5
Buyers are too conservative and suspicious of anything new or different	2
Other	7

[a]Question: Here is a list of possible reasons for consumer resistance to energy conservation features. [HAND CARD M.] Which do you think is the best explanation of why consumers may hesitate to invest in energy conservation features? (one and only one answer allowed.)

Awareness and Knowledge. Awareness and knowledge ranked third, behind cost and marketing factors, as a stimulus to consider installing energy conservation features in new houses (Table 6-5, above). Twenty-one percent of the builders cited these as factors with respect to their own most recent speculatively-built house, and 25 percent cited them as stimuli for builders in general in their market area. Although well below the percentages of builders who cited marketing and cost factors, awareness and knowledge fall well ahead of other explanations.

Exploring this interpretation a bit further, we find that a high proportion of builders say they are aware of and concerned about the energy situation. Sixty-one percent thought that the need to save energy is very serious, and 68 percent felt that people do not have the right to use as much energy as they can pay for.[6] However, builders get mixed grades on their knowledge of sources of unwanted heat gain and loss in a house. Ninety-one percent know that the standards of the North Carolina Uniform Residential Building Code are required by law and not just recommended. Eighty-nine percent answered correctly that windows are the greatest source of heat loss, compared to the roof, walls or floor. However, only 63 percent answered correctly that cutting infiltration around windows and doors is more effective than adding more insulation over the ceiling.

Still fewer (only 40 percent) realized that a conventional fireplace does not reduce winter heating requirements in a typical house in North Carolina—that in fact, it is a source of heat loss if operated while the heating system is on.

In spite of its high rank (third) among factors cited by builders, a greater knowledge of the causes of unwanted heat gain and loss does not lead to increased use of energy conservation features in new houses. Further, there is no evidence that builders who hold stronger energy conservation attitudes are more likely to use energy-conserving features in the houses they build. In fact, the greater the knowledge of conservation and the stronger the attitude toward it, the less likely were builders to use energy-saving features, although the associations are not statistically significant. The overall conclusion is that builder behavior is unrelated to general attitude and knowledge.

Other Stimuli. Two other factors were mentioned by a significant number of respondents (Table 6-5, above). First, there was technical efficiency (e.g., "better R-values", "cleaner heat") in connection with the builder's most recently built house. The other was government regulations. In addition to indicating that builders in general were influenced by local regulations, most builders cited government regulations when asked what public policy had the most effect on their own firm. The fact that few cited regulations in terms of the application of specific features in their most recent speculative house, however, suggests that after costs and market factors, the use of different energy conservation features may be affected by varying stimuli.

Technical efficiency and regulations are close to being opposite explanations of energy conservation behavior by builders. The first is rooted in a desire to improve voluntarily one's own product, and the second suggests that builders need to be forced to build more energy-conserving houses. Probably both are motivating factors in the decisionmaking process. Regulations are a bigger influence on his own behavior than the builder will admit, and voluntary product improvement is a more important motivation in the industry at large than is indicated in Table 6-5.

In summary, it is clear that marketing and cost considerations are the primary motivations in the adoption of energy-saving features. Other factors, such as attitudes toward conservation, technical knowledge, governmental regulations, and the desire to improve one's product, probably play significant supporting roles. The obvious policy implications are straightforward: (1) encourage buyers to demand energy-efficient houses; (2) reduce the cost of conservation features; (3) make it possible for buyers to pay for such houses more easily; (4) raise the cost of the energy that could be saved by employing conservation features.

The Adoption Process: Final Decision Criteria

Size and Price of the House. Certainly one of the most important factors in the decision of whether or not to use energy conservation features in new construction is the size and price of the house to be marketed. Although only 50 percent of the builders directly stated that the price range of the house was important, Table 6-7 shows clearly that cost does make a difference.

Expensive and/or large homes, and two-story houses, are much more likely to incorporate energy conservation features. For example, over twice as many houses above $55,000 have eight or more energy conservation features as those priced below $55,000.

The principle behind the installation and marketing of energy conservation features is that, although they add to the initial cost, they save money in the longer run. Unfortunately, they add more proportionately to the cost of lower-priced houses, where initial cost is also much more critical in the customer's purchase decision. Thus, it is those least able to afford higher operating costs later who are unable to avoid them by investing in a more energy-efficient house to begin with.

Table 6-7. The Influence of the Size and Price of the House Being Built on the Number of Energy Conservation Features Incorporated

| | Dependent Variable | | |
| | Number of Features Used[a] (N = 50) | | |
Independent Variables: Type of House	Energy-efficient Equipment	Thermal Efficiency Features	Total Number of Features
Two story vs. other (mostly one story)	NS	.26	.23
Size (number of square feet)	.24	.20	.28
Sales price	.23	.21	.28

[a]The statistics shown are Kendall's Tau$_c$.

NS = Not statistically significant at .05 level.

Other Decision Criteria. Builders were also asked explicitly about criteria they used in making the final decision about whether or not to incorporate a feature (as opposed to initial stimulus to consider a feature). Uppermost in their minds at the time of the final decision was marketability, expressed as consumer demand, interest or at least acceptance. As shown in Table 6-8, marketability was mentioned by almost 90 percent of the builders. Furthermore, almost half felt it was the single most important criterion in their final decision. Performance reliability was also an important criterion when it came to the final decision about incorporation of an energy efficiency feature.

Another way to consider decision criteria is to examine a builder's concerns about the risks involved in making decisions about whether or not to use a particular house design or new equipment and materials. From this perspective, initial costs, particularly unexpected costs, emerge as the most important criterion. As shown in Table 6-9, over 50 percent of the respondents listed "incurring higher costs

Table 6-8. Decision Criteria Used in Making Final Decision about Use of Energy Conservation Feature

	Percent of Builders (N = 75)	
Decision Criteria	*Used as a Criterion Perhaps among Others*[a]	*Most Important Criterion*[b]
Likely consumer demand, interest, acceptance	89	47
Performance reliability	69	28
Availability	40	1
Ease of installation	40	0
Cost in comparison with alternatives	36	4
Degree of change from houses company was building	28	1
Use by competition	27	0
Willingness/unwillingness of subcontractors to participate	24	0
Building regulations	20	8
Profit margin	19	1
Others	23	9

[a]*Question:* Thinking back when you were deciding whether to use (NAME OF FEATURE), which of the following factors did you consider in making up your mind about it? [HAND CARD J]

[b]*Question:* Again thinking about the factors you considered in deciding to adopt (NAME OF FEATURE), which factor was the most important in your decision?

Table 6-9. Relative Importance of Five Risk Factors in Using Energy-efficient Features[a]

Risk	Percent Ranking the Risk as (N = 100)	
	Most Important	Second Most Important
Incurring higher costs than expected	51	25
Difficulty in selling the house	19	21
Problems in getting the feature properly installed in the house	13	24
Delay in getting the house completed	11	23
Having to respond to consumer complaints after the sale	6	7

[a]*Question:* These cards list some risks involved in making decisions about house design, materials, and equipment. [HAND CARD DECK TO RESPONDENT] Please look at each of these cards and then stack them in their order of importance in your mind when considering whether to do something different from what you have done in the past. Put the most serious risk on top, then the next most serious, with the least serious on the bottom.

than expected" as the most important of five possible risks in trying something different. Another 25 percent ranked it second in importance. "Difficulty in selling the house", i.e., marketability, was the second most important of these risks, followed closely by "problems in getting the feature properly installed" and "delay in getting the house completed."

To summarize the discussion about final decision criteria, marketability and costs are again the vital considerations for the builder. Whether or not the added costs of the conservation features will be justifiable to the consumer is a question uppermost in his mind. Cost and marketability become especially critical and more difficult to keep under control, as the price of the house goes down. In other words, it is more difficult to market energy conservation features in less expensive houses. Improving the availability, ease of installation and reliability of energy conservation features would further reduce the financial risk to the builder.

Sources of Information about Energy Conservation Features

As shown earlier in Figure 6-1, sources of information for builders are expected to influence the adoption of energy conservation features. If we can (1) identify the sources builders use to find out about energy and determine which are relied upon in making the final adoption/nonadoption decisions, and (2) isolate those sources which are most related statistically to the number of energy-efficient features incorporated into the houses that are built, we will have a powerful tool for channelling information to builders and for further stimulating energy efficiency in new housing.

Builders were asked which of sixteen possible sources they used in finding out about energy conservation features for residential buildings. Table 6-10 shows the extent to which each of a number of sources is used, and the strength of the statistical association between the use of that source and the number of energy-conserving features eventually adopted.

As shown by the first column of figures, builders make use of a wide range of published materials and personal contacts. Every source offered as a possibility was used by at least 40 percent of the builders, and ten of the sixteen sources were used by more than half of the respondents. The three sources marked by asterisks are the ones which builders reported they relied on most in their final decisions about the use of energy conservation features, regardless of how many other sources they used or how often they used them. These three key information sources are the electric power company, the consumer, and the National Association of Home Builders' handbook on energy conservation.

The remaining three columns of the table show the statistical relationship (Tau_c) between the use of each source and the number of energy-conserving features incorporated in the most recent speculatively built house. While the electric company, popular magazines, TV, newspapers, the consumer, and trade publications were all cited by 60 percent or more of the builders, exposure to these sources does not seem to be related statistically to whether or not energy efficiency features are built into new homes. Of the more commonly used sources, only the use of suppliers appears to be strongly related to eventual adoption of energy conservation features. Many of the sources that are used by fewer builders, on the other hand, appear to be much more strongly related to adoption by those who do use them. These include the National Association of Home Builders' handbook on designing, building and selling energy-conserving homes (National Association of Home Builders, 1978), as well as other books, and information from architects. The NAHB handbook is also one of the three sources most relied upon by builders in making their final decision about whether or not to use an energy-conserving feature.

Overall, it seems that the design of a simple yet efficient informa-

Table 6-10. Builders' Use of Sources of Information about Energy Conservation Features and Their Influence on Adoption

Independent Variable: Source of Information about Energy Conservation Features	Percent of Sample Using the Information Source[a] (N = 100)	Dependent Variable: Number of Features Used[b] (N = 80)		
		Energy-efficient Equipment	Thermal Efficiency Features	Total Number of Features
*Electric utility company	79	NS	NS	NS
Suppliers	67	NS	.23	.24
Popular magazines, TV, newspaper	67	NS	NS	NS
*Consumers	61	NS	NS	NS
Trade publications, generally	60	NS	.24	NS
Seminars and meetings on energy	59	NS	NS	NS
Subcontractors	59	NS	NS	NS
Federal government publications	53	NS	NS	NS
*National Association of Home Builders' handbook on energy	51	.29	.27	.34
State government officials	50	.28	NS	NS
Local government officials	46	NS	NS	NS
Other builders	45	NS	NS	NS
Consultant engineers	45	.27	NS	NS
Books	43	.23	.34	.36
Architects	41	.37	.22	.36
Gas utility company	40	NS	.21	.22

NS = Not statistically significant at .05 level.

*Sources builders relied on most in making final decisions about the use of energy conservation features.

[a] Question: Here is a list of possible sources of information about energy conservation features. [HAND CARD H] For each, I want you to tell me whether or not you used it during the past year in finding out about energy conservation features you would include in the houses you have built?

[b] The figures in the table are Kendall's Tau_c.

114

tion program to reach builders is complicated by the wide range of information sources they are exposed to and the fact that those sources most widely used are not the ones most strongly related to the application of energy conservation features. A well conceived handbook by a credible source (like the NAHB handbook) seems to influence considerably those who use it, but only about half the builders cited that particular example. Perhaps the promotion of such a handbook in numerous other sources is advisable.

SATISFACTION, PROBLEMS, OBSTACLES

In addition to the above findings, other factors influencing the continued adoption or nonadoption of conservation features in new homes must be mentioned. They are: (1) the satisfaction of builders with the energy-saving features they have tried; (2) the problems they have had with certain of them; and (3) the obstacles that builders see, or that the analysis indicates, as road blocks to further gains in the level of energy efficiency in new house construction.

Builders were overwhelmingly satisfied with the energy features used in their most recent house. Sixty-three percent were "very" satisfied and 32 percent were "somewhat" satisfied, leaving only 5 percent dissatisfied.

This is not to say that builders experience no problems with energy conservation features. The most commonly experienced problems were higher costs than expected (27 percent); unavailability of material or equipment (22 percent); and improper installation (19 percent). With one exception, problems were not associated with one particular feature more than another. The exception was the unavailability of material. This was a problem for 36 percent of the builders who installed extra insulation, versus 12 percent of the builders who used other energy conservation features.

Satisfaction may itself be an obstacle to improved energy efficiency. For example, air infiltration is a bigger source of unwanted heat loss/gain than conduction through walls, ceilings and floors, even in relatively well constructed houses. A slight crack all the way around a window or door, for example, can be equivalent to a hole four inches in diameter cut through an outside wall. Unfortunately, 96 percent of North Carolina builders said they are satisfied with the "tightness" of their own construction. Even when asked to suggest what steps might lessen air infiltration, 20 percent responded that such steps were not needed. Otherwise, as shown in Table 6-11 most suggestions focus appropriately on cutting down infiltration through and around windows and doors by improving caulking, weatherstripping and insulation around them, and by using fewer, smaller, and better constructed windows and doors.

Thus, while the research has focused mainly on the adoption or nonadoption of energy conservation features in the house, the quality of construction is also vitally important. The way in which equipment and windows are installed and the care with which a dwelling is framed, caulked, weatherstripped and insulated are as important as the type and amount of equipment, windows and insulation used. Quality of construction is one of the difficult issues of energy conservation which the industry and government must address.

While the quality of construction is one barrier to more energy-efficient dwellings, builders identified others in response to direct questioning. As shown in Table 6-12, the primary obstacle from the builders' perspectives appears to be cost—primarily the initial

Table 6-11. Builder-suggested Steps to Insure "Tighter" Houses[a]

Recommended Step	Percent of Respondents Suggesting the Step (N = 100)
Improve weatherstripping, caulking and insulation around doors and windows, and in framing	32
Use storm windows and/or fewer windows	30
Improve quality of workmanship, supervision, inspection to tighten the building generally	30
Add more insulation to attic and walls	19
Use storm doors, insulated doors, and/or do not use sliding glass doors	16
Modify government codes and incentives	8
Improve quality of building products	6
Modify fireplace	4
Modify attic	3
Other modifications to structure, other than those specifically included above	19
Builder believes that reduced air infiltration is not needed	20

[a]Question: Because reducing air infiltration is so important in achieving an energy-efficient house, the quality of construction is critical. What steps do you think could be taken to insure that "tighter" houses are constructed than seem to the case at the present time? (Responses were recorded verbatim and coded at the office into the predetermined categories above.)

Table 6-12. Obstacles to the Building of Energy-efficient Homes[a]

Obstacle	Percent of Builders Who Cited Obstacles (N = 100)
Cost factors (mostly initial cost)	72
Lack of awareness/knowledge (mostly builder, not consumer knowledge)	11
Shortages/unavailability of materials and supplies	9
Inadequate building code or other regulations	3
Marketing factors (lack of consumer demand, consumer preferences, etc.)	3
Technology lacking	3
Other	10

[a]*Question:* What do you think is the biggest obstacle to the building of energy-efficient homes? (An open-ended question, coded later in the office, not limited to one obstacle if several mentioned.)

expense of energy conservation features. This was cited by 72 percent of the sample. Lack of awareness and knowledge, and unavailability of materials and equipment follow, but far behind the cost factor. It should also be observed that, while 41 percent of the builders cited market demand as a key stimulus to more energy-efficient new homes (Tables 6-5 and 6-8), only 3 percent saw lack of such demand as an obstacle (Table 6-12).

SUMMARY OF FINDINGS
AND CONCLUSIONS

Nine major findings regarding energy conservation decisions for new housing emerge from the data and analyses presented in this chapter:

1. Although builders have yet to embrace solar energy widely, high proportions are using a variety of more conventional energy conservation features.
2. Builders are perhaps too satisfied with the air-tightness with which they construct their homes. This is still a major source of potential improvement in the thermal efficiency of new houses.
3. Most do not regard the adoption of energy conservation features as innovative behavior in the sense of creating a new product to reach new markets. Rather, it is adaptive behavior geared to maintain adequate sales and marketability of a

product they are already selling in a market they are already reaching.

4. Marketability and cost considerations (both initial costs and operating expenses) are the key factors in determining whether energy conservation features are included in a house.

5. While most builders have positive attitudes about the need to save energy and many are knowledgeable about how to do so effectively, knowledge and attitudes have little or nothing to do with what they build.

6. Builders appear to be business-minded men who are responding to the marketplace. They build what they think will sell. Whether or not that product is energy-efficient is a result of the marketplace decision to build what will sell.

7. Some builders are more likely to use energy conservation features than others. Those utilizing more energy conservation features in their houses often have smaller firms and tend to be younger and less experienced but better educated. They are innovators in the sense that they are more inclined to try new products than wait to find out how well they work for others. They build more expensive houses on the average and become more actively involved in determining the type and design of the heating/cooling system instead of leaving these decisions to a subcontractor.

8. The size and the price of the house being built are important factors in the likelihood of more energy conservation features being included. Larger, more expensive, generally two-story houses are much more likely than others to have more energy conservation features.

9. Builders use a wide range of sources of information about energy conservation. However, they rely mainly on electric power companies, consumers, and the National Association of Home Builders' handbook on designing, building and selling energy-conserving homes in making final decisions about whether or not to include a feature. Use of the handbook, other books, and information from architects and suppliers are also significantly related, statistically, to the number of energy-conserving features in the builder's most recent speculatively built house.

What are the implications for policy? The findings suggest that educational programs aimed at changing a builder's level of technical knowledge and his attitudes toward energy conservation will have little direct effect. Such educational programs perhaps should be focused on the consumer, to whom the builder responds. Builder-oriented educational programs might instead be better aimed at defining what will and will not sell and showing how to keep down the cost of energy conservation practices so that they can be included in less expensive houses as well as those at the "top of the line." More directly, policies should be generated which (1) make conservation economically attractive by offering financial incentives, (2) reduce the price tag on energy conservation features, and (3) increase the cost of the energy which the features might save. Further suggestions for building industry policy follow in Chapter 7.

NOTES

1. Although comparative national statistics are rare, it appears that with the exception of a much higher use of heat pumps, North Carolina builders' use of energy conservation features is similar to that of builders in other states. For example, a national survey of homebuilders conducted by the Bureau of Building Marketing Research in the spring of 1977 indicated that 95 percent (vs. 93 percent of North Carolina builders) were using storm windows or double/triple glazing; 29 percent (vs. 25 percent) were installing attic fans; 19 percent (vs. 8 percent) were using 2 x 6 framing; and 8 percent (vs. 4 percent) were using solar hot water heating ("How Good Is Your ESP," 1977).

2. The conceptual framework was developed from our own previous research on the residential development industry (Kaiser 1968; Kaiser and Weiss, 1970); research conducted elsewhere on the adoption of innovations (Rogers, 1962; Hunt, 1965; Loy, 1969; Darley, 1978); and a preliminary review of the literature on energy conservation in residential environments.

3. Builder characteristics that exhibited no significant relationship to the use of energy conservation features include: type of business organization; number of employees; number of counties in which the firm operates; years of experience; proportion of the firm's production in speculative homes compared to custom-built homes; number of homebuilders with whom the builder socializes or is acquainted; membership in trade associations; reading of trade journals; and attendance at trade association meetings.

4. Contextual characteristics that exhibited no significant relationship to the use of energy conservation features include: city and county population, county median education, county median home value, level of urbanization in the county, rate of building in the county, and climatic factors such as heating degree days and full-load cooling hours.

5. This statement is based on the response pattern to the following question in the interview: "Which of the following statements comes closer to explaining why you used (NAME OF FEATURE) in the first house you tried it in? (HAND CARD I)

To maintain adequate sales and marketability of my houses

To create a different housing product in order to expand beyond my previous market

More than twice as many chose the first statement (54 percent) rather than the second statement (24 percent); 19 percent chose neither, replying that marketing was not a factor.
6. These percentages compare to 55 percent and 74 percent respectively for consumers in response to the same question.

REFERENCES

Darley, John M. 1978. "Energy Conservation Techniques as Innovations and Their Diffusion." *Energy and Building*, Vol 1, (April), 339-343.

Hemphill, Marion L. 1977. "Urban Form and Energy Conservation." *Energy and the City*, Hearings Before the Subcommittee on the City of the Committee on Banking, Finance and Urban Affairs, House of Representatives, Ninety-fifth Congress, First Session, September 14, 15, and 16, 1977. Washington: U.S. Government Printing Office, pp. 99-130.

Hittman Associates, Inc. 1978. *Residential Energy Consumption Detailed Geographical Analysis. Summary Report.* Office of the Assistant Secretary for Policy Development and Research, Department of Housing and Urban Development. Washington: U.S. Government Printing Office.

"How Good Is Your ESP." 1977. *Professional Builder* (June), pp. 112-126.

Hunt, Lawrence John. 1965. "An Analysis of the Role Communications Agents Play in Influencing Innovation Acceptance Among Home Building Contractors in Eugene-Springfield, Oregon Area." D.B.A. Dissertation, School of Business Administration, University of Oregon.

Jaffe, Martin. 1978. "Protecting Solar Access." *Environmental Comment* (May), pp. 12-14.

Kaiser, Edward J. 1968. *A Producer Model for Residential Growth.* Chapel Hill, N.C.: Center for Urban and Regional Studies, University of North Carolina at Chapel Hill.

Kaiser, Edward J., and Shirley F. Weiss. 1970. "Public Policy and the Residential Development Process." *Journal of the American Institute of Planners*, Vol. 36 (January), pp. 30-37.

Leighton, Gerald S. 1977. "Statement." *Energy and the City.* Hearings Before the Subcommittee on the City of the Committee on Banking, Finance and Urban Affairs, House of Representatives, Ninety-fifth Congress, First Session, September 14, 15 and 16, 1977. Washington: U.S. Government Printing Office, pp. 208-228.

Loy, John W. 1969. "Social Psychological Characteristics of Innovators." *American Sociological Review*, Vol. 34, pp. 73-82.

National Association of Home Builders. 1978. *Designing, Building and Selling Energy-Conserving Homes.* Washington: The Association.

Real Estate Research Corporation. 1974. *The Cost of Sprawl: Environmental and Economic Costs of Alternative Residential Development Patterns at the Urban Fringe: Detailed Cost Analysis.* Washington: U.S. Government Printing Office, April.
Rogers, Everett M. 1962. *Diffusion of Innovations.* New York: The Free Press.

PART III

Residential Energy Conservation Policy and State Government

Chapter 7

State Energy Policy for the Residential Sector

Raymond J. Burby and Mary Ellen Marsden

,

State policies directed toward energy conservation in the residential sector can provide a strong supplement to those outlined in the president's National Energy Plan. Making conservation and efficiency the cornerstone of federal energy policy, the recently passed energy plan included several policies particularly affecting consumption in the residential sector—energy performance standards for new buildings; tax credits for homeowners for retrofitting existing housing; minimum efficiency standards for appliances; direct subsidies to low-income persons for retrofitting; and the establishment of rate structures to encourage energy conservation (U.S. Department of Energy, 1978; Council on Environmental Quality, 1979, pp. 35-39).

These major policy pronouncements are reinforced by those set forth in state energy management plans and by a number of other federal programs. Broadly, these current policies, and those likely to be in effect in the future, fall into several categories: price strategies; supply restriction or allocation plans; regulatory programs; incentive strategies; and information programs (Healy and Hertzfeld, 1975, p. 7). This chapter outlines existing and potential conservation policy in the residential sector, first concentrating on existing housing, and then moving to the new housing market. Since price strategies and supply or allocation strategies are more generally the province of the federal government, here the emphasis is placed on the role of the states in instituting information, incentive, and regulatory strategies.

STATE ENERGY CONSERVATION POLICIES FOR EXISTING HOUSING

Energy conservation in existing housing may be promoted by increasing the number of energy-efficient dwellings that may be selected by consumers, by convincing the populace to retrofit existing homes, or by changing consumer behavior in the direction of less energy-consumptive living patterns. Although energy conservation in existing housing may of course be affected by building practices, it is the state policies affecting consumer energy conservation which are examined here. The next section of this chapter more closely scrutinizes policies for promoting energy efficiency in new homes. Before addressing specific policy proposals emerging from the research findings, we first review the current status of federal and state policies and programs for existing housing. Discussion focuses around the effectiveness of informational, incentive, and regulatory policies for existing housing in the residential sector.

Current Federal and State Policies and Programs for Existing Housing

The current system of informational, incentive, and regulatory policies for the residential sector is based primarily on the Emergency Petroleum Allocation Act of 1973, supplemented by the Energy Conservation and Production Act (ECPA) of 1976 and the National Energy Act (NEA) of 1978 (Healy and Hertzfeld, 1975, p. 8; U.S. Department of Energy, 1978). Under provisions of the ECPA, the states were asked to join with the federal government to reduce energy use by 5 percent by 1980. The responses to this act among the fifty states were assessed here by means of a survey of state energy offices and appear in Supplementary Analysis III appended to this volume. Other strategies set forth under the NEA are discussed in conjunction with the ECPA provisions below.

A central focus of energy policy in the fifty states is the provision of broad-based educational and *information programs* for household residents. Major aspects of the information programs of most states include an energy hotline and clearinghouse for conservation information; community outreach programs such as workshops, training courses, and special interest group presentations; special public school programs; and mass media campaigns. Although the impact of the educational programs is difficult to assess, the states are currently providing a broad range of educational services to residents. An improved energy information base, combined with economic incentives and disincentives, will bring about increased participation in energy conservation.

As outlined in Chapter 3, and in Kaiser, Marsden, and Burby (1979), knowledge of energy conservation techniques is associated with a greater likelihood of conservation practice in existing housing. Informed homeowners are likely to reduce the amount of heating and air conditioning, to use appliances less, and to retrofit their homes. A moderately strong association between energy knowledge and awareness of the energy crisis, and involvement in conservation behavior, was also found by Gottlieb and Matre (1976, p. 26). Thus, information programs may have substantial positive effects in increasing energy conservation, even if the impact of those programs is to increase the energy awareness of residents. Analyses in Chapter 3 reveal that information programs are those most favored by households, with 94 percent of those interviewed favoring government involvement in such programs. In contrast, price, rationing, and regulatory programs receive little public support. In the short term, and in the absence of rationing or radically increased prices, these programs may contribute significantly to energy conservation in the residential sector.

Incentive strategies advanced by federal and state governments include both subsidies for energy conservation practices and taxes on continued energy-wasteful patterns of behavior. The primary focus of many state incentive programs has been the provision of state income tax credits for the retrofitting of homes with solar space or hot water heating or with insulation; fifteen state energy offices interviewed in the supplementary survey noted they had tax credit programs. In addition, twenty-one states had either retrofit or new source loans. These energy conservation loan programs are backed up by extensive financial support from the federal government for home improvements, particularly for the elderly or for moderate-income families.

While previous research has found incentive programs highly effective (Cunningham and Lopreato, 1976, p. 100), those segments of the population most in need of energy savings have participated least in the programs. In North Carolina, figures obtained in the household survey indicate that approximately 7 percent of eligible households took advantage of the tax credit in 1977, the first year it was offered, and 32 percent stated they planned to do so in the future. Participants were disproportionately more affluent and better educated. Although these figures may slightly overestimate the proportion of actual and potential participants due to bias introduced by the telephone survey, it is clear that only a small proportion of eligible households have used the tax credit. Since less than 1 percent of homes in the state are heated by solar energy, it is also a safe assumption that most of the 7 percent used the tax credit to add insulation to their homes. It is expected, however, that as energy supplies become more scarce, incentive programs will play an increasing role in state and federal energy policies.

Regulatory programs are those which place constraints on how energy is used. They set minimum standards for appliances, heating or cooling systems, or the quality of workmanship. Regulatory programs for existing housing are a less integral part of state energy conservation programs than informational or incentive programs; most regulatory programs focus on new or renovated housing. However, fully 73 percent of residents interviewed favored government involvement in setting insulation standards for homes. Other studies suggest that support for regulatory policies increases as awareness of the need to conserve increases (Cunningham and Lopreato, 1976, p. 103). Therefore, regulatory programs may become a more acceptable and effective part of energy conservation planning for states.

Other energy conservation plans available to the states are not readily classifiable as information, incentive, or regulatory programs although they may serve some of these functions. Of the state energy offices interviewed, twenty-eight revealed they provided weatherization of low-income homes, twenty-three provided energy audits, and twelve offered aerial thermal photographs of homes. While the weatherization program to insulate low-income homes is supported financially by the federal government, the other two programs are less extensively used in the residential sector and are offered more on a demonstration basis. These programs are supplemented by others mandated by the NEA—(1) efficiency standards for major home appliances; (2) federally insured loans for conservation improvements in multi-family housing; and (3) voluntary regulatory standards for rate design (U.S. Department of Energy, 1978).

These federal and state energy conservation programs for existing housing will advance the trend toward increasing energy efficiency and conservation. However, a number of other information, incentive, and regulatory programs outlined below will further energy conservation in the residential sector. These proposed programs both extend current programs and offer alternatives for the states to follow.

Proposed Information and Education Policies and Programs

Consumers fully support government involvement in energy information programs, and those programs are in the short run the most effective means of hastening energy conservation in the residential sector. The major policy suggestion based on analyses presented in this report is to expand considerably the energy education effort in the states. Such efforts should be focused on those segments of the population which live in less energy-efficient housing or which could most benefit from information about energy savings from retrofitting investments or conservation behavior. Based on data presented in Chapter 3 regarding sources of energy knowledge, the changes would be most effectively introduced by means of flyers with utility bills, television, or newspapers and magazines. Proposed focuses of energy education programs in the states include the following.

Address Educational Efforts to the Low-Income, Nonmetropolitan Segments of the Population. Analyses presented in Chapter 2 revealed that the least energy-efficient housing existed in lower socioeconomic status and nonmetropolitan households. Although energy consumption tends to be lower for those segments of the population, they could benefit from additional information regarding the means of retrofitting structures, the availability of weatherization programs, the existence of low-interest loans for retrofitting and tax credits for solar heating or insulation, and techniques of further reducing the heating bill via conservation measures. These information programs could be associated with expanded use of home energy audits administered by state energy offices or utility companies.

Publicize Financial Savings from Retrofitting or Energy Conservation Behavior. Information on the estimated financial savings from improvements to the structure or from conservation behavior may speed energy conservation, as indicated in the data in the supplementary analysis by MacRae appended to this volume. A large proportion of respondents underestimated the savings that would accompany energy conservation actions and so hesitated to make investments in retrofitting; that segment of the population might easily become investors if given more accurate information on energy savings. In addition, information on the savings derived from switching from resistance heat to heat pumps and from purchasing life-cycle cost appliances could encourage greater conservation.

Publicize Energy Savings in Alternatives to the Single-Family Detached or in the Smaller Home. The housing stock of most states is largely composed of single-family detached homes, the most energy-consumptive form of housing. As the price of heating and cooling homes increases, educational efforts could effectively publicize the energy savings inherent in multiple-family housing or smaller homes or those with energy-efficient floor plans.

These policy suggestions mark a shift in energy conservation from a primary focus on the need to conserve energy to a new focus on the means of conserving, coupled with the financial benefits of conservation behavior. The proposed changes are ones of emphasis toward those segments of the population most in need of relief from rising energy prices.

Proposed Incentive Policies

Based on the energy savings to be gained from the retrofitting of energy-inefficient homes as well as the substantial proportion of eligible homeowners who plan to use the tax credit in the future, the following proposals are advanced. Although incentive strategies are not a focal point of many state energy plans, energy conservation incentives offer effective means of generating public support for energy conservation.

Initiate or Continue State Tax Credits for Insulation and Solar Retrofitting. As energy prices increase and more homeowners become aware of the availability of tax credits, more are certain to take advantage of such credits and other state incentives. The impact of tax credits on investment behavior, as well as the cost to the states, should however receive extensive study.

Expand Tax Credits to Cover Other Forms of Investment Behavior. Additional savings in energy could be gained by including as part of state tax credit programs such items as the conversion from electric resistance heat to heat pumps, and the addition of woodstoves for major heating uses.

Extend the Availability of Low-Cost Loans. To supplement the above programs, low-cost loans could be made available to more moderate-income households.

Proposed Regulatory Policies

There should be increasing governmental involvement in fostering energy conservation in the area of regulatory policies, which offer highly effective approaches for the residential sector. Although most current regulatory programs focus on new housing, the programs suggested below are designed to supplement the more stringent requirements for new homes.

Institute Disclosure Regulations for the Cost of Heating and Cooling. For both rental and owner-occupied dwelling units, information for new residents on the costs of heating and cooling the dwelling unit during the past year could ease the financial burden of increasing energy costs. However, since the behavior of past residents can significantly influence the amount of energy consumed, disclosure regulations may offer a misleading picture of the energy efficiency of the structure. Clearly, a means must be found to arrive at consistent, standardized estimates based on structural characteristics of housing to supplement information provided by heating and cooling bills.

Institute a Consumer Protection Plan for Quality of Retrofitting. As the proportion of households improving the thermal efficiency of their homes increases, the need for control over the quality of such improvements also increases. The quality of installation may be more important than the amount of insulation added. In this state, 73 percent of households interviewed favored greater governmental regulation of insulation standards.

Establish Utility Rate Structures to Reward Conservation. Although voluntary rate structures are an integral part of the National Energy Plan, the states could encourage changes in rate structures or pricing for electricity and gas utilities, nonregulated utilities, and home heating suppliers, in order to hasten the move toward the goal of reduction in energy use.

The programs outlined above are not exhaustive, but they are indicative of the type of programs that could be instituted or expanded at the state level to increase energy conservation in existing housing. Although the necessary stage of the calculation of costs and benefits must be completed prior to the establishment of these programs, they would appear to meet a necessary criterion of consumer acceptance. Further criteria to be evaluated include program effectiveness, efficiency, and the equity of program impact across segments of the population (Healy and Hertzfeld, 1975; Olsen and Goodnight, 1977). Previous research has suggested that these programs can effectively bring about energy conservation. In addition, each program addresses the problem of providing equitably for the needs of all segments of the population as rising energy prices negatively influence lower-income households.

STATE POLICIES FOR ENERGY CONSERVATION IN NEW HOUSING

In addition to addressing household use and conservation of energy, the states have also attempted to save energy through policies and programs focused on the new housing segment of the residential sector. In this section, we briefly review current federal and state policies for new housing and then draw on the findings of our research to suggest a number of additional policy and program initiatives.

These suggestions have not been subjected to a rigorous policy analysis. They are ideas that may prove to be effective ways of promoting energy conservation in the residential sector based on the current attitudes and business behavior of consumers and builders. Before the states proceed further with them, the proposed policies should be subjected to at least two additional sets of analyses. First, while we believe each of the policies and programs we suggest will result in additional energy savings, better estimates of the magnitude of the potential savings are needed. Second, estimates will also be needed of the cost, both to government and to the private sector, of implementing each of the proposed policies and programs. Given these two caveats, we believe the research reported in this volume provides a much improved foundation for the formulation of the next round of energy policies for new housing in the states.

Current Federal and State Policies and Programs for New Housing

Any new policy initiatives for new housing must build on the existing federal and state policy framework for this segment of the residential sector. At the federal level, three sets of policies seem particularly important. First, any new state policies designed to improve the thermal efficiency of new housing must take into account federal standards mandated by the Energy Conservation and Production Act of 1976. Standards are being developed by the U.S. Department of Housing and Urban Development and U.S. Department of Energy and are to be adopted by the states by 1980. Second, the National Energy Act of 1978 strengthened appliance standards legislation originally adopted in 1975. A number of appliances installed in new housing, including furnaces, water heaters, room and central air conditioners, kitchen ranges and ovens, and refrigerators, will now be subject to federal minimum efficiency standards. According to Hirst and Carney (1978), the federal thermal efficiency and appliance programs will result in significant reductions in the growth of energy consumption in the United States. The third federal program of note, the Solar Demonstration Effort of the Department of Housing and Urban Development, has long-term implications for energy conservation in the residential sector. The program offers grants for approved solar systems as a means of encouraging widespread use of solar energy in new housing. Through the first four of five proposed cycles, 558 grants were awarded.

Energy policy for new housing in the states has also followed three major thrusts: (1) thermal efficiency standards for new construction; (2) information and education programs pursued under the Energy Policy and Conservation Act/Energy Conservation and Production Act programs; and (3) tax incentives to stimulate the adoption of solar energy systems. In the case of North Carolina, it is noteworthy that over 90 percent of the homebuilders we interviewed were aware that building standards existed and were required by law. Almost nine out of ten (89 percent) of the builders who were aware of them thought that the standards were being enforced effectively in the communities in which they were building homes.

Taken together, federal and state energy conservation programs affecting new construction should result in the production of more energy-efficient new housing. One indicator of the impact of these programs is builders' reports of policies which in their opinion have influenced their use of energy conservation features. When asked about policy impacts, almost half of the builders we interviewed (45 percent) indicated that building code standards had the most effect on their use of energy conservation features. Another 6 percent cited not the code itself, but its enforcement. Far fewer builders felt that other state or federal policies had had the most effect on their use of energy conservation features. Ten percent mentioned the availability of information dealing with energy conservation, and 4 percent cited FHA, FmHA, and other federal minimum-property standards. Further influence factors (less directly tied to specific public policies) that were mentioned included utility company standards and energy conservation advertising (14 percent); consumer demand (10 percent); and the cost of energy or of energy conservation features (6 percent). Only 22 percent of the builders felt that government programs were having no effect at all on their use of energy conservation features.

Proposed Information and Education Policies and Programs

As noted above, 10 percent of the builders we interviewed thought that information provided by agencies was the one factor most responsible for their use of energy conservation features. We asked builders what *kinds* of information they needed in order to make better decisions regarding the adoption of energy conservation features in the homes they built. The most frequent responses were:

1. information about building product characteristics, including their reliability and effectiveness (mentioned by 34 percent)
2. details of the cost implications of energy conservation features, including the added expense of using a feature and the cost and amount of energy saved by the feature—its overall cost effectiveness (34 percent)
3. information on consumer demand for energy conservation features (9 percent)
4. instruction on solar energy (9 percent)
5. the provision of one reliable source of information about energy in housing (4 percent).

Only 10 percent of the builders volunteered that they already had all of the information they needed about the energy efficiency of housing.

Expand Workshops, Seminars, Educational Material. Builder interest in obtaining additional information about conservation features suggests that the states could play a very useful role in assembling, packaging, and distributing information about energy conservation in homebuilding. Although energy-related information is available from the major national trade association—the National Association of Home Builders (NAHB)—a sizable proportion of builders (at least a third in North Carolina, for example) are not members and so are unlikely to be aware of the NAHB publications. However, even members of the national association would benefit from a state-run energy information service. Information related to energy conservation in homebuilding is currently being issued by a vast array of sources, ranging from federal agencies to craft unions to building materials suppliers to associations of suppliers. A continuing workshop and seminar series, backed up with easily digested summaries of the latest developments in energy and homebuilding, would provide a means for all builders in a state to keep pace with this rapidly changing field.

Establish a Lending Library of Publications Related to Energy and Homebuilding. Builders, architects, subcontractors and others concerned with the energy efficiency of housing need a single, central source of information about this field. Each state could greatly assist in the dissemination of energy-related information if one unit was funded specifically to acquire information related to energy in homebuilding, provide catalogs and lists of available publications, and distribute materials on a lending basis to firms and individuals throughout the state.

Establish State Institutes for Builders. In addition to easy access to more information, homebuilders need an organization that can assemble information about energy conservation and other aspects of building, process the data in terms of builder needs in each state, and issue authoritative advice and recommendations about the effectiveness and dependability of new building and development materials, processes, and techniques. At the conclusion of our homebuilder interview, we asked builders whether they thought there was a need for a state institute for builders and whether they would be willing to support financially such an institution. Almost half of the builders (48 percent) thought that the need was great and said that they would pay $100 a year to support such an effort. Another 27 percent thought the need high, but were not willing to pay $100 a year for such an institute's services. Only a quarter of the builders felt that there was little need for a builders' institute at this time. Given the perceived need for such a service and builder interest in it, state governments should actively explore the establishment of individual state building institutes.

Establish a Market Research Service. Providing better information about energy conservation features is one method of reducing the risk involved in their use and speeding up builder adoption of the features. As our research indicates, however, builders are also often concerned about the market for them. In particular, they need to know about the kinds of energy conservation features consumers are interested in and how much consumers are willing to pay for houses equipped with them. In addition, builders seek information on the market segments that are most likely to be buyers of particular energy-efficient housing types (such as the $10,000 - $14,999 income bracket that may be a major market for cluster housing) and of particular energy conservation features. Because of the localized nature of the building industry and the housing markets the industry serves, statewide market information is not likely to be of much help. Builders need better information about the markets they serve, which are usually restricted to one or two counties (or even portions of counties in the case of metropolitan areas of a state).

As another means of promoting the construction of energy-efficient homes, the states could provide market research services for homebuilders. Possibly at first on a trial basis, the states would finance the preparation of "Housing Energy Market Reports" for each county or other housing market area. The reports would be made available, at a nominal price, to homebuilders, subcontractors, building materials suppliers, architects, and others involved in the homebuilding industry so that these groups could more accurately gauge the demand by consumers for energy-efficient homes and housing products and their willingness to pay for them. The reports would be updated periodically. In addition to providing needed information to the housing industry, the Housing Energy Market Reports would over time enable state energy officials, utility companies, and others promoting the energy consciousness of households to gauge the success of their efforts to stimulate consumer demand for energy-efficient housing.

Continue Research and Demonstration Programs on Energy Conservation in the Residential Sector. In order that energy conservation ideas be adopted by the homebuilding industry, their value needs to be clearly illustrated. While some builders will adopt a new feature or building technique based on what they have read about it, many others need to see the feature in place or in use. Thus, in the promotion of energy conservation in the homebuilding industry, there is a clear place for continuing demonstration efforts. Any demonstrations funded should include steps to inform builders of the demonstration, to show it to them, and to discuss it in terms that are relevant to builder concerns regarding cost, ease of installation, dependability, and consumer reaction.

Based on the results of our research, the energy conservation technology most in need of further demonstration is solar energy. As shown in Chapter 6, homebuilders have yet to use solar energy features in new construction in any great numbers. Demonstrations of solar housing should be designed not only to indicate the technical feasibility of particular solar energy systems, but also to show how major consumer reservations can be overcome. Aspects of solar energy of particular concern to homebuilders include high initial costs (99 percent of the builders interviewed rated this as a major consumer reservation); the need for a supplemental heating system (77 percent thought this was a major consumer objection); and the question of the reliability of the system (71 percent rated it a major consumer reservation).

Beyond the funding of demonstrations of solar energy and other new energy conservation technologies, there is a clear need for continued research related to the production of residential environments. Homebuilding is an extremely complex industry involving scores of different types of firms. While the present study provides a foundation for policies which would affect the homebuilding firm itself, we know relatively little about the various supporting firms and the decisionmakers whose actions are equally critical to the production of energy-efficient housing. These include:

1. land developers, who prepare residential sites for building
2. site planners (planners, architects, landscape architects, civil engineers, and surveyors), who are employed by development firms to design specific projects
3. craft and specialty subcontractors, who put together various parts of housing and whose actions have major impacts on the energy efficiency of the finished product
4. representatives of building material firms and appliance supply and manufacturing companies, who are instrumental in the distribution of energy-efficient products to homebuilders and subcontractors
5. realtors, who market finished houses and who may sensitize consumers to the energy conservation features of housing.

Finally, the research reported in this volume focuses on only one segment—ownership housing—of the residential sector. The rental market also is critical to the energy efficiency of housing in the United States. Studies must be performed on the attention investors give to the energy efficiency of new rental housing and on the ways in which landlords can be induced to improve the energy efficiency of existing rental housing units in the states.

Proposed Incentive Policies

Incentives are a second major class of policies that can be used to stimulate the production of energy-efficient housing. Because of the highly competitive nature of the homebuilding industry and its consequent sensitivity to the "first costs" of energy conservation investments, incentives are a particularly appropriate class of policies to bring about change in the industry.

Tax Credits for New Construction. Existing tax credit programs in the states could be expanded and modified to address more directly the new construction segment of the residential sector. For example, if solar energy tax credits or incentive grants were available directly to the builder, builders could lower the prices of solar houses to make them more competitive with housing equipped with conventional heating systems. This might reduce some of the uncertainty involved with, for example, the tax credits, so that they have a more direct effect on consumer demand. In addition, where restricted to active systems, eligibility for solar tax credits could be expanded to include passive solar systems. Even though the definition of such systems may create administrative difficulties, the most effective active solar systems often cannot be designed unless they incorporate various passive solar energy principles. If the required passive features increase construction costs but are not eligible for tax credits, builders may have to design and install less than optimal solar systems or they may be discouraged from using solar energy at all. In addition, since the cost effectiveness of active solar space heating in many states has yet to be demonstrated, passive solar energy applications may have the greatest potential for reducing consumption of conventional fuels and electricity.

As shown in Chapters 5 and 6, homebuilders often install wood-burning fireplaces, thus making use of a plentiful fuel in many states. However, the fireplaces often have little value in home heating. The technology does exist to construct and install energy-efficient fireplaces, woodstoves, fireplace insert heaters, and furnaces for use as primary and supplemental heating systems. However, because these systems add more to the cost of the home, builders are apparently reluctant to use them to any great degree. In order to stimulate builders to construct and install energy-efficent forms of woodburning home heating devices, consideration should be given to extending a modified tax credit (modified to make it claimable by the builder) for them.

100-Percent Financing of Energy Conservation Features. Builder concern about the cost of energy conservation features (Chapter 6) might be overcome if such costs did not add to the equity investment required to purchase a new home. For example, if builders could show that annual savings in the costs of operating the home were greater than the increased principal and interest payments required to finance the installation of a package of energy-saving features, such features would make a positive contribution to home sales. In order to induce builders to take this approach, the states should consider establishing a revolving second mortgage loan fund applicable to the increased costs arising from the use of selected energy conservation features. Standard "extra" costs could be established for various energy conservation features, with second mortgage funds made available to home purchasers to cover these costs. If interest rates were set at a rate equal to the cost of money to the state, plus administration of the program, it might be highly attractive to home purchasers and builders alike.

Alternatively, of course, if lending institutions took home operating costs into account in determining required loan to home value ratios and other loan terms, a similar result might be obtained without the establishment of major new state programs. For example, if energy conservation investments reduced utility costs more than they increased interest payments, households would have an enhanced ability to meet their mortgage payments, so that a lower down payment (equity investment) might be justified.

Raise Price of Energy Used in Housing. According to the Council on Environmental Quality (1979, p. 41), recent studies show that the elasticity of demand for energy is much more sensitive to price than had been thought previously. Therefore, policies which use increased prices to promote energy conservation may now be more effective (and less subject to criticism for contributing to inflation) than they have in the past. One means of promoting energy conservation in the residential sector, of course, is to increase further the costs of heating, cooling, and other household uses of energy through the imposition of state taxes on electricity, fuel oil, and natural gas. As the price of energy increases, households will make stronger demands on builders for homes that minimize the use of expensive energy. Equity problems—increased hardships placed on lower-income households—might be overcome if the receipts from such a tax were used to finance low-income weatherization programs at a scale more in keeping with the housing problems of the urban and rural poor in the United States.

Tax Energy-Inefficient Housing Characteristics. A case might be made for requiring households to pay the true social costs of their preferred ways of life. As shown earlier in this report, households overwhelmingly prefer single-family detached houses even though such houses use more energy per square foot than dwellings built at higher densities. Like the gas-guzzling automobile, the energy-guzzling house could be taxed at a higher rate than more energy-efficient houses. In addition to housing type, such a tax could be based on other characteristics that have demonstrated energy waste implications, such as the type of heating and cooling system, the orientation on the lot, and the amount of insulation. Alternatively, energy consumption per square foot could be calculated using standard models based on housing size and structural characteristics, and the tax could be based on estimated Btu per gross square foot per year. The housing energy use tax could be administered through the county-level property tax system, with energy-use estimates for houses adjusted each year to take into account retrofit investments. Presumably, as the cost of owning and operating energy-inefficient housing increased, households would create an effective demand for housing that incorporated various energy conservation features. As with the tax on electricity and home heating fuels, proceeds of the "energy-guzzling house tax" could be used to weatherize houses owned or rented by poorer families, thereby reducing some of the inequities that such a tax would create for households least able to afford decent housing. These inequities might also be reduced if the "energy-guzzling house tax" were applied only to new housing; on the other hand, this would further reduce the ability of low- and moderate-income households to afford a new home.

Proposed Regulatory Policies

A third approach to improving the energy efficiency of new housing is through mandatory regulations. As noted above, homebuilders themselves rated building codes as the major factor inducing them to use various energy conservation features. Building codes could be modified to require the use of additional features that have been shown to be cost-effective in reducing energy consumption. In addition, regulations could be adopted to improve the energy performance of other segments of the housing industry, such as subcontractors and developers, and to increase consumer ability to exert an effective market demand for energy-efficient housing products.

Add Additional Energy-Saving Ideas to Features Required in Building Code. Most state building codes, as they apply to single-family detached houses, are like a cookbook—an energy-efficient house requires various ingredients, such as a certain amount of insulation, a certain amount of glass surface area and the like. Given this approach, it makes sense to add to the "recipe" any energy conservation features that have been shown to be cost-effective in most applications. For example, it was reported in Chapter 6 that less than half of the builders interviewed were using each of ten features that appear to save more in energy costs than they cost to purchase (fabricate) and install. These include:

attic fan
clock thermostat
fireplace which uses outside air for combustion and provides
  supplemental space heating
reduced glass area
insulated hot water pipes
2 X 6 framing to allow extra insulation and tighter intersections
insulated shutters
reflective glass
microwave oven
roof overhang for shade in summer.

Other suggestions of devices which would reduce consumption (NAHB Research Foundation, 1979, pp. 51-57) include storm doors, 24-inch o.c. wall framing, appropriate roof colors, insulated ducts, and the use of fluorescent lights for selected areas of the home. While not all of these are appropriate for inclusion in the statewide building code, consideration should be given to the use of the code as a device for promoting the widespread use of those which have a very high benefit/cost ratio and which are clearly in the best interests of the people of a state.

Address the Quality of Construction in the Building Code/Provide

State Technical and Financial Assistance for Local Building Inspection. Studies have shown that air infiltration is a serious problem in energy conservation. According to Harrje (1978), for example, about one-third of the total energy is lost as air moves into a house, is heated or cooled, and then moves out of the house. A key means of reducing air infiltration is through tighter construction. According to Seidel, Plotkin and Reck (1973, p. 55)

> Exfiltration loss could be reduced 50 percent if regulations were written and enforced to include quality of installation as well as quality of material.
>
> Modifications to insure proper fitting of doors and window frames and caulking of leaks, could also result in major reductions of infiltration losses.

Presumably, standards for acceptable rates of air infiltration could be established and made part of a building code. Alternatively, by means of the cookbook approach, standards related to the performance quality of various operations needed to build a tight house could be developed, with simple indicators formulated so that the standards could be enforced by inspectors in the field. If more complex building code standards are adopted, the state should explore methods of insuring that the standards are adequately enforced at the local level. These methods could range from state-generated training programs to state monitoring of the quality of local inspection to the provision of state financial assistance to enable localities to employ qualified persons for this vital task.

Establish Energy Conservation Standards for Used Housing. One means of encouraging home retrofitting is to require existing homes to meet state-specified energy conservation standards for thermal efficiency and heating and cooling equipment when ownership is transferred. While such a policy has obvious benefits in terms of the energy efficiency of the existing housing stock, it should also promote the production of energy-efficient new homes. If used houses have to meet standards similar to those required of new houses, homebuilders will not suffer as great a cost disadvantage in competing with used housing coming on the market. As a result, they should be less likely to turn away from various energy conservation features because of cost considerations.

Mandatory Disclosure of Home Energy Operating Costs. In order to increase consumer awareness of the energy costs involved in home operation and to provide a means for households to consider energy-related operating costs when choosing a house to purchase or rent, the state could require that energy operating costs be disclosed when housing ownership is transferred. These costs could be expressed in terms of the actual or estimated fuel and electricity use for a preceding or a future time period (the last or the next twelve months) or in terms of estimated Btu expended per gross square foot per year. As noted in Chapter 5, half of the homebuilders interviewed favored such a policy for new housing. If it also applied to used housing, consumers would be able to choose between new and used housing on the basis of energy efficiency as well as cost and other residential choice factors.

Promote Adoption of Passive Solar Energy Principles. In Chapter 6, the potential energy savings of a variety of passive solar energy concepts in landscaping, housing orientation, and neighborhood design were documented. However, it was also noted that relatively few builders or developers were incorporating passive solar energy principles in either the homes they constructed or the subdivisions they were developing. Careful consideration should be given to several means whereby the states can promote accelerated use of passive solar energy in the residential sector. As a start, the states could amend their subdivision regulation enabling legislation to make energy conservation a valid purpose of subdivision regulation. Second, model subdivision regulations incorporating various passive solar energy and other "neighborhood" energy conservation concepts could be developed and promoted among local governmental officials in a state, along with documentation of the energy savings possible through passive solar design. Third, building codes could be amended so that builders were required to consider the potential for passive solar energy in the orientation of housing units, design of roof overhangs, size and location of windows, use of landscaping, and other characteristics of residential sites and structures.

Consider Mandatory Licensing. In order to insure that solar and conventional HVAC equipment is designed and installed properly, that insulation, caulking and weatherstripping are properly installed, and that other energy-efficient construction procedures are followed, licenses could be required of various installers, subcontractors, and craftsmen involved in the homebuilding industry. Before a license were issued, the applicant could be required to demonstrate knowledge of the energy-related aspects of the particular job or procedure for which the license was being sought. In addition, to keep licenses current, holders and applicants could be required to participate in short courses and occasional training sessions to acquaint them with new developments and techniques.

Builders' Evaluations of Energy Policy Options

During the interviews with homebuilders, the respondents were asked to consider a range of public policies for new housing, including many of those discussed above, and to indicate which *one* policy they thought would be most effective in producing more energy-efficient new home construction. Although some policies drew more support than others, there was no consensus that any one policy would be most effective. Those deemed likely to be most effective, and the proportion of builders who thought so, were:

bigger tax credits for homeowners (22 percent)
100-percent financing of energy-saving features—i.e., no down payment (19 percent)
development of practical solar heating systems (18 percent)
better enforcement of building code requirements (15 percent)
higher prices for fuel and electricity (10 percent)
education of lenders to accept life-cycle costing principles (8 percent)
retraining programs for builders (6 percent)
retraining programs for subcontractors (1 percent).

The variety of viewpoints about the *most* effective policy to promote energy conservation in new home construction reflects the diversity and complexity of the homebuilding industry. In addition, it may indicate that the states cannot rely on any one policy or even a small group of policies to achieve their residential energy conservation objectives. Instead, a mix of policies, spanning the entire range discussed above, might be appropriate. Finally, it seems worth reiterating that given the complexity of the homebuilding industry, randomly selected policies for promoting improved energy efficiency in new housing will probably produce less than satisfactory results. Policies must be selected and formulated so that they combine into a coherent program of energy conservation for the homebuilding industry.

CONCLUSION

The trend toward building for energy efficiency in the residential sector has been explored in this book by examining the current status of the thermal efficiency of existing housing and builder practices in new housing. Residential structures are becoming more energy-efficient as a result of both advances in building technology and consumers' improvement to their homes. However, the process of improving the thermal efficiency of residential structures may be hastened.

The states can play a significant role in this process by continuing and expanding current energy conservation programs in three areas—information, incentives, and regulations. Such programs can increase consumer awareness and hence consumer investment in more energy-efficient structures. People's demand for energy-efficient structures, in turn, will increase builder use of energy-saving features in new homes. The end result is the increased availability of energy-efficient structures, and progress toward meeting state energy conservation goals.

This study has revealed a number of obstacles toward the more efficient use of energy in the residential sector. Consumers are notably resistant to change in the type and design of residential structures. They prefer the more energy consumptive single-family detached dwelling. Builders tend to respond not to advances in construction practices, but to consumer demand. Thus, consumers and builders act to perpetuate the building of the more conventional, energy-inefficient structures. However, skyrocketing energy costs are fostering consumer demand for energy-efficient structures and will increasingly encourage the building of more efficient structures.

State policy can mold this trend toward energy-efficient structures by providing insulation standards, information on conservation techniques and retrofitting, and incentive programs. In each of these programs the states can encourage the production of less energy-consumptive dwellings and can attempt to provide equitably for the needs of all segments of the residential sector. This chapter has indicated current and potential programs to accomplish these goals.

We have identified a number of new avenues for the study of the diffusion of innovation of energy-saving features in the residential sector. Although these analyses have primarily examined energy conservation in new housing and the retrofitting of existing housing, an important topic of future study is the status of energy conservation in the rental sector and the means of increasing conservation here. Such a study would focus on both the residents and investors in rental housing. Another fruitful line of inquiry is a more intensive study of the adoption of alternative technologies, such as solar energy, in the housing industry. A parallel study of solar builders and homeowners could provide useful information on means of increasing the rate of adoption of solar space or hot water heating.

Finally, the fragmentation of the building industry brings to bear a number of key decision agents in the process of adoption of innovation in the industry. This fragmentation also necessitates the further study of subcontractors or investors who may either facilitate or inhibit the process of building for energy efficiency.

REFERENCES

Bultena, Gordon. 1976. *Public Response to the Energy Crisis: A Study of Citizens' Attitudes and Adaptive Behaviors*. Ames, Iowa: Iowa State University, Department of Sociology.

Council on Environmental Quality. 1979. *The Good News About Energy*. Washington: U.S. Government Printing Office.

Cunningham, William H., and Sally Cook Lopreato. 1976. *Energy Use and Conservation Incentives: A Study of the Southwestern United States*. New York: Praeger Publishers.

Gladhart, Peter Michael, James J. Zuiches, and Bonnie Maas Morrison. 1978. *Energy Policy in the United States: Social and Behavioral Dimensions*. New York: Praeger Publishers.

Gottlieb, David, and Marc Matre. 1976. *Sociological Dimensions of the Energy Crisis: A Follow-up Study*. Houston, Texas: University of Houston, The Energy Institute.

Harrje, David T. 1978. "The Twin Rivers Experiments in Home Energy Conservation." In Raymond J. Burby and A. Fleming Bell, eds., *Energy and the Community*. Cambridge, Mass.: Ballinger Publishing Company, pp. 19-23.

Healy, Robert A., and Henry R. Hertzfeld. 1975. *Energy Conservation Strategies*. An Issue Report. Washington: The Conservation Foundation.

Hirst, Eric, and Janet Carney. 1978. "Effects of Federal Residential Energy Conservation Programs." *Science*, Vol. 199 (24 February), pp. 845-851.

Kaiser, Edward J., Mary Ellen Marsden, and Raymond J. Burby. 1979. "Energy Conservation Practices in the Production and Use of Residences in North Carolina." Paper presented at the First Annual Urban Affairs Conference, Asheville, North Carolina.

Minan, John H., and William H. Lawrence. 1978. "State Tax Incentives to Promote the Use of Solar Energy." *Texas Law Review*, Vol. 56, pp. 835-859.

NAHB Research Foundation, Inc. 1979. *Insulation Manual: Homes, Apartments*. Rockville, Md.: The Foundation.

Olsen, Marvin E., and Jill A. Goodnight. 1977. *Social Aspects of Energy Conservation*. Seattle, Washington: Battelle Human Affairs Research Centers.

Seidel, Marquis R., Steven E. Plotkin, and Robert O. Reck. 1973. *Energy Conservation Strategies*. Socioeconomic Environmental Studies Series, EPA-R5-73-021, 1973. Washington: U.S. Government Printing Office.

United States Department of Energy. 1978. *The National Energy Act*. Washington: The Department of Energy.

Supplementary Analyses

Rational Models for Consumer Energy Conservation[1]

Duncan MacRae, Jr.

As energy supplies dwindle, we increasingly consider not only alternative sources of energy but also the more efficient use of what we have. Among the possible sources of efficiency are changes in consumer behavior, or considered more broadly, in styles of life. We may buy more efficient cars and homes, add insulation, join car pools, ride bicycles or walk, dress more warmly and keep our residences cooler in winter, and take other steps to conserve.

Changes of this sort may be brought about not only by individual actions, but also as the result of government policies. Governments may restrict energy supplies, encourage the development of new products, regulate and inspect those that are sold, tax some products and provide rebates on others, or inform or persuade the public (Burby and Marsden, Chapter 1 of this volume). This last type of activity—information or persuasion—is of particular interest because in a free society it must be kept within limits. If abused, governmental persuasion can be a means for circumventing democratic processes and maintaining an incumbent government in power. Even the power to provide information, as by control of a national television network, has similar risks. Governmental information systems are nevertheless widely used—an example being the information provided by the U.S. Department of Agriculture to farmers.

The purpose of this section is to explore conditions under which North Carolina citizens might be amenable to energy conservation through the furnishing of information—by state or local government, utility companies, or other sources. The information in question would center about the monetary savings that citizens could expect to obtain by allowing their homes to remain cooler in winter or by buying more energy-efficient refrigerators, homes, or cars.

A second and related purpose is to compare with other models the economic model of human behavior, which assumes rational maximization. I shall assume at the start, as economists often do, that people are rational maximizers of income.[2] This may be an extreme assumption for our household survey respondents; but because it is widely used yet seldom tested by surveys, such a test is desirable. From this assumption I shall draw conclusions as to how survey respondents might be expected to behave in setting home temperature. I shall also draw conclusions as to how they should respond to one question about investment for conservation, in view of their responses to other questions.

The comparison of rational models with other models for inducing changes in behavior relates to various sorts of public policies. Energy shortages and population growth, both aspects of a global problem, actually confront governments with similar choices. Governmental policies may be first directed at providing information, in hopes that the citizen's or the consumer's self-interest will lead to the conservation of energy or to the curtailment of fertility. If, however, self-interest is not a sufficient motive to provide the changes that society needs, governments (and citizens through them) may consider models of altruistic behavior (Leik and Kolman, 1978) or stronger methods for altering behavior. Because of this similarity, the analysis of policies for energy conservation should be able to benefit from the literature on policies for fertility control, in which rational economic models have also been advanced (Becker, 1976, Ch. 9).

Questions of the sort studied here, requiring respondents to answer tradeoff items in monetary terms, are not often asked in surveys; here and in other such studies (McKinney and MacRae, 1978) a considerable proportion of non-response has been obtained. For this reason our results are based on a small proportion of the overall sample, as we shall indicate in the tables. Corresponding caution in interpretation is required.

This analysis will consist of two major parts: (1) an examination of how much money respondents would require to reduce their home temperatures from 65° to 62° in the winter, in comparison with the estimated amount that they would actually save; and (2) a study of what rates of monthly or annual return respondents would require in order to invest in various energy-conserving devices. The main conclusion from the first part will be that 33 percent of those who responded should be willing to lower their home temperatures if given the relevant information. The second part, however, leads us to question whether respondents are making rational choices of investment in view of the expected rates of return.

REDUCING HOME TEMPERATURE IN WINTER

Savings Reported to be Necessary

The North Carolina Energy Survey contains two questions that are particularly useful for estimating how much money respondents would require in order to keep their homes cooler:

> Q. 74 (part 1) (SAVING1): One way to save on energy bills is to turn down your heat in the winter. How much money would you have to save on your heating bill to make it worthwhile to keep your house at 65 degrees?

> Q. 74 (part 2) (SAVING2): How much would you have to save on your heating bill to make it worthwhile to keep your house at 62 degrees?

Answers to both questions were coded in dollars per month, in two digits. Frequency distributions of the responses to these questions are shown in Table I-1. Fewer than one-fourth of the respondents gave monetary amounts in response to each of these questions; about two-thirds of the sample said either that they already kept the temperature at the indicated level, or that they didn't know how much they would require.

These questions did not specify whether daytime or nighttime temperature was involved, but we may assume that the respondent considered conditions to be the same for both questions. In that case, the *difference* (SAVING2 - SAVING1) between the monthly amounts given in response to the two questions may be used as an estimate of the monthly saving required for respondents to lower the temperature from 65° to 62°, which we might call a "price of discomfort." We compute this difference for all respondents who specified monetary values for the two "saving" questions, including those who said they already kept their houses at 65°.

Table I-1. Frequencies of Response for Amounts Needed to Keep House
at 65° or 62°

	Number of Respondents Asking Indicated Amount to Keep House at	
	65° F	62° F
Amount Required:		
$ 1-5	22	14
6-10	25	32
11-15	14	16
16-20	11	14
21-25	20	13
26-30	2	8
31-35	2	3
36-50	14	20
Over 50	6	20
Subtotal (mean)	116 ($21.77)	140 ($28.54)
Already keep at indicated temperature	217	89
Would not turn down	20	42
Cannot turn down—health	29	41
Don't know	222	292
Total	604	604

In this preliminary analysis I shall assume that the respondent, as a responsible adult, was taking into account the preferences of other family members as well as him/her self. Other analyses show, however, that couples with children do not engage in conservation behavior as much as do childless couples.[3] If in families comparable to each other but differing in the number of children, the parents respond similarly to the above questions but actually conserve differently, we shall have to estimate the total need for compensation for the entire family, including consideration of the discomfort and health of other family members.

If we could show respondents (or residential energy consumers more generally) that turning down the heat would in fact save them *more* than they would require, then they would presumably have rational grounds for turning the heat down and saving energy.

The following analysis will be a first approximation to stating the conditions for such rational persuasion. In the course of the discussion we shall note assumptions that may be refined so that the analysis may be made more exact.

Heat Loss, Temperature, and the Price of Discomfort

We wish to compare respondents' required savings with their expected savings, which can be shown to be related to their actual heating bills. The relations among these quantities can be approximated by a simple model.

The thermal leakage from a residence, and the corresponding heating needs, are approximately proportional directly to the temperature difference between inside and outside,[4] and inversely to the resistance provided by the walls, windows, etc. This latter resistance is incorporated in the heating bill, however; thus if we knew the average temperature differential between inside and outside during the winter, then halving this temperature differential would cut the heat bill in half. Reducing the temperature differential by $3°$ would reduce the heat bill by the same fraction that $3°$, or ($65°$-$62°$), is of the inside-outside differential.

As long as the outside temperature is always below the inside temperature of the dwelling, we need only know the average inside-outside differential. For, if we let

T_i = internal temperature,

T_e = external temperature, and

k = the constant of proportionality, for a particular dwelling, between temperature differential and rate of heat loss,

then the rate of heat loss will be

$$k(T_i - T_e)$$

A similar relation holds for the heat flow when air conditioning is used. If T_i is held at a constant value while the external temperature varies with weather conditions, then the total heat loss during the winter will be

$$k \int_{t_0}^{t_1} (T_i - T_e)\, dt = kT_i(t_1 - t_0) - k \int_{t_0}^{t_1} T_e\, dt \qquad (1)$$

where t_0 and t_1 are the starting and ending dates of the heating period. The right-hand expression in (1) consists of two parts:

kT_i $(t_1 - t_0)$, which depends only on the internal temperature T_i of the residence, multipled by the heat-loss constant k for that residence and the length of time $(t_1 - t_0)$ during which heating takes place; and

$$-k \int_{t_0}^{t_1} T_e \, dt,$$ which depends on the external temperature;

this expression can also be written as $-k\overline{T}_e$ $(t_1 - t_0)$, where $\overline{T}_e$ is the average external temperature during the heating period.

On the left-hand side of (1), the integral itself (exclusive of k) gives the total number of heating degree-days required relative to internal temperature T_i, a characteristic of the locality and the weather conditions which can be used in calculations for residences with various values of k. The number of heating degree-days is frequently used in analysis of energy savings (Schipper, 1979, p. 363).

If the price of energy is p, the total heating bill for an individual residence can be written as a modification of (1). If we replace the right-hand integral by $-k\overline{T}_e(t_1 - t_0)$, the heat bill may be expressed as

$$H = pk(T_i - \overline{T}_e) \, (t_1 - t_0) \tag{2}$$

Expression (2) embodies the proportional relation between the heat bill and the average inside-outside differential, which we referred to above; the heat bill is proportional to $(T_i - \overline{T}_e)$, if we assume that the time period $(t_1 - t_0)$ does not change appreciably as the resident varies T_i.

In the survey, respondents were asked to report last year's heating bill in response to the following question:

Q. 30 (HEATBILL): (If pays for fuel and lived in current home last year) Thinking back to *last winter*, about how much did you spend heating your house?

The coding categories used, the numerical values we shall assign to them, and the frequencies of response are shown in Table I-2.[5]

We wish to express the respondent's required monthly saving, or "price of discomfort," in terms that are comparable with the entire winter heat bill. Whereas the heat bill fluctuates with T_e, being less in the fall and spring than in the winter, the "price of discomfort" does not; rather, it is a uniform effect for the entire

Table I-2. Coding Categories, Assigned Monetary Values, and Frequencies for Respondent's Report of Heat Bill

Coding Category	Assigned Value	Frequency
1. Less than $100	$ 50	20
2. $100-$200	$150	78
3. $200-$300	$250	135
4. $300-$400	$350	99
5. $400-$500	$450	54
6. $500-$750	$625	42
7. Over $750	$900	8
	Subtotal	436
	Not applicable	91
	Nothing or don't know	77
		604

period during which heating may take place. If we make the simplifying assumption that $(t_1 - t_0)$ does not change with the respondent's choice of T_1, then the price of discomfort for the winter is $(t_1 - t_0)$ (in months) times the price per month, and we need to estimate $(t_1 - t_0)$. At the same time we need to estimate $\overline{T}_e$ as it enters into (2). Both of these estimations depend on North Carolina weather data, which we present for Raleigh and Charlotte in Table I-3.

We first estimate $(t_1 - t_0)$ on the assumption that heating is required as long as T_e is 65° or less. For this purpose we use the average of Raleigh and Charlotte temperatures, assuming that each holds for the middle day of the month, and using a linear approximation to the variation of temperature between adjacent months. This leads to a total time interval of almost exactly *seven months*, since a temperature of 65° occurs 3.5 days into October and 3.6 days into May.[6] We can therefore multiply the respondent's monthly required difference in monetary savings by seven to obtain his total required saving for the winter.

We next estimate $\overline{T}_e$ for this seven-month period from the average temperatures in Table I-3. With small compensating linear adjustments for October and May, it is 49.7°.

We are now able to compare the respondent's required savings with his/her heat bill. We further assume that for last year's heat bill, respondents had kept their residences at 68°; we assume a uniform temperature to simplify calculations. The average inside-outside differential would then have been 18.3° and the fraction

Table I-3. Normal Monthly Average Temperatures (°F) for Two North Carolina Cities

	Sept.	Oct.	Nov.	Dec.	Jan.	Feb.	Mar.	Apr.	May
Charlotte	72.0	61.7	51.0	42.5	42.1	44.0	50.6	60.8	68.8
Raleigh	70.6	60.2	50.0	41.2	40.5	42.2	49.2	59.5	67.4
Average	71.3	60.95	50.5	41.85	41.3	43.1	49.9	60.15	68.1

[a]Source: U.S. Bureau of the Census (1976, p. 191)

of the heat bill saved by a 3° reduction would have been 3/18.3 or .164. The fraction of the heat bill that would have been saved per month is .164/7 or .0234. Thus we classify a respondent whose required monthly saving is less than .0234 of this winter's heat bill as a "gainer" from lowering the temperature by 3°. If he behaved rationally, we should expect the "gainer" to lower the temperature in response to heat bill savings. In these subjective terms, a respondent whose required monthly saving is greater than .0234 times the heat bill will be classified as a "loser" from lowering the temperature.

Table I-4 shows the division of respondents between gainers and losers, cross-tabulated by reported heat bill. Of the 103 respondents who gave monetary responses, thirty-four (33 percent) would be apparent gainers; the gainers, relative to the losers, tended to have lower family income and blue-collar occupations. Among those with

Table I-4. Potential Gainers and Losers from 3° Temperature Reduction, by Winter Heat Bill

		Heat Bill						
	<$100	$100-$200	$200-$300	$300-$400	$400-$500	$500-$750	Over $750	Total
Midpoint	$ 50	150	250	350	450	625	900	
Gainers	—	6	7	12	6	3	—	34
Losers[a]	3	16	15	14	11	9	1	69
Subtotal giving monetary responses	3	22	22	26	17	12	1	103

[a]Including a few for whom gains and losses were equal.

low heat bills, a substantial proportion already kept their residences at 62° or less; those who did so included a disproportionate number of persons aged over 65.

If all respondents had reached rational individual decisions about their home temperatures, we should expect to find no "gainers" (except for measurement error). Insofar as there are prospective gainers, we may imagine that the survey has provided a snapshot of a process in which consumers are adjusting their behavior to equilibrium. Alternatively, they may have been deciding in terms of family preferences, a situation which would require more compensation for discomfort than would the respondent's preference alone.

Insofar as these data are reliable and the sample representative, it appears that information campaigns telling citizens how much they would save by turning the temperature down could have a modest effect. If the data were more precise, we might proceed to estimate amounts saved rather than merely to classify gainers and losers. The results of past energy conservation information campaigns have been mixed (Cunningham and Lopreato, 1977, pp. 20-24); possibly such campaigns could be improved by focusing more accurately on persons who might be expected to gain from conservation.

INVESTMENT IN CONSERVATION AND RATES OF RETURN

So far we have considered the tradeoffs by respondents between lower temperature and monetary gain. If they consider investment in energy-saving equipment, however, their tradeoff is between present consumption on the one hand, and delayed consumption with economies over time on the other. If we could tell consumers how much a given device would save them over time, they could then judge whether this saving would be worth the investment.

We have assumed that the respondents' tradeoff, when they consider investment, is between using a given sum for investment (postponing consumption) and for consumption. However, a consumer may compare various sorts of investments. If he/she has resources to invest, he may be able to place them in investments that yield various rates of return. At present these rates range from 5 percent (in savings accounts) to 10 percent or more (in income-yielding property), depending on circumstances and on how inflation is taken into account. Effective available rates at a given time vary with the degree of liquidity desired, the degree of risk, the investor's breadth of knowledge of opportunities, and his tax situation. At any given time, however, we should expect a rational consumer/investor to invest at the best rate obtainable. We should expect him not to invest at highly disparate rates when different purchases are involved, but rather to transfer funds so that all investments are yielding about the same marginal rate of return. We shall here compare only investments that make income available for other purposes; but for citizens in higher tax brackets, this available income will be tax-free in comparison with most other investments.

The following analysis will attempt to estimate the particular rates of return, or discount rates, that individual respondents require for investment in energy conservation. The goal of such an analysis, as in our previous study of home temperatures, is to ascertain whether respondents in general, or particular types of respondents, might be willing to make these investments if there was a realistic expectation of the amount of return (savings) required. We shall see, however, that individual respondents do not seem to have well-defined and consistent rates of return (discount rates) that they require for various sorts of investment.

Individual Discount Rates

Most of the tradeoff questions in this survey dealt with the respondent's willingness to invest money at one time in return for a stream of additional available income after that time. If the initial investment is I, and the annual income that would result is S, then we shall say that the individual who will accept just that return and no less has a personal discount rate of $R = (S/I)$. Such a formulation ignores depreciation and assumes that the investor can recover the initial value of the investment later; but as we shall see, this simplification is not the greatest problem involved.

An economic analysis, assuming rational consumers, might conclude that individuals would be similar in their discount rates, having adjusted their previous investments in view of the interest rates available in the market so that their marginal rate of return was equal to the market rate. Persons whose individual rate of discount was low might thus invest as much as they could in the future; however, having done so, they might eventually come to value the present more for their marginal dollars, and their current investments might correspond more nearly to the market interest rate. Conversely, persons with high individual discount rates (e.g., elderly persons without heirs) might spend much of their resources on immediate consumption; though having done so, they might come to value consumption less and investment more for the remainder of their resources.

In this analysis, however, we shall start by postulating that each individual has a distinct but consistent discount rate and by examining the truth of this postulate. There is some literature on individual differences in time-perspective (Back and Gergen, 1963), and conceivably we might test the hypotheses presented there. As we shall see, however, the consistency of estimates of this discount rate is a precondition for the precise analysis that we require to predict rational choices.

The questions we use are of two kinds. First are *direct* estimates of the respondent's discount rate, in which a specific monetary investment is compared with a rate of return expressed (or asked) in dollars per time interval. Second are *indirect* estimates, in which the amount saved is expressed as a fraction of some other flow of expenses.

Consistency of Direct Estimates of Individual Discount Rates

The interview schedule included three questions providing direct information on discount rates:

Q. 51 (TOREFRIG): Suppose you were buying a new refrigerator and could get one that cost $100 more but saved on electric bills. How much would you have to save per month to spend the extra $100 for the refrigerator?

$____ (SPECIFY ANY OTHER RESPONSE) _____

(If no answer) Would $2.00 a month be enough? ___ Yes ___ No
                  Would $4.00 a month be enough? ___ Yes ___ No
                  (Continue with $1 increments
                  until you get an answer) $____ final amount
                                   ____ DK

Q. 71 (part 1) (ADD200): (if plan to buy a home in next two or three years) If you were able to save $50 per year on heating bills, would you be willing to spend $200 more for your new home?

Q. 71 (part 2) (ADD600): (if plan to buy) If you were able to save $100 per year on heating bills, would you be willing to spend $600 on additional construction costs for energy-saving devices in your next home?

The first of these questions asked the respondent to specify an amount; the second and third asked only whether he/she would accept a specified rate of return. A difficulty with the first question concerns the excessive amounts ($2, $4, etc.) specified in the probes—this may have led to exaggerated estimates of discount rates.

Table I-5 shows the interrelations between the second and third of these questions, which show the greatest consistency. Data are shown for the small subsample who answered these questions dealing with home investment. Out of the total sample of 604, only those who said they planned to buy a home enter into these tabulations.

Of the seventy-eight respondents in the table, sixty-eight answered "yes" to both questions, five answered "no" to both, and the remaining five answered "yes" to one and "no" to the other. Most of these respondents would therefore seem to have individual discount rates of 16-2/3 percent or less. For the last five, a "consistent" pattern of responses, based on a single individual discount rate, would be to reject the rate of 16-2/3 percent but accept 25 percent. Four of the five fall in this category; only one rejected the higher rate and accepted the lower. Note that in our interpretation of Table I-5, unlike a conventional Guttman scale comparison, the sequence of questions is given by their wording and not simply by the marginals. We thus refer to "consistency" rather than "reliability," which is conventionally based on correlation coefficients rather than on exact correspondence.

Table I-6 shows the relationship between the first (refrigerator) question and the other two. Note first that the responses to Q. 51 (refrigerator) are concentrated in the $2 and $4 per month categories (see "approximate total") because of the probes used. Rates of return asked by most respondents were 60 percent or less annually (seemingly a rather high figure), but some requested rates over 100 percent per year.

Table I-5. Interrelation of Home Investment Questions (Q. 71).

		Would Accept 25% Savings ($50 for $200)?		
		Yes	No	Total
Would accept $16\frac{2}{3}$ savings ($100 for $600)?	Yes	68	1[a]	69
	No	4	5	9
		72	6	78

[a]Apparently inconsistent response.

Table I-6. Discount Rates for Refrigerator and for Home Investment

		Refrigerator Savings (Q. 51)												Monthly
		$1	$2	$3	$4	$5	$6	$7	$8	$9	$10	$11-$25	$30-$50	Annual
		12%	24%	36%	48%	60%	72%	84%	96%	108%	120%	216%	480%	
25% Home Investment	Yes	3	30	4	10	9	–	–	2	–	2	3	1 [a]	64
	No	–	2	–	–	–	–	–	–	–	–	–	–	2
16⅔% Savings (Q. 71)	Yes	3	30	3	9	8	–	–	2	–	1	2	1 [a]	59
	No	–	1	–	1	1	–	–	–	–	1	1	–	5
Approx. total		3	32	4	10	9	–	–	2	–	2	3	1	

[a] Apparently inconsistent responses; estimated refrigerator savings are higher than estimated home investment savings.

In judging consistency among these responses, we must hypothesize at the start that each response represents a careful balancing of alternatives. Thus a response to the refrigerator question would be interpreted as meaning that the specified rate of return was the least which that respondent would require, i.e., the equilibrium rate R. In reality the discrete nature of the categories and the character of the probes might permit an error of, say, $2; however, within a margin of this sort, we might assume that Q. 51 provided an estimate of R. If this is so, a respondent who required a rate of 36 percent—or certainly 48 percent—would have been expected to say "no" when offered a rate of only 25 percent on a home investment. In actuality, a high proportion of the respondents (see boxes in the table) responded inconsistently in this sense. One possible interpretation is that they did not convert monthly savings into annual savings—and, thinking in terms of an absolute number, asked for a monthly amount greater than one-twelfth of what they would have asked annually. A second interpretation is that numerous answers were in error by one category in the sequence of probes—two dollars or 24 percent. In this case the number of clear errors would decline to about one-fourth of the number of respondents in the upper part of the table.[7]

We see from Table I-6 that asking about numerical amounts and looking for consistency in these amounts imposes far more stringent conditions on the data than do the customary methods of comparing items for scalability. The methodology of survey analysis (and psychometrics) with which I am familiar tacitly assumes that the responses to attitude questions may be subjected to a monotonic transformation (certainly a linear transformation) without loss of information.

This apparent inconsistency can be interpreted in several ways:

1. We may take the responses at face value and assume that they represent accurate indicators of what respondents would do. Since respondents require a greater rate of return on the refrigerator, public policymakers and manufacturers must see whether the actual return available on refrigerators is as great as this. If not, they should either seek stronger motives for saving on refrigerators than sheer self-interest would provide, or concentrate their efforts on reducing energy consumption in homes rather than in refrigerators.

2. We may try to change people's responses so as to induce them to be more consistent as we view consistency. By pointing out to respondents that they are asking quite different rates

of return in two situations, we may try to persuade them that they are in effect asking for an exceedingly high rate of return on the efficient refrigerator relative to what they expect in other investments.

3. We may look to the survey procedure itself as possibly yielding invalid results. In the refrigerator question (and even more in later questions to be discussed) we may be asking respondents to perform a calculation that is too complex for a telephone interview—translating monthly rates into annual rates. It may also be that the frame of reference involved in possibly buying a home can lead the same respondents to think in terms of rates of return nearer to the market rate (or to mortgage rates). In further surveys or experiments, therefore, it may be possible to combine approaches (1) and (2) and provide respondents with information about rates of return and discount rates before obtaining their judgments as to what they would require.

Consistency of Indirect Estimates

Table I-6, based on direct measures of discount rates, gives little support to our hypothesis that respondents were rational calculators in terms of personal discount rates. We shall now see that similar or greater disconfirmations result from our analysis of indirect estimates. The additional questions available for this purpose (with mean responses) are:
Gasoline:

Q. 75 (part 2) (PAYCAR): (If thought about buying a car that gets better gas mileage) Would you be willing to pay $500 more for a car that gets 5 miles a gallon more than the car you drive now?

Q. 14a (MPG): (If own or use a car) On the average how many miles per gallon do you get on the car *most often* driven? (Mean = 17 for N = 463)

Q. 14b (MPYEAR): About how many thousand miles was this car driven over the last year? (Mean = 13.0 thousand for N = 427)

Q. 14c (GASMONEY): About how much do you spend on gasoline each week for that car? (Mean = $10.57 for N = 474)

The above questions were included in the same survey for another sponsor. In combination, they permit us to define a rate of return that the respondent says he or she will accept or refuse.
Heat pump:

Q. 72 (part 1) (ADD1200): (If plan to buy home) Would you consider buying a new home with an electric heat pump which would cost $1,200 more to purchase, but would save you one-third on your heating bills?

Q. 30 (HEATBILL): (If pays for fuel and lived in current home last year) Thinking back to *last winter*, about how much did you spend heating your house?

Subject to certain assumptions, these questions also provide an estimate of a rate of return that respondent would or would not be willing to accept. Frequencies for the second of these questions were given in Table I-2.

Our procedure will be to estimate the rate of return corresponding to the dichotomous questions for gasoline and the heat pump, and then to see whether the responses for each dichotomy are consistent with those for the refrigerator question.

For the gasoline questions we compute the rate of return which the respondent chooses as follows. We first compute two estimates of annual expenditures on gasoline:

$$\text{GASYR\$1} = 52 \times \text{(weekly expenditure on gasoline)}$$

$$\text{GASYR\$2} = \text{(miles per year/miles per gallon)} \times .70$$

where a gallon of gasoline was assumed to cost 70 cents at the time of the survey. The correlation between these two measures was .54, and their means were of the same order of magnitude. The two estimates were then averaged:

$$\text{GASYR\$AV} = (\text{GASYR\$1} + \text{GASYR\$2})/2$$

We next computed the savings from an increase of 5 miles per gallon and divided this by $500, multiplying by 100 to get a percentage figure:

$$\text{GASDISC} = \frac{100}{500} \times \text{GASYR\$AV} \left[1 - \frac{\text{MPG}}{(\text{MPG} + 5)} \right]$$

$$= \text{GASYR\$AV}/(\text{MPG} + 5)$$

If we substitute the mean figures given above, we obtain a discount rate of 25 percent. Our hypothesis of rational calculation implies that consciously or unconsciously, the respondent carried out a similar computation. Such a hypothesis is similar to the assumption that seems to be made in much economic analysis.

The sample of respondents was then separated into two sub-samples, as in the preceding analysis—those who would accept their individually specified threshold rate of return (GASDISC) by buying the gasoline-efficient car, and those who would not. For each of the two subsets, the rate in question was compared with that given by the respondent for the refrigerator. Table I-7A shows these comparisons. We expect those respondents who say they would buy the gasoline-efficient car to have a personal discount rate equal to or lower than GASDISC, or a value of GASDISC *higher* than their refrigerator rate; however, sixty-five of ninety-one respondents failed to meet this condition. For respondents who would not buy the more efficient car, we expect the opposite; by a small majority, the respondents in the second column of Table I-7A conform to our hypothesis. Taken together, however, the two columns of Table I-7A give little support to the hypothesis. Even if we allowed one dichotomy to have an arbitrary additive constant relative to the other, and treated the table as a table of association, the direction of the association would be opposite to that expected.

For the heat pump question our logic will be similar but simpler. The discount rate that the respondent accepts or rejects is (1/3 of heat bill)/$1200, multiplied by 100 for expression as a percentage.

Table I-7. Direct vs. Indirect Estimates of Discount Rates

A. Gasoline vs. Refrigerator Discount Rates

		Would *buy* efficient car	Would *not* buy	Total
Gasoline rate at least as high as refrigerator rate?	Yes	26	$\boxed{23}$ [a]	49
	No	$\boxed{65}$ [a]	28	93
		91	51	142

B. Heat Pump vs. Refrigerator Discount Rates

		Would *buy* heat pump	Would *not* buy	Total
Heat pump rate at least as high as refrigerator rate?	Yes	1	$\boxed{-}$ [a]	1
	No	$\boxed{32}$ [a]	10	42
		33	10	43

[a]"Inconsistent" responses.

The heat pump discount rate is thus (1/36) of the estimated heat bill for a year. For a heat bill of $150 this would be 4.2 percent; for $625, 17.4 percent. Table I-7B shows the relation between this rate and the respondent's refrigerator discount rate for the two sub-samples who say they would buy, or would not buy, the heat pump.

Table I-7B shows that only one respondent set the discount rate higher for the heat pump than for the refrigerator; all the rest set it lower. Thirty-two respondents thus said they would buy the heat pump at discount rates *lower* than the rate they required for the refrigerator—inconsistent responses. Note also that even though the "average" discount rate on the car was higher than that on the heat pump, a higher proportion of the small heat pump subsample said they would buy it than the proportion of the car subsample who said they would buy the car.

Interpretation

In Tables I-6 and I-7 we have seen two types of apparent inconsistency between the same individuals' judgments of acceptable discount rates for one investment and another. The first sort of inconsistency concerns the magnitude of the rate required, and may be seen from the totals in Table I-7. For 93 of 142 respondents, the rate of return on the gasoline-efficient car was lower than that which they required for the refrigerator; for 42 of 43 respondents, the rate of return on the heat pump was lower than that required for the refrigerator. Possibly the greater the amount of money involved in the purchase (for a home, a car, or a refrigerator), the lower the expected rate of return considered by the same person. (It may be that those respondents who think in terms of larger sums also consider lower discount rates.) This differential was in fact built into the gasoline and heat pump questions. It is interesting to note that a substantial majority said they would buy each. In order to see whether the respondent is engaging in economic calculation, we need to ask questions about willingness to invest in the same type of product at *several* levels of return.

Similar phenomena have been reported in a recent study by Hausman (1979), based on actual consumer behavior in the purchase of home air conditioners. From data on the price of air conditioners, their cooling capacity, and their energy efficiency, he infers consumer tradeoffs between operating costs and purchase price. The result, for an assumed durability at the mean of the sample, is a discount rate of 26.4 percent (1979, p. 51), higher than the available rate of interest. He points out that "previous estimates of consumer

demand for energy-saving appliances, which are usually characterized by higher initial price, may be overly optimistic." This conclusion suggests that consumers' discount rates may be greater
for lower-priced appliances.

Hausman also analyzes data on individual purchasers of various
income groups and finds discount rates ranging from 39 percent
(for incomes between $6,000 and $10,000) down to 8.9 percent
(for incomes between $35,000 and $50,000). Rates for more extreme incomes are estimated to be even more disparate, though
these estimates are less certain. The magnitudes of some of these
rates and their variation among types of purchases resemble some
of our findings. Responses to our refrigerator question also showed
a tendency for lower-income and nonwhite respondents to ask for
higher rates of return.

The second sort of inconsistency relates to the reversed direction
of association in Table I-7A. Those respondents who said they
would buy the efficient car, relative to those who would not, tended
to have discount rates for gasoline that were *lower* than their specified rates for the refrigerator. If the refrigerator rates were accurate
estimates of their personal discount rates, they should not have said
they would buy the efficient car. Possibly other considerations
entered into their decision to purchase the car.

The apparent inconsistencies among respondents' answers to
various questions on discount rates in our study resemble those in
unpublished research by Turchi and Udry (1979). These authors
asked two questions intended to measure individual discount rates:

> 92. Suppose you were guaranteed to receive $100 one year from
> today. How much *less* would you be willing to take in order
> to get the money *today?*
> 213. Suppose you could get $100 today or wait one year and be
> guaranteed more money. How much more money would
> you demand next year in order to wait?

The first of these questions imposes a lower bound on responses; the
second does not have an upper bound. They were nevertheless expected to be alternative measures of the same variable. In response
to the first of these questions, the mean discount rate for a sample
of 800 women in seventeen U.S. cities, interviewed in 1977, was 13.7
percent. Nonwhite respondents asked somewhat higher rates than
white.

A striking result from this study, however, was the low association between answers to the two questions. The correlation between
the discount rates given by the two questions was only 0.02. The

distribution of answers to the second question was positively skewed, as some respondents (like ours) required discount rates over 100 percent. A logarithmic transformation was then performed on answers to both questions, and the correlation rose to 0.16.

This lack of consistent or reliable measurement suggests that our own similar findings are not peculiar to our study, but express a more general problem.

CONCLUSION

An important contribution to energy conservation can presumably be made by changes in consumer behavior—either through direct use of energy, as in adjustment of home temperature, or through purchases of energy-efficient devices. We need to be able to predict the conditions under which such changes in behavior will occur. Two major research approaches are available for this prediction: (1) the economic approach, which assumes rational consumer behavior aimed at personal benefit; and (2) the sociological or psychological approach, which seeks determinants of behavior other than effective prices, such as attitudes. Economists tend to test their theories with reference to aggregate behavior in the marketplace; sociologists are more inclined to use sample surveys as indications of potential behavior.

The North Carolina Energy Survey contains a number of questions intended to estimate dollar values that respondents placed on aspects of energy conservation—temperature adjustments in homes and various sorts of investments in relation to later streams of savings. These questions, introduced by Michael McKinney and myself, constitute part of a longer-term effort to explore the possibility of survey measurement of variables that play a part in economic theories of human behavior (McKinney and MacRae, 1978). We have two goals in analyzing them: first, to see whether there is evidence of consistency in response; and second, if there is consistency, to estimate the values that will flow to respondents from various decisions by themselves or by government. If we can estimate those values, we may be able to aid the process of public choice (through policy analysis) or private choice (through supplying information as to the rewards or returns that consumers can expect).

Although there are increasing efforts by survey techniques to estimate consumer willingness to pay, this approach has still not proved its reliability for policy purposes. For the most part, it has been ignored by economists, who prefer to estimate demand from preferences revealed in the market rather than from responses to hypothetical questions. Sociologists and political scientists, on the other hand, are accustomed to using multi-point scales rather than monetary amounts in the survey questions they design. Such scales do not, however, provide sufficient information for policymakers to estimate how much expenditure on a public program is justified. Our experiments with tradeoff questions are intended to bridge this gap. It may, however, be difficult to bridge; some of the findings reported here reveal the difficulty not only of getting answers to such novel questions, but also of deriving consistent estimates of value from them.

We have observed little consistency among the choices that a respondent makes regarding discount rates. Further survey analysis might reveal conditions for greater consistency, or it might reveal systematic variations in respondents' discount rates with type of purchase. It is also possible that a telephone survey is an inappropriate method of testing such rational tradeoffs. Conceivably highly educated respondents will reveal more consistency than others, and more detailed series of carefully worded questions will yield better responses, but a more promising approach would seem to be to allow respondents more time to learn a response and to confront them with related judgments in close succession. Carefully designed personal interviews may reveal greater consistency. The experimental laboratory may also be a useful alternative to the survey for this purpose.

The questions analyzed here (apart from the refrigerator question) do suggest a substantial willingness among the group of respondents analyzed to conserve energy by investment in efficient devices. We need to be sure, however, that these responses are reliable predictors of actual behavior in response to public policies or private initiatives. Such assurance of course requires that the sample be representative. It also requires that the questions be valid indicators of potential behavior. Internal consistency of response would be a necessary condition of that validity. Beyond the survey method lies the necessity of testing actual responses to policies. Such testing can best be done through controlled experiments, perhaps on communities as well as individuals.

NOTES

1. I am indebted to Michael W. McKinney, Mary Ellen Marsden, Raymond J. Burby, Susan Clarke, other members of the research group, and readers

from Carolina Power and Light Company for helpful comments. David Crowley and David Falk assisted in computer work for this report.

2. This distinction between economic and noneconomic models of behavior is also made by Kaiser, Marsden, and Burby (1979), who argue that builders are relatively more concerned with market conditions and profit, while household respondents react relatively more in terms of attitudes and knowledge.

3. See Klausner (1978).

4. This proportionality expresses a steady-state relationship. Actual net heat losses are also affected by wind and radiation, and involve more complex dynamic responses (Kusuda, 1975).

5. We assume that the report of last winter's heat bill provides the best information available to us as to how the respondent would calculate rationally the potential savings from reducing the temperature. More accurate information as to the heat bill may be available, however, from the suppliers of fuel, provided that one type of fuel is used for heating only. In this case the supplier might be able to inform the consumer as to how much savings could be expected from lowering home temperature. The questionnaire also contained information on the physical characteristics of the residential unit, which could be used together with weather characteristics of regions of the state for a rough alternative estimate of heating expenses.

6. This interval is sensitive to the assumed value of Ti; for a value of $70°$ it would extend approximately from mid-September to mid-May and be about eight months.

7. It is also conceivable that respondents expect a higher rate of depreciation on a refrigerator than on the other investments about which they were asked, or that the cost of time spent in calculation would lead respondents to require larger rates of return on smaller investments.

8. Udry and Morris (1971, p. 780) hypothesize that "individual discount rates are inversely proportional to the discretionary resources available to the individual." J. Richard Udry and Ellen Fried also find, in an unpublished report, that "Discount rates for blacks were higher than those for whites."

REFERENCES

Back, Kurt W., and Kenneth J. Gergen. 1963. "Apocalyptic and Serial Time Orientations and the Structure of Opinions." *Public Opinion Quarterly* 27 #3 (Fall): pp. 427-442.

Becker, Gary S. 1976. *The Economic Approach to Human Behavior*. Chicago, Ill.: University of Chicago Press.

Cunningham, William A., and Sally Cook Lopreato. 1977. *Energy Use and Conservation Incentives: A Study of the Southwestern United States*. New York: Praeger Publishers.

Hausman, Jerry A. 1979. "Individual Discount Rates and the Purchase and Utilization of Energy-Using Durables." *Bell Journal of Economics* 10 #1 (Spring): pp. 33-54.

Kaiser, Edward J., Mary Ellen Marsden, and Raymond J. Burby. 1979. "Energy Conservation Practices in the Production and Use of Residences in North

Carolina." Presented at the First Annual Urban Affairs Conference of the University of North Carolina, Asheville, N.C., April 29-May 1.

Klausner, Samuel F. 1978. "Household Organization and the Use of Electricity." In Seymour Warkov, ed. *Energy Policy in the United States: Social and Behavioral Dimensions.* New York: Praeger Publishers.

Kusuda, Tamami. 1975 "The NBSLD Program." In Jack B. Chaddock, ed. *Energy Conservation in Buildings.* Proceedings of the United States—Australia Joint Seminar at Duke University, June 9-11, 1975. Durham, N.C.: Duke University Center for the Study of Energy Conservation.

Leik, Robert K., and Anita Sue Kolman. 1978. "Isn't It Rational to be Wasteful?" In Seymour Warkov, ed., *Energy Policy in the United States.* New York: Praeger Publishers, pp. 148-163.

McKinney, Michael W., and Duncan MacRae, Jr. 1978. "Survey Assessments of Consumer Demand for Publicly Supplied Goods: Recreation Facilities." Institute for Research in Social Science Discussion Papers, No. 5, University of North Carolina at Chapel Hill.

Schipper, Lee. 1979. "Another Look at Energy Conservation." *American Economic Review* 69 #2 (May): pp. 362-368.

Turchi, Boone A., and J. Richard Udry. 1979. Unpublished research at the University of North Carolina at Chapel Hill.

Udry, J. Richard, and Naomi M. Morris, 1971. "A Spoonful of Sugar Helps the Medicine Go Down," *American Journal of Public Health* 61, #4 (April), pp. 776-785.

U.S. Bureau of the Census. 1976. *Statistical Abstract of the United States.* Washington: U.S. Government Printing Office.

Solar Homebuilders

William W. Hill

The results of the random sample of 100 homebuilders across North Carolina described in Chapters 5 and 6 provide useful information concerning characteristics of the homebuilding industry in the state, the extent to which energy-conserving features are being incorporated into new housing, and the reasons that some features are more likely to be adopted than others. The fact that the survey was carefully designed to produce a random sample of the current status of residential housing construction makes it particularly useful in that it provides base data against which future survey results can be compared to see how various state and federal policies and other factors are affecting the use of energy conservation features.

The random sampling procedure appears to have produced a data set very representative of North Carolina's residential building industry. The spatial variation of the sample corresponds extremely well with the spatial variation of residential building permits issued in 1977. On the other hand, the random sampling procedure and the data thus obtained did not produce much information on innovators in the residential homebuilding industry. This was particularly true with respect to the use of solar features in new housing constructed for the speculative housing market. In the random sample of 100 homebuilders, there were only nine who could be classified as using solar. Moreover, solar builders were loosely defined to include those using "a maximum of south-facing glass" (a passive solar application). The random sample included seven of these "passive solar" builders and two who had used solar domestic hot water (DHW) systems in their speculative houses.

Because there were so few solar builders in the random sample of 100 builders (henceforth referred to as the "general survey"), a decision was made in February 1979 to construct a follow-up survey of speculative solar homebuilders in order to obtain information on those who might be considered at the cutting edge with respect to the diffusion of new energy conservation technologies in the residential homebuilding market. In this analysis, characteristics of twenty solar builders in North Carolina and the housing they are producing are described and compared with those of North Carolina's homebuilding industry in general. Additional data were gathered which address builder decisions to adopt solar features, incentives and disincentives facing the solar homebuilding industry, and solar builders' views regarding solar energy policy options. Analyses of these data will be reported at a future date.

Nine of the twenty solar builders included in the sample were identified in the original random survey. In these nine cases call-backs were made, and additional short interviews conducted, to get responses to further questions. The additional eleven builders included in this solar survey were identified by means of a systematic telephone survey. In the process of identifying these solar builders, it was quickly ascertained that there are very few speculative solar homebuilders in North Carolina and that generally the builders know one another. The list took shape very quickly in that solar builders, when asked to identify others, very often gave us names that we had already obtained. The number of sources used and telephone contacts made suggests that the sample discussed in this analysis probably includes almost all speculative solar builders in the state. While this number may appear small, the reader should bear in mind that the sample included only those firms building *speculative* solar homes. The number of firms building custom solar homes in North Carolina is no doubt much larger.

Because of the small sample size of the solar survey and the fact that it was not randomly drawn, it is not possible to perform statistical analyses on the differences between the two groups. On the other hand, if the reader accepts the contention that the sample of speculative solar builders represents very nearly the "universe" (i.e., all such builders), no statistical analyses are needed. If in fact the sample of 20 speculative builders represents nearly all such builders in the state, then *any* difference between this sample and the random sample of 100 builders is significant.

CHARACTERISTICS OF SOLAR HOMEBUILDING FIRMS

This section examines the sample of firms building speculative solar homes (hereafter referred to as the "solar survey") along the same lines as those used to examine the random sample of 100 homebuilding firms (the "general survey"). Our intent is to determine if there are any characteristics of these solar firms that set them apart from general homebuilding firms—specifically characteristics that might have policy implications for hastening the adoption of solar features by the residential building industry in North Carolina.

Type of Firm

Chapter 5 differentiates between merchant (or speculative) builders and general contractors (or custom builders). As shown in Table 5-1 above, the majority (59 percent) of the builders in the general survey could not be classified as either pure merchant builders or pure general contractors, but rather were engaged in both types of construction activities. In the solar survey this was true of all twenty builders; all firms in the solar sample built both custom and speculative homes.

One of the hypotheses tested in the solar survey was the following. Since solar home construction represents a new and unproven technology with uncertain market potential, builders would be most likely to try it first on a custom home before building for the speculative market. The survey data appear to bear out this hypothesis.

Eighty percent of the respondents in the solar survey had built a custom solar home before testing solar in the speculative home market. One implication of this finding is that future research addressing the incorporation of innovative technologies in the homebuilding industry would do well to examine custom homebuilders. With respect to state energy policy, this finding suggests that any programs aimed at educating builders should be targeted at both merchant builders and general contractors—the assumptions being that (1) (in light of the data of Table 5-2) merchant builders construct the majority of new homes in North Carolina, but (2) new ideas such as solar are likely to be used in a custom home built by a general contractor before being tested in the speculative housing market.

Size and Organization of Solar Home Building Firms

As discussed above in Chapter 5, the homebuilding industry in North Carolina follows the national pattern with respect to the size of the firm. Table II-1 below shows that solar firms do not differ significantly in size from the general sample in terms of numbers of housing units constructed in 1978. The median number of units constructed by solar builders was ten, the same as the median for the general sample. The only difference is that there were fewer large builders in the solar survey; one firm had built 62 homes in 1978 and another had built 69. No firms building solar homes had built over 100 homes in 1978.

While the lack of large-volume firms building solar homes may not appear to be significant, it could have policy implications in light of the discussion in Chapter 5. While only 5 percent of the firms in the general survey built more than 100 housing units in 1978, this 5 percent accounted for 41 percent of all new housing. Thus state programs to promote the use of solar design and solar systems might best be directed toward the larger firms to maximize their

Table II-1. Size of Homebuilding Firms (Construction Volume): Solar Builders vs. General

Number of Housing Units Constructed, 1978	Percent of Homebuilders		Percent of Homes Built, by Sample	
	Solar (N = 20)	General (N = 100)	Solar (N = 310)	General (N = 2260)
1-4	30	29	5	3
5-9	20	16	8	4
10-14	20	17	15	8
15-24	10	17	10	13
25-49	10	10	19	13
50-99	10	6	42	18
100 or more	0	5	0	41
Total	100	100	99[a]	100

[a]Does not add to 100% due to rounding.

effectiveness. While it may be premature to expect large firms to be engaged in the construction of solar homes at the present time, the data show that it is imperative that these larger firms do start incorporating solar design features into their houses soon if solar is to have a significant effect in energy conservation in the residential housing sector.

As discussed in Chapter 5, the size of the firm is related to its organizational structure. Of the twenty firms interviewed for the solar survey, 25 percent were single proprietorships, 15 percent were partnerships or joint ventures, 20 percent were family-owned corporations, and 30 percent were closely held but nonfamily corporations. Again there is little difference between the firms building solar homes and the general sample in this regard. The only difference is that there were three publicly owned corporations in the general survey and none in the solar survey. This could be significant in that these publicly owned corporations have access to broader sources of equity capital and thus, potentially, could have a greater effect if they were to incorporate solar design features into their new housing.

Solar Homebuilding Firms'
Modes of Operation

The homebuilding industry is noted for fragmentation of the production process in that firms do not have a large number of in-house employees but instead subcontract many of the tasks entailed in the production of a house. As shown in Table II-2, the number of permanent and part-time persons employed by firms in the solar sample is virtually identical to that in the general sample of all builders. Only

Table II-2. Number of Employees: Solar Builders vs. General

| | *Percent of Homebuilders* | |
Number of Persons Employed *Full- and Part-Time, Sept. 1978*	*Solar* *(N = 20)*	*General* *(N = 100)*
1-3	35	28
4-6	25	21
7-9	20	20
10-19	10	20
20 or more	10	11
Total	100	100

two firms employed more than twenty persons, with twenty-six
being the largest number employed by any single firm.

As noted above and discussed at length in Chapter 5, most firms in
the homebuilding industry subcontract many building operations
rather than maintaining the necessary expertise in-house. Table II-3
(identical in form to Table 5-4) summarizes, for both the solar
survey and the general survey, the extent to which these firms depend on subcontractors for each of eight key building and marketing
tasks. The table indicates the percentage of builders in each survey
who (1) perform the task in-house, (2) perform it in conjunction
with a subcontractor, or (3) subcontract the task completely. As the
data in Table II-3 show, there is little difference between the firms
in the solar survey and those in the general survey in this regard.
The only task in which there appears to be any significant difference
is the installing of insulation. Forty percent of the firms in the solar
survey install the insulation themselves, as opposed to 23 percent of

Table II-3. Use of Subcontractors to Perform Selected Homebuilding Operations:
Solar Builders vs. General[a]

	Percent of Home Builders					
	Task Performed by Own Employees		Task Performed by Own Employees and Subcontractors		Task Performed by Subcontractors	
Homebuilding Operation	Solar (N = 20)	General (N = 99)	Solar (N = 20)	General (N = 99)	Solar (N = 20)	General (N = 99)
Electrical work	5	1	5	2	90	97
Framing	60	58	0	4	40	38
Grading the lot	25	20	5	3	70	77
Heating, ventilating, and air conditioning (HVAC)	5	1	10	1	85	98
Insulation	40	23	5	10	55	67
Landscaping the lot	35	27	5	5	60	68
Marketing and sales	45	62	30	16	25	22
Plumbing	5	6	5	1	90	93

[a]Question: Now, getting back to your company. In building (single-family detached)
homes, which of the following activities do you usually do within your firm with your own
employees and which are usually subcontracted or otherwise done outside of your firm?
[HAND CARD C] First, what about. . . .

the firms in the general survey. The significance of this is taken up in greater detail below.

Chapter 5 reveals that the practice of subcontracting many operations has important implications for state energy policy. These implications stem from the lack of quality control that a builder has over a subcontractor and the difficulty in introducing innovations into an industry where so many different groups have a great deal of control over important decisions affecting energy conservation.

While heating, ventilating and air conditioning (HVAC) subcontractors and installers of insulation are the two most obvious groups to single out for their potential role in the construction of energy-efficient housing, it is important to note that many of the other subcontractors can play a major part. For example, it is quite possible for a builder to construct a "tight" house (i.e., one with little infiltration) through careful construction practices, only to have the electrical or plumbing subcontractor come in and damage the "thermal integrity of the building envelope" by injudicious placement of holes and electrical boxes. It is also possible for the subcontractor doing the interior plastering to damage the thermal integrity by removing insulation which gets in his way. Thus, in order for a builder to be assured that he is producing an energy-efficient house, it is important that he maintain close supervision and quality control over all his subcontractors.

As noted above, the HVAC and insulation subcontractors probably have the greatest potential effect on the energy efficiency of a house. For this reason two questions were included in the surveys to determine who had the major responsibility for key decisions concerning these operations. The results of these questions are summarized in Table II-4 for both the solar and general surveys.

With respect to HVAC systems, the data show very little difference between the builders in the solar survey and those in the general survey. Builders are more likely to play a role in decisions concerning the type of the heating system than its size or capacity. This is unfortunate in that an oversized heating system is less efficient than one sized to match the heating load. Moreover, HVAC subcontractors have no incentive for installing smaller heating and cooling systems; in fact, there may be motives for installing systems which are larger than necessary. Nearly half (45 percent) of the builders in the general survey left this decision concerning system capacity entirely to the HVAC contractor. Builders in the solar survey exercised somewhat more control in this decision, with only 30 percent leaving the decision entirely to the HVAC subcontractor.

Table II-4. Locus of Responsibility for Decisions about HVAC Systems and Installation of Insulation: Solar Builders vs. General

	Percent of Builders					
	Builder Specifies[a]		Joint Decision		Subcontractor Specifies	
Decision	Solar (N = 20)	General (N = 100)	Solar (N = 20)	General (N = 100)	Solar (N = 20)	General (N = 100)
HVAC Systems						
1. Type of heating equipment	55	55	45	38	0	7
2. Capacity of heating equipment	20	14	50	41	30	45
Insulation						
1. Type of insulation	95	66	5	16	0	18
2. Amount of insulation	95	87	5	10	0	3

[a]Includes builders who performed function within the firm and builders who subcontracted the function, but made decisions regarding heating and insulation.

With respect to decisions concerning insulation, builders in both surveys tended to exercise more control over the type and amount of insulation used. Two-thirds of the builders in the general survey indicated that they were responsible for the decisions about the type of insulation used, and 87 percent reported that they determined the amount. In the solar survey only one of the twenty builders did not assume sole responsibility for both of these decisions. Perhaps more importantly, none of the solar builders relegated either of these decisions concerning insulation entirely to the subcontractor.

In summary, the data suggest that solar builders are in fact taking somewhat more responsibility than builders in general in these important decisions concerning insulation and HVAC systems. This is no doubt the preferred procedure to insure the construction of more energy-efficient housing. However, if decisions on the sizing of HVAC systems continue to be left to the subcontractors, as will likely be the case, the conclusions of Chapter 5 still hold. State efforts to promote the use of energy-efficient HVAC equipment matched to design loads must be directed at both homebuilding firms and HVAC contractors if they are to be successful.

Location of Production

A third noteworthy characteristic of the homebuilding industry reported in Chapter 5 is the localization of production. This characteristic, which holds true nationwide, was found in the general survey, with 55 percent of the builders interviewed reporting they had limited their homebuilding operations in 1977 and 1978 to one county, and another 27 percent reporting they operated in two counties. The same trend was found in the solar survey, with 45 percent operating in one county and another 35 percent operating in two counties.

The implications of this localization of production vis-a-vis the adoption of new energy technologies are discussed at length in Chapter 5 and need not be repeated here. Suffice it to say that the implications are probably even more pronounced for the adoption of solar systems, where the technology is both newer and less well understood.

Diversity of Functions

The final characteristic of homebuilding firms discussed in Chapter 5 is the diversity of functions they perform. There was little difference between builders in the solar survey and builders in the general survey with respect to this characteristic. Half the solar builders were also involved in nonresidential construction, 65 percent were engaged in residential land development, 40 percent were involved in real estate brokerage, and 35 percent provided property management services. The only difference between the solar builders and those in the general survey that appears at all significant is the number engaged in the construction of multi-family residential buildings (i.e., apartments). Only 15 percent of the solar builders were engaged in this activity, versus 36 percent of the builders in the general survey. This may be merely a reflection of the smaller number of large building firms in the solar survey. On the other hand, it may be a reflection of market demand. Since landlords can pass higher energy costs on to their renters, there is less demand for energy efficiency in the multi-family sector of the housing market. If one assumes that the builders in the solar survey are generally committed to building more energy-efficient housing than those in the random sample, it stands to reason that there would be less demand for their services in this sector of the residential housing market.

THE SOLAR BUILDERS

This section continues to follow the format of Chapter 5 by describing selected characteristics of the principals in the home-building firms interviewed for the solar survey. As noted above, the homebuilding industry is characterized by small firms in which decision-making authority is generally highly centralized (i.e., often vested in one person). The interviews were specifically directed at the one person who has ultimate responsibility about the kinds of homes built, and specifically the accountability for the energy-related aspects. As with the section above, the focus here will be on identifying similarities and differences between the solar builders and builders in the random survey.

Age, Education, and Experience

Table II-5 summarizes the age, education, and experience in home-building, and number of counties of residence for the 20 builders in the solar survey and the 100 builders in the general survey. There do appear to be some significant differences between solar and general survey builders with respect to the first three characteristics.

First, solar builders appear to be somewhat younger overall than builders in the general survey. Thirty-five percent of the solar builders were under the age of thirty-five, as opposed to 22 percent of those in the general survey. Only one solar builder was over fifty-five, whereas about one-quarter (26 percent) of the general survey builders were in this age group. This finding is consistent with theories of innovation diffusion which suggest that younger persons are more likely to experiment with innovative technologies.

The age difference is reflected in the builders' length of experience in the homebuilding industry. Almost half (45 percent) of the solar builders had been involved in homebuilding for less than ten years, as opposed to 31 percent of builders in the general survey. At the other end of the spectrum, 25 percent of solar builders had been involved in the industry for twenty years or more, versus 39 percent of builders in the general survey.

The most noticeable difference between the two groups concerns the level of education. Only one builder in the solar survey had not had some college education; 40 percent were college graduates and another 10 percent had some graduate education beyond the baccalaureate. In contrast, 42 percent of builders in the general survey had not attended college, 26 percent had some college education, 27 percent were college graduates, and another 5 percent

Table II-5. Selected Characteristics of Homebuilding Executives: Solar Builders vs. General

Characteristic	Percent of Executives	
	Solar (N = 20)	*General (N = 100)*
Age		
Under 35	35	22
35-44	25	30
45-54	35	22
55 or older	5	26
Total	100	100
Education		
Less than high school	5	8
High school graduate	0	34
Some college	45	26
College graduate	50	32
Total	100	100
Experience in Homebuilding		
Less than 10 years	45	31
10-19 years	30	30
20 or more years	25	39
Total	100	100
Counties of Residence in North Carolina		
One	45	48
Two	40	33
Three or more	15	19
Total	100	100

had some graduate or professional training beyond an undergraduate degree. These data suggest that builders incorporating solar design features into new homes at the present time tend to be somewhat better educated than the average homebuilder.

The final builder characteristic shown in Table II-5, the number of counties of residence, reflects the localized nature of the homebuilding industry in the state for both solar and nonsolar builders. Nearly half the builders in both samples had lived in only one North Carolina county; only 15 percent and 19 percent of the builders in the solar survey and general survey, respectively, had lived in more than two counties. Thus, as noted in Chapter 5, builder expertise, whether it be in solar or nonsolar construction, tends to come from living and working in one market area.

Integration into the Homebuilding Industry

The implications for state energy policy concerning builders integration into the homebuilding industry are discussed in this section. One finding from research on the adoption of innovation in a particular field is that in industries such as homebuilding which are conservative and generally resistant to change, persons who are strongly integrated into the industry tend to be slow to adopt new ideas; the innovators tend to be "loners." Although this hypothesis is not formally tested here, data on the extent to which solar builders are integrated into their industry are examined, and salient differences between solar builders and nonsolar builders with respect to this characteristic are presented.

Table II-6 summarizes four indicators of the integration of homebuilders into the industry for both the solar and the general surveys. Most of the measures suggest that both sets of builders tend to be well integrated into their industry. All builders in the solar survey regularly read trade magazines; 70 percent are members of a building trade association; and 85 percent have attended conventions or other meetings of builder, developer, or real estate associations, half of these within the last year. All of these percentages are slightly higher than the corresponding percentages for builders in the general survey, though not appreciably so. What the data do appear to indicate is that solar builders are keeping up with developments in the homebuilding industry through the reading of trade magazines and attendance at building association meetings. One policy implication is that information on new energy-conserving features or design practices and the use of solar energy features can be communicated to a majority of homebuilders in a state through their trade associations.

The question on the number of builders known on a first-name basis is probably the best indicator of whether or not a builder tends to be a "loner." If the above hypothesis were true, one might expect to see more loners among the builders in the solar sample. While solar builders tend to know slightly fewer other homebuilders on a first name basis, the difference is not great enough to be significant. Moreover, this difference could be explained by the fact that builders in the solar survey were younger and had not been involved in the industry for as long.

Attitudes Toward the Energy Situation

Chapter 5 compared the outlooks of homebuilders toward the energy problem in the United States with the attitudes held by households

Table II-6. Executives' Integration into the Homebuilding Industry: Solar
Builders vs. General

Indicator	Percent of Executives	
	Solar	*General*
Regularly Read Building Trade Magazines		
Yes	100	83
No	0	17
Total	100	100
	(*N* = 20)	(*N* = 100)
Number of Homebuilders Know by First Name		
1-10	33	20
11-20	33	33
21 or more	33	47
Total	99[a]	100
	(*N* = 18)	(*N* = 100)
Membership in Building Trade Association		
Yes	70	62
No	30	38
Total	100	100
	(*N* = 20)	(*N* = 100)
Attendance at Trade Association Meeting/Convention		
Yes	85	72
No	15	28
Total	100	100
	(*N* = 20)	(*N* = 100)

[a]Total does not add to 100% due to rounding.

in North Carolina (Chapter 3) and found them to be generally
similar. Below, attitudes of builders in the solar survey are compared to those of the general survey builders. One might surmise
that solar builders would tend to view the energy situation as more
serious than homebuilders in general, since the former are doing
something about it. The logic behind this is that builders getting
into the speculative solar home market must perceive a market
demand for their product; this perceived demand may be in part
based on their own assessment of the seriousness of the energy
situation.

Eighty percent of builders in the solar survey felt that the need
to save energy was "very serious," while another 20 percent saw
it as "somewhat serious;" none felt that it was "not at all serious."

The corresponding percentage for builders in the general survey were 61 percent, 33 percent and 6 percent. Thus solar builders do appear to see the energy situation as somewhat more serious than home-builders in general.

The attitudes of builders in the two surveys on the question of whether ". . . people's efforts to save energy in homes and driving can help reduce our total energy use" were very similar—basically not overly optimistic. Forty percent of solar builders and 48 percent of general sample builders felt that such efforts could reduce our total energy use a "great deal;" 50 percent of solar builders and 43 percent of other builders said "a fair amount;" 10 percent of solar builders and 6 percent of other builders said "very little." Three percent of builders in the general survey felt that such efforts would have "no impact at all;" no respondents in the solar survey were equally pessimistic.

A final question asked the respondents whether they thought that ". . . people have the right to use as much energy as they can pay for." Sixty percent of the solar builders did not believe that people had this right—a view shared by builders in the general survey (68 percent) and respondents in the household survey (73 percent).

HOUSING PRODUCT MIX

In the following section, the overview of salient characteristics of firms and builders in the solar survey as compared to those of the typical homebuilder is concluded. This section briefly examines the mix of products that the two groups are producing for the speculative housing market. These data, summarized in Table II-7, were obtained by asking builders about the characteristics of the most recent speculative home their firm had constructed.

Types of Housing Being Built

As shown in Table II-7, there is not a great deal of difference between the types of homes being built by solar versus general builders. The most recent speculative home constructed by over three-quarters of the builders in both surveys was either a one-story ranch home or two-story home. It is noteworthy that solar builders were constructing fewer ranch-style homes and more two-story homes than were the builders in the general survey. A two-story home is generally more energy-efficient than a ranch-style home in that the

Table II-7. Selected Characteristics of New Speculative Housing in North
Carolina: Solar Builders vs. General

Characteristic	Percent of Speculative Houses[a]	
	Solar (N = 20)	*General (N = 100)*
Housing Style		
One story (ranch)	50	66
Split level	15	7
Two story	30	20
Three story	5	3
Other	0	4
Total	100	100
Size of Houses		
Under 1250 sq. ft.	0	21
1250-1499 sq. ft.	30	19
1500-1749 sq. ft.	30	20
1750-1999 sq. ft.	5	7
2000 or more sq. ft.	35	33
Total	100	100
Price of Houses		
Under $35,000	5	9
$35,000-$44,999	15	23
$45,000-$54,999	15	17
$55,000-$64,999	10	13
$65,000-$79,999	35	21
$80,000 or more	20	17
Total	100	100
Features Utilized		
Rangehood with fan	90	100
Two or more bathrooms	90	91
Central air conditioning	95	89
Fireplace	80	85
Dishwasher	85	85
Separate family room	50	73
Separate dining room	75	69
Patio or deck	80	69
Garage	60	64
Garbage disposal	50	53
Bathroom heater	30	23
Trash compactor	20	11
Enclosed/screened porch	10	10
Microwave oven	10	10
Central vacuum system	10	5

[a]Data refer to "most recent speculative house" built by homebuilders.

former has a smaller ratio of surface area to volume (or useful square feet of floor area).

Size and Price Range of New Housing

The sizes of the homes being constructed by builders in the two samples is quite similar, with one exception. Twenty-one percent of the most recent speculative homes constructed by builders in the general survey were "budget housing" with less than 1250 square feet. No such homes were being constructed for the speculative solar market. The median size of the most recent speculative home constructed by builders in both surveys was essentially the same—approximately 1600 square feet. Furthermore, there was little difference in the price range of the homes in the two samples. The median price was also about the same.

Features Installed in New Housing

The features provided in the most recent speculative home constructed by builders in both surveys were remarkably similar, as shown at the bottom of Table II-7. In fact, the relative frequency of features used in homes in the two samples was identical. The use of some of these features in solar homes was somewhat surprising. For example, 85 percent of the solar homes contained a fireplace even though 85 percent of the solar builders had given the "correct" response to another question on the survey—that conventional fireplaces would have negative or insignificant effects on reducing the winter heating requirements of a typical house. (It is hoped that the fireplaces in these recent speculative solar homes are not of "conventional" design.) Similarly it was somewhat surprising to see approximately the same number of bathroom heaters and trash compactors being installed in the solar homes. What these data suggest is that builders, whether solar or nonsolar, are responding to market demands. To compete successfully in the speculative housing market, solar homes must contain the same amenities as nonsolar homes. It is apparent from these data that speculative solar homes are not being built for sale to a specialized market of "energy-conserving zealots" interested in abandoning life's amenities and returning to a spartan self-sufficient lifestyle.

SUMMARY AND CONCLUSIONS

This analysis has summarized part of a survey of twenty builders constructing solar homes for the speculative housing market in North Carolina. The survey was conducted in the spring of 1979 as a follow-up to the random survey of the state's residential homebuilders conducted in the fall of 1978. The data presented herein described characteristics of solar builders, their firms, and the houses they produce. Beyond providing a descriptive analysis of speculative solar homebuilding, the study attempted to identify significant differences which set these solar builders apart from the typical homebuilder. Other data collected in this "solar survey" included what factors motivate builders to enter the speculative market with solar homes, what impediments they now face, and what their views are regarding various policy options designed to promote the use of solar energy in the residential housing sector. Analyses of these data will be presented at a future date.

In general, the differences between solar builders and builders in the random survey of the entire North Carolina homebuilding industry were small. There were few differences which appeared to be significant concerning the builders themselves, their firms, or the mix of houses they produced. Observed differences which may have implications for state energy policy are summarized below.

In general, solar builders tended to be younger, better educated, and slightly less experienced than the typical homebuilder. These findings are consistent with the theories of innovation diffusion; these are all characteristics of persons who are more likely to try new, unproven technologies. However, the data do suggest that solar builders are not prone to enter the speculative market without first gaining some experience with a custom home. Eighty percent of the builders in the survey had built a custom solar home before building a solar home for the speculative market. One implication of this finding is that state energy policy efforts aimed at encouraging the construction of solar homes should be targeted at builders constructing custom homes.

The homebuilding industry is noted for fragmentation of the production process, and no exception to this general trend was found among either solar builders or builders in general. The majority of firms subcontract most of the major tasks other than the framing of the house. The implication of this for state energy policy is that any policies aimed at producing more energy-efficient housing must be targeted at a diverse group of small subcontracting firms. Furthermore, a builder intent on constructing energy-efficient homes must exercise a great deal of quality control to insure that his/her intentions are not thwarted by the subcontractors. Two of the more important decisions which directly affect the energy efficiency of new housing concern the type and capacity of the heating, ventilating and air conditioning (HVAC) system, and the kind and amount of insulation installed. Solar builders tended to assume somewhat greater responsibility for these decisions than did the typical homebuilder. This was especially true with respect to decisions concerning insulation—none of the solar builders relegated the decision concerning the type and amount of insulation solely to the subcontractor. For this reason, it is likely that the solar builders will be insured of more energy-efficient homes.

Two possible options for state energy policy are suggested by these findings. First, programs to improve the energy efficiency of new homes must be directed at both builders and subcontractors (especially HVAC). Second, builders should be encouraged to assume a larger role in these decisions and to oversee the work of their subcontractors to insure adequate quality control.

A final finding of note concerns the types of features being installed in speculative solar homes as compared to the typical speculative home built in North Carolina. The relative frequency with which fifteen different features were being utilized was identical in the two samples. Features such as fireplaces, bathroom heaters and trash compactors—features which one might not expect to find in a solar home—were in fact used to essentially the same extent in solar homes as in nonsolar. The implication is that solar builders are not building for a select market; they are responding to the same market forces as any builder constructing speculative homes in North Carolina. The only difference in the homes is the energy source for space heating or hot water—solar or conventional. These data suggest that the market for solar is potentially widespread; it is not limited to a small number of potential homeowners interested in self-sufficient lifestyles. The implications for state energy policy in this regard are clear: the market exists; it is incumbent upon state policymakers to insure that existing or potential institutional barriers to solar are removed and that builders and homebuyers alike are educated to recognize that solar utilization in residential home construction is technically and economically viable today.

Energy Policy in the Fifty States

David W. Orr and
Jeanne T. Hernandez

Residential energy use, which is approximately 20 percent of the U.S. energy budget, has been traditionally regarded as a strictly private matter left to individual homeowners and builders. With the Arab oil embargo of 1973-1974, however, it became clear to many that this area and others needed to come under closer governmental control in order to encourage greater efficiency and economy. The initial effort to stimulate residential conservation was contained in the Energy Policy and Conservation Act of 1975 (EPCA) as amended by the Energy Conservation and Production Act (ECPA) of 1976. Under provisions of EPCA, states were encouraged to join voluntarily with the federal government to reduce energy use in specific ways by 5 percent by 1980. In return for developing plans for conservation, the Department of Energy (which took over from the Federal Energy Administration on October 1, 1977) was entitled to make grants to aid in the implementation of the plan.

As of September 30, 1977, all the states had submitted plans under EPCA and had been awarded grants totalling $22,500,000. By the end of 1977, all fifty states had further submitted supplementary programs describing implementation procedures under the provisions of ECPA and were awarded funds totalling an additional

$11,930,000. The national impact of the EPCA program will result, according to DOE estimates, in a reduction of energy consumption of about 5.55 quadrillion Btu of energy or approximately 6.7 percent of the amount of energy that would have been used in 1980 if no conservation effort had been made. Of this 6.7 percent, conservation in the residential sector is supposed to contribute 1.3 percent.

Under the terms of EPCA and ECPA each state was required to create programs covering five areas. Of these, only the requirement for thermal efficiency standards and insulation requirements in new and renovated housing directly impacts on the residential sector. However, all states were encouraged to promote conservation through a variety of other ways, including the creation of loan guarantees for energy conservation investment, and the redesign of electric rates. In short, EPCA and ECPA provided a broad, if modest, stimulus toward energy conservation and set minimal requirements to qualify for federal funds. The mandatory provisions of ECPA were slight enough such that no state eventually failed to qualify.

While it will not be clear for at least two more years whether the goals established in EPCA have been met, it is not too early to review the various responses of the states to EPCA and the challenge provided by the energy crisis in general. This response was clearly hindered by the traditional belief that energy policy was a federal problem and that energy consumption decisions were a private matter. In either view, there was little for states to do beyond serving as an administrative liaison between the public and Washington. Consequently, before 1975 there was little thought about what the states could do either to encourage energy production or to control consumption. This problem was compounded by the fact that political power in most sectors increasingly gravitated to Washington, leaving states paralyzed on a variety of issues.

For analytical convenience, response to the "new realities" of the energy situation can be broken into three types: (1) government regulation and taxation; (2) the operations of the market; and (3) exhortation or education. In practice these often overlap, as in the case of government-imposed taxes which affect market decisions. In terms of the EPCA requirements for the residential sector, the only major attempt to impose government control is in the adoption of more stringent building codes. More often states have attempted to encourage energy conservation through the adoption of programs to inform citizens of why and how to develop energy savings in their own homes; incentives in the form of services such as energy audits;

and encouragement to private lending institutions and utilities to establish low-interest loans for conservation.

Given the sizeable difficulty of passing national energy legislation and the questionable effect of that legislation, it is reasonable to suggest that states will play an increasingly important role in energy policy. To some degree this is already apparent in several states that have adopted energy programs that are more ambitious in several important respects than that which President Carter submitted to the Congress in April of 1977. This development is aided by the growing interest in local and on-site technologies using solar, wind, or biomass. In these cases, states are probably better equipped to create a flexible energy program than is the federal government. Administratively, states are also closer to the target population and presumably better equipped to determine and respond to particular needs imposed by circumstances or geography.

In the text that follows, we will review state energy conservation plans in the residential sector. The information was solicited from each state by a letter sent in June 1978 to the administrative heads of each of the state energy offices (see the appendix). Follow-up letters and telephone calls were made through November. In particular, each state was asked to submit information about:

1. the use of incentives and disincentives in the residential sector (e.g., tax credits, low-interest loans, etc.)
2. regulatory programs (e.g., building codes)
3. public education programs
4. surveys and other attempts to monitor public awareness as well as the overall success of the energy program
5. annual reports and overall descriptions of state energy policy.

As of spring 1979, we had received responses from forty-four states. These varied in completeness from a single-page letter to extensive reports, surveys, and samples of public education programs. The range of replies suggests that there is a rather wide range of responses to the ECPA legislation, and that many states have done little more than comply with the minimum guidelines necessary to receive federal funds. Next we will briefly describe the programs of the responding states, giving particular attention to the following eight programs that were frequently adopted:

tighter building codes (mandatory)
public information programs
flyovers

energy audits
low-interest loans for conservation and solar energy usage
tax credits for conservation and solar usage
weatherization programs
the use of public surveys.

The availability of these and other programs in fifty states and the District of Columbia is summarized in Table III-1.

Although the programs may appear to be similar, they often differ in what their specific goals are and whether they are administered by the state or private agencies, including utilities and universities. The greatest difficulty we encountered in the study was the degree of unevenness both in the substance of state programs and in the way in which programs were described in reports. Less than half of the states have some sort of an annual report, and these varied widely in thoroughness.

Alabama

The Alabama Energy Management Board is responsible for a program which will reduce its 1980 energy needs by 5¾ percent. Its 1976 allotment for the inauguration of the program was $205,000.

1. Alabama has adopted the ASHRAE 90-75 code for thermal and lighting efficiency.
2. The management board cooperates with the power and gas companies to encourage construction of energy-efficient homes. In 1977, 700 such homes were constructed. In addition, a conference program was organized between the Home Builders Association and the utilities; financiers, builders and suppliers were surveyed to aid in development of promotional material; and training programs in conservation were made available to the above groups.
3. The management board is aiding lending institutions in establishing low-interest loans for retrofitting.
4. Legislation demands disclosure of operational costs of home heating and cooling systems. Plans are to extend disclosure of costs to freezers, air conditioners, heat pumps, and other major appliances.
5. The state maintains a film library of conservation materials for use by teachers and civic organizations.
6. The state follows Project Conserve in offering class B energy audits for homeowners; a 75-percent response rate from homeowners is anticipated.

7. A program of public school teacher workshops has been implemented for the development of public school curricula on conservation.

Alaska

The Alaska Division of Energy and Power Development was opened in 1974. It oversees a handful of conservation programs, a few of which affect the residential sector.

1. With a grant from the ACTION agency, the state initiated the Energy Conservation Advocates, a grass roots program in ten small communities. The groups work with energy audits, school curriculum development, and public presentations.
2. A weatherization program for low-income homes is in progress.
3. An energy extension service is planned but not operable at this time.
4. The state has initiated a revolving fund for offering low-interest loans to homeowners for adding alternative power sources to their dwellings.
5. The state allows homeowners a state income tax credit for 10 percent of the cost of retrofitting their homes.

Arizona

The Arizona energy program is modest in all respects. It is described in little over two pages in a document from the Office of Economic Planning and Development. There is every indication that the program under EPCA was considered a one shot deal. The state has offered a solar tax credit of 25 percent to a maximum of $1,000. The credit declines beginning in 1979 and terminates in 1984. Solar equipment is also exempted from the state sales tax until 1984. The state has not attempted to develop information material on its own, nor does it have an extensive outreach program.

Arkansas

Arkansas does not publish a report of its conservation program. According to the DOE Annual Report, however, Arkansas did submit a program which included the mandatory EPCA programs, as well as three other programs. The foremost program involving the residential sector is legislation allowing tax exemptions for the cash purchase of energy-saving equipment and its installation in homes.

Table III-1. Presence of Energy Conservation Programs in States, 1978-1979

	Hotline	Weatherization	Audits	Building Code	Community Outreach	Extension Services	Public School Curricula	Mass Media Campaigns
Alabama							✓	
Alaska								
Arizona	✓	✓	✓	✓	✓	✓		✓
Arkansas	✓	✓		✓	✓	✓		✓
California		✓	✓	✓	✓	✓	✓	✓
Colorado	no response							
Connecticut					✓			✓
Delaware	no response				✓			
District of Columbia						✓		
Florida		✓		✓	✓	✓	✓	✓
Georgia	no response	✓	✓	✓	✓	✓	✓	✓
Hawaii	✓	✓	✓	✓			✓	✓
Idaho	no response		✓	✓	✓	✓		✓
Illinois	no response	✓		✓	✓	✓	✓	✓
Indiana	no response		✓	✓	✓		✓	✓
Iowa			✓					
Kansas						✓		
Kentucky			✓	✓		✓		
Louisiana	no usable response			✓	✓	✓		
Maine	no response			✓	✓	✓		
Maryland	✓	✓	✓	✓	✓	✓	✓	✓
Massachusetts	✓	✓	✓				✓	✓
Michigan	✓	✓					✓	✓
Minnesota	✓	✓						✓
Mississippi								

Table III-1. *(continued)*

	Hotline	Weather-ization	Audits	Building Code	Community Outreach	Extension Services	Public School Curricula	Mass Media Campaigns
Missouri	✓	✓	✓	✓		✓		✓
Montana		✓		✓			✓	✓
Nebraska	✓	✓	✓	✓	✓			✓
Nevada		✓	✓	✓	✓	✓	✓	✓
New Hampshire	✓	✓		✓	✓		✓	✓
New Jersey	no response	✓	✓		✓			✓
New Mexico	✓	✓	✓	✓				✓
New York	✓		✓	✓		✓		✓
North Carolina		✓		✓	✓	✓	✓	
North Dakota		✓						
Ohio	✓	✓	✓	✓	✓	✓		✓
Oklahoma	✓		✓	✓	✓	✓	✓	
Oregon		✓		✓		✓	✓	✓
Pennsylvania	no response							
Rhode Island				✓				
South Carolina		✓	✓					
South Dakota		✓	✓	✓	✓	✓	✓	✓
Tennessee	✓		✓	✓	✓	✓	✓	
Texas		✓	✓					
Utah	✓	✓	✓					✓
Vermont	no response	✓		✓	✓	✓		
Virginia			✓	✓	✓	✓		✓
Washington	✓	✓	✓	✓	✓	✓	✓	✓
West Virginia		✓	✓	✓	✓	✓		
Wisconsin		✓					✓	
Wyoming							✓	✓

Table III-1. (continued)

	Tax Credit	Demonstrations	Aerial Thermal Photos	Retrofit and New Source Loans	Encouraging Alternate Systems	Program Evaluation	Periodicals
Alabama		✓				✓	
Alaska	✓			✓	✓		
Arizona	✓			✓	✓		
Arkansas	✓						
California	✓	✓		✓	✓		✓
Colorado	✓				✓	✓	
Connecticut							✓
Delaware						✓	
District of Columbia							✓
Florida		✓		✓		✓	✓
Georgia		✓					
Hawaii		✓					
Idaho	✓	✓		✓	✓	✓	
Illinois							
Indiana							
Iowa	✓	✓		✓	✓	✓	
Kansas	✓	✓		✓	✓	✓	
Kentucky			✓				
Louisiana							
Maine							
Maryland				✓	✓	✓	
Massachusetts		✓		✓	✓	✓	
Michigan		✓	✓	✓		✓	
Minnesota		✓	✓	✓		✓	
Mississippi		✓		✓			

Table III-1. *(continued)*

	Tax Credit	Demonstrations	Aerial Thermal Photos	Retrofit and New Source Loans	Encouraging Alternate Systems	Program Evaluation	Periodicals
Missouri	✓					✓	✓
Montana		✓				✓	✓
Nebraska	✓	✓	✓				
Nevada	✓	✓		✓		✓	
New Hampshire		✓		✓	✓	✓	
New Jersey	✓	✓	✓	✓	✓	✓	✓
New Mexico				✓	✓	✓	
New York			✓	✓	✓		✓
North Carolina	✓	✓	✓	✓	✓	✓	
North Dakota	✓					✓	
Ohio	✓						
Oklahoma		✓	✓		✓	✓	✓
Oregon	✓	✓	✓	✓	✓		
Pennsylvania						✓	
Rhode Island							
South Carolina			✓				
South Dakota			✓		✓		
Tennessee				✓			
Texas							
Utah						✓	
Vermont							
Virginia		✓	✓				✓
Washington				✓	✓	✓	
West Virginia				✓	✓		
Wisconsin	✓	✓	✓		✓	✓	
Wyoming		✓			✓	✓	✓

199

There have been no surveys of the public on knowledge or attitudes towards conservation. There is an energy information hotline, and conservation has been advertised through television and radio announcements, and at booths at state fairs. Further legislation will be enacted in 1979, to meet State Energy Conservation Plan requirements.

California

Of the states surveyed, California has established the most ambitious program to encourage adoption of the renewable energy sources of solar (direct and passive), wind, and biomass. Beyond this, California set four major goals that affect the residential sector: (1) to upgrade building codes; (2) to expand information and technical assistance; (3) to train and license energy analysts; (4) to retrofit all "feasible" residences by 1982. In addition to these goals which paralleled or exceeded those set by the NEP in 1977, California also began to consider the complex issue of energy pricing, rate structures, and a means to encourage alternative energy sources. From the staff reports obtained from the California Energy Resources Conservation and Development Commission, we would rate the California plan as one of the best that we surveyed.

The primary focus of the California program is on education rather than regulation or economic incentives (excluding the one major exception of solar tax credits). As indicated by Table 1 which lists specific state programs, California has tightened building codes and encouraged installation of insulation in existing buildings. The extent of these programs was not, however, evident from the material available. The Energy Commission recommended in 1977 that utilities be required to provide information and loans for installation of conservation retrofits, but we were unable to determine whether this had become state law. California has also established an "Office of Appropriate Technology" which provides public information in the form of brochures, pamphlets, and trailer exhibits to encourage alternative energy devices.

The main thrust of the California program lies in the attempt to encourage the adoption of solar energy on a widespread basis. The credit adopted in September 1977 is available to builders and homeowners alike. The law allows a credit of 55 percent of the cost of solar equipment up to $3,000, covering both the purchase and installation costs. For buildings other than single family residences, the credit is 25 percent of up to $3,000. This applies to both active and passive solar systems. In addition, the state has created a solar agency (Solar Cal) to actively encourage the development of a solar fabrication industry as a new base of economic development and jobs. Overall, the state has a goal of installing solar space conditioning and hot water heating systems in 20 percent of all residential and commercial buildings by 1985. This is equivalent to 1.5 million homes. The Energy Commission staff estimates that this program will create 50,000 new year-round jobs.

The educational outreach part of the California program is done by the existing utilities, all of which have both some form of information on, and a marketing program for, residential insulation. However, this has, by their estimates, been a slow process which will take from five to thirteen years to reach half of the potential market. Consequently, the Energy Commission recommended in late 1976 that standards be raised for residential insulation and that utilities be required to expand their insulation marketing programs. To our knowledge, the first of these is now law, but we do not have information on the second. At the same time, the commission recommended the development of low-cost utility financing programs and modest tax credits for residential retrofits.

Colorado

The Colorado Office of Energy Conservation (OEC) plans to use its DOE allocations ($457,000 for 1977, $918,000 for 1978 and 1979, $644,000 for 1980) to reduce its energy needs by 5.4 percent. Several of its programs apply to the residential sector. The public information and service programs are as follows.

1. The state supports lifestyle audits for residents including home environment, appliance use and transportation.
2. A TV program supporting and explaining the mass-distributed audits is being organized.
3. The Regional Energy/Environment Information Center has been established in the Conservation Library of the Denver Public Library as a comprehensive information source.
4. A toll-free hotline to the above source has been established.
5. The OEC prepares and distributes fact sheets, news releases, a monthly newsletter, and brochures on conservation. Weekly five-minute TV spots on conservation are also produced.
6. The Domestic Technology Institute will establish local conservation centers across the state and will coordinate with local organizations on action-oriented programs. An independent firm will evaluate the success of the community centers

system in delivering information. A private contract is being formulated to provide the regional centers with publications and lists of programs and references.

7. The Cooperative Extension Service, set up at Colorado State University, will distribute DTI's energy program and provide conservation technology in-service training programs.

8. A special impact TV series of four thirty-minute programs will deal with energy problems of the poor, elderly and minority populations. Programs will be leadoffs for community discussion meetings or longer TV programs. They are produced for use across a six-state region (Colorado, Wyoming, Montana, Utah, South Dakota and North Dakota).

9. OEC distributes material, written with the help of an attorney to help consumers protect themselves against fraudulent conservation and solar materials and equipment sales schemes.

10. The state (with DOE money) will establish a $17,000 weatherization drawing for ten Colorado families.

11. The Colorado Office of Human Resources provides energy conservation information to all participants in its weatherization program.

12. The OEC's data collection analysis section is a clearinghouse and referral center for energy information and data. This office serves to monitor conservation programs and provides bases for policy analysis and impact.

13. In the area of alternative sources, OEC has produced a Solar Information Handbook and is participating in the thirteen-state Western Regional Solar Network, which encourages the use of solar energy.

14. The state will coordinate conservation efforts on a local, federal, and state basis, so as to provide equal distribution of programs throughout the state.

15. OEC has written and enacted its own building code for thermal and lighting efficiency.

16. Three types of tax benefits are available. Taxpayers receive a state income tax adjustment on the purchase and installation of alternative energy devices and heat pumps, comparable to their rate of tax payment. Buildings using solar energy are properly taxed at a 5-percent rate rather than the normal 30-percent rate. Also, homeowners retrofitting their thirty- or more-year old homes may delay reassessments for five years.

Delaware

The State Office of Management, Budget and Planning is responsible for the implementation and monitoring of their conservation plan, which includes five mandatory programs and twelve others. Savings by 1980 are projected to be $143,000 and over 5 percent in Btu. The largest savings are predicted through adopting and enforcing the ASHRAE 90-75 standards for thermal and lighting efficiency, which have already been included in the building codes in all but three political jurisdictions in the state. A public education program will inform the public of the ASHRAE requirements to encourage compliance. If standard legislation becomes necessary, it will begin with a study of similar legislation in other states. Plans are underway for involving the private sector in retrofitting by designing manuals and materials for training programs, educating the public and legislating passive energy conservation standards in building design, and developing programs encouraging voluntary retrofitting, such as giving tax credits to apartment house owners. A monitoring and report system for retrofitting activities will be developed.

Of the optional programs, five apply to the residential sector.

1. The Delmarva Power Company uses a peak load pricing rate for residents with electric heating. It has also stopped accepting any new residential gas customers, as of 1971.
2. The power company is considering retrofitting gas furnaces with smaller orifices to reduce gas consumption.
3. The Public Utilities Commission has approved the promotional advertising of electric heat pumps.
4. Insulation seminars have been sponsored regionally to answer citizens' questions directly.
5. An education program is being designed specifically to encourage pilot light turnoff in the summer.
6. Project Conserve will be implemented to give homeowners concrete facts on conservation techniques, prices and savings. The University of Delaware will manage the project. A survey of builders and contractors will first be done to ascertain costs and availability of materials. There will then be a complete mass media distribution of the results. Community service groups will be asked to encourage public participation. The state may offer a service award to clubs which most actively promote Project Conserve. Workshops and a hotline will be established to answer individual questions.
7. The Fuel Oil Distributors Association will be legislatively backed in its campaign to service oil furnaces annually. The state will advertise the program and the distributors will report the numbers of serviced burners to the state as a method of monitoring program success.

204 / Supplementary Analyses

Florida

Florida was not among the ten states selected by EPCA for pilot programs, but with its seed money it monitored noteworthy programs conducted by two county extension services.

For the fiscal year 1977, Florida received $1,481,027 from the U.S. Government. The state energy office has two major divisions relating to the residential sector—the Energy Supply and Demand Section, which provides some statistical publications; and the Conservation Management Section, which provides a training and registration program for energy auditors and the public encouragement of energy audits. Florida's energy consumption by the residential sector is 24 percent of its total, whereas the national average is 11 percent. The emphasis needs to be on the transportation of people and goods, and on changes in lifestyle. The Residential Energy Conservation Program has an energy savings calculation of at least 5 percent by 1980.

In addition, the Planning and Information Section of the state energy office contains the Residential Conservation Program.

1. Through a series of publications, issues of ventilation, shading, alternative energy sources, servicing, cooling and other conservation techniques will be addressed.

2. The Technical Information Development Program monitors test homes and compares standard energy techniques with conservation techniques. The resulting data are then presented to the public.

3. County Energy Information Centers provide information for individuals and for public addresses; the centers will later be expanded to become part of the Energy Extension Service. At present there are regional offices responsible for keeping contact with the citizens.

4. Considerable attention was given to formal energy education in public schools in that every school has an environmental educator to carry out energy-related programs. Florida first held a statewide informational conference for educators, then regional workshops, and finally school district programs, so as to involve local citizens and make material relevant on the community level.

5. In the area of alternative sources, residential conservation exhibits have been set up for community leaders.

6. Florida State University has produced a cost-effectiveness analysis of solar hot water retrofitting.

7. The 1978 fiscal budget includes plans for nine new solar retrofit projects.
8. In the area of media presentation of research findings and other energy-related information, the energy office contracted with a commercial advertising firm to promote conservation materials on a statewide basis.
9. A noteworthy survey of energy use and knowledge was prepared by the Pinella County Extension Service. Results of that survey were not sent to us.

Georgia

The Georgia program is a relatively modest one. The state has upgraded building codes and has empowered local governments to exempt the value of solar equipment from property taxes. Beyond this, Georgia does not publish an annual report, nor has it attempted to survey public attitudes and knowledge of energy-saving measures.

The state has developed a program to provide energy information to homebuilders and buyers. The present program is funded by the state and is run by Georgia Tech University through a series of workshops. Also, the Office of Energy Resources has developed a program of information, including a newsletter, audio-visual materials, workshops, and a speakers' bureau. Total funding for this program is $132,102. Finally, the state has also funded ($32,000) a program for training energy auditors through the Georgia Society of Professional Engineers. Presently the outreach program is run by the University of Georgia, Georgia Technical, and the Home Builders Association, with the state in a supervisory role.

Idaho

Idaho's Office of Energy developed an energy plan by asking its citizens on a one-to-one basis and in community meetings what they wanted their state to do to help them conserve energy. The plan was designed to conserve 5 percent of the projected 1980 energy consumption.

1. The mandatory lighting and thermal efficiency plan was specific to the state, following the ASHRAE 90-75 guidelines.
2. A Home Audit Program is offered; the audits are performed by engineering graduate students. The audit program also provides demonstrations on residential measurement of heat

loss; local forums for the sharing between homeowners of effective weatherization techniques; and demonstrations of new weatherization materials. Thus it provides general energy information as well as information specific to each dwelling.

3. Idaho allows a state income tax deduction of 100 percent of the cost of installing insulation materials or renewable energy systems up to $5,000.

4. The state has a plan for educating children on energy issues through the public schools. The program includes units in public libraries, assembly programs, a youth training program, and college courses in conservation measures.

5. The state energy office distributes to all media sources the *Idaho Energy Background* looseleaf binder, which contains data on energy issues and programs.

6. A monthly newsletter on energy is distributed to residents of Idaho upon request.

7. Idaho cooperates with Washington and Oregon in preparing energy programs for radio and television stations.

8. The office distributes to anyone, upon request, information on the efficiency and economics of energy-consuming appliances.

9. The office maintains a Speaker's Bureau and a film/slide library on energy issues.

10. A statewide energy hotline is maintained.

11. A weatherization program winterizes the homes of low-income and elderly state residents; the program is carried out by any of seven Community Action agencies.

12. Idaho's evaluation of each program specifies a two-pronged approach; it quantitatively evaluates the program economically and mechanically, to improve its effectiveness, and it qualitatively evaluates its problems and constraints, which would affect its acceptance and implementation.

Indiana

Indiana responded only by letter, suggesting that the state had done little beyond EPCA requirements. For example, Indiana does not have any program of incentives for either solar or conservation retrofits. Nor has the state attempted to survey public attitudes and knowledge of energy issues. New thermal standards have been adopted, but as of June had not yet been enforced. Indiana has developed a minimal outreach education program, which includes presentations at fairs, a system of community coordinators, and "energy days."

Iowa

Iowa's Energy Policy Council has enacted a conservation plan to reduce energy usage by 8 percent by 1980. The plan includes the five mandatory practices and five others, many of which involve education and information to the public.

1. The Kill-a-Watt campaign was a major mass media educational effort to provide information on conservation. News releases on the project were sent to radio and TV stations. Newspapers carried Kill-a-Watt ads, four features stories, daily conservation tips, and project explanations. Particular stress was on peak loading in the summer of 1978.
2. Public speakers and slide shows are available.
3. The state publishes a monthly energy bulletin of approximately eight pages.
4. To encourage more community action, the state distributes $5,000 in grants presented by the governor, of up to $500 each, for community self-improvement projects.
5. An annotated bibliography of public school curricula on conservation is available for kindergarten through sixth grade.
6. Energy Efficiency Sharing Workshops are carried out in manufacturing firms so that workers can share conservation ideas on an individual basis as well as on an industry-organized level. This project won the FEA outstanding Conservation Program award.
7. The State Weatherization Program provides money ($120,000 in 1976) for weatherization of homes of low-income and elderly persons.
8. The state has prepared its own home energy audit sheet, which is given out to homeowners on a one-to-one basis at malls, fairs, and energy demonstrations; it is distributed by the State University Cooperative Extension Service.
9. The state provides $50,000 for low-interest loans to lower-income persons for the retrofitting of single-family dwellings.
10. Legislation requires that all existing homes meet thermal efficiency standards before the transfer of ownership.
11. Legislation bans the sale of new gas appliances with pilot lights.

12. The following tax benefits were legislated—Solar and wind energy devices and methane gas production systems are exempt from property tax; the sale of fuels used for residential purposes are exempt from sales tax; income tax credit may be received for the purchase and installation of solar heating devices and materials.
13. A lifeline electrical service demonstration program has been established for elderly low-income people.
14. The state is promoting the use of solar energy by encouraging research on all aspects of its usage.
15. The state is enforcing efficiency standards on all appliances sold in Iowa.

Kansas

Kansas has indicated that it is following the ASHRAE 90-75 thermal building codes. As of 1978 there were no formal conservation plans outlined for the residential sector. However, three pieces of legislation had been adopted to give financial assistance to the homeowner.

1. State income tax credit is given for purchase and installation of solar energy equipment.
2. A 35- percent state property tax rebate is given for solar energy systems capable of meeting at least 70 percent of a homeowner's heating and cooling needs. A plan has also been outlined for securing access to sunlight through easements.
3. Homeowners may take a deduction of 50 percent, or $500, of the cost of labor and materials for installation of home weatherization equipment.

Kentucky

A state energy conservation plan was developed in 1975 by Kentucky's Department of Energy. In 1977, $367,000 was made available for carrying out the program. Of the fifty-two plans proposed and set up, only sixteen could be fully implemented with the money provided.

The state has developed its own mandatory lighting and building standards which are at least as stringent as the ASHRAE 90-75; the monitoring of this program as well as a full-scale education program are the responsibility of the state fire marshall.

A cooperative extension service has been established to disseminate printed information to the public, both by mail and by personal contact. There are home energy workshops, local exhibits, seminars, and lectures for special interest groups; and short courses are available through the extension service. A mobile van carries programs, exhibits, and printed material to the counties. Telelectures and radio programs are also prepared. The extension service provides home energy audit forms for computer processing and/or self-auditing.

The Department of Education has developed a written curriculum for the promotion of conservation attitudes in the schools. Teacher training within universities and on-the-job is being provided and there are yearly general awareness workshops for teachers and administrators. Additional material is made available through a computer-based resource unit and an energy education television program system. The program is evaluated on a regular basis.

The extension service also provides public awareness programs through the 4H Clubs' Energy Awareness Week and other public awareness programs, such as an energy awards banquet.

As a forerunner of a tax incentive program for the installation and the use of solar energy equipment in the household, the state began a thorough study of tax incentive systems in 1976.

In addition to these programs, a "bottle bill" and a weatherization program were being studied for future inclusion.

Though not described here, Kentucky's involvement with the public in setting up a car pool program tailored to each city has been impressive.

Maryland

Maryland is presently in the process of revising its building codes to comply with EPCA. The state presently offers no incentives in the form of tax credits for solar or conservation investments, although private lending institutions do offer low-interest loans. The state has run an educational program which includes the dissemination of information and an energy hotline. Maryland does promote weatherization programs through utilities. The state also has conducted a survey of residential energy use, but did not include results.

Massachusetts

The Massachusetts energy program is reportedly among the better organized ones. The State Energy Office is divided into three parts: Public Information; Program and Policy Development; and Energy Conservation and Extension. Residential conservation is run through

"Project Conserve," which includes thirty separate programs and is budgeted at $1.7 million. The state has developed a low-interest loan program for conservation and has encouraged "life cycle costing" in the housing sector. In addition, the Massachusetts program includes a solar component. The state has established a Solar Action Office, which is attempting to fund a solar installation and training program. Massachusetts also grants a real estate tax exemption for solar or wind systems.

The Massachusetts public information program includes educational materials for public schools and an "energy phone" manned by students from Clark University. The state is also working to improve its energy audit program with the University of Massachusetts. To encourage the adoption of energy conservation, 115 banks have agreed to reduce their interest rates for energy retrofits. Finally, Massachusetts has used public opinion surveys to determine the success of particular programs.

Michigan

Michigan has set up an Energy Administration geared to save 7.8 percent of the 1980 projected energy usage; during 1978 its budget from EPCA has been $1,624,000. The state appears to have a well-organized network of offices which administer its programs. In addition, many more programs aimed at conservation are in the process of being legislated.

1. The state had adopted the ASHRAE 90-75 code for thermal efficiency.
2. It is using the ASHRAE 90-75 code for efficiency in lighting.
3. The Project Conserve home audit is used; it has been modified to be specific to Michigan.
4. The state is using federal funds for infrared photos of private homes.
5. Weatherization of low-income homes is administered jointly by the Energy Administration and the Bureau of Community Action agencies.
6. The state is formulating a law requiring mandatory installation of furnace orifices and fuel restrictors before transfer of property.
7. The administration supports a program for training local building code officials in the new building code.
8. The new Consumer Protection Fraud Prevention Program provides information to homeowners which will arm them

against fraudulent salesmen of conservation devices.

9. The state supports an Energy Extension Service which provides 160 brochures on energy conservation, some of which are specific to Michigan and others of which are provided through links with the DOE, Lockheed, and New York Times Clearinghouses. Also, Michigan State University has a computerized file of energy information.

10. A statewide energy hotline is maintained through the extension service.

11. The state supports a Youth Education Program which provides educational activities and learning-by-doing experiences for young people and their parents. Activities include small group discussions, fairs, poster exhibits, and youth-oriented home and transportation audits.

12. The Energy Administration puts considerable effort into its Local Government Program. It provides grants, technical assistance and incentives for the establishment of local offices. Some local units have dwelt on government operations; most are concerned with providing knowledge and organization to the residential sector. The Local Government Unit currently operates a Multiple Option Publicity Campaign; in this program, it has chosen one large city for the dissemination of all types of awareness material, the major purpose being to evaluate the effectiveness of the various materials for use in other communities. The unit encourages the use of volunteer groups for conservation awareness campaigning at the local level.

13. The state is enacting legislation for the provision of low-interest loans for energy-saving devices.

14. A state solar energy coordinating council is being established. Legislation is in operation to permit a 50-percent reduction of cost and the installation of alternate source energy units.

15. Legislation is in progress to permit a 100-percent tax deduction for the retrofitting of insulation, $200 for the retrofitting of gas furnaces, and tax credits for other homestead improvements for conservation.

16. Proposed legislation would mandate the adoption of peak load rate structures for utility companies.

17. A residential Utility Consumer Action Group is being established through the Committee on Public Utilities.

18. Various pieces of legislation to provide and encourage fuel conservation devices on furnaces are under consideration.

19. The state does not now have a public school curriculum for

energy conservation, but a Committee on Education is currently preparing one.

20. Michigan now provides bonds for the retrofitting of moderate-and low-income housing.

Minnesota

The Minnesota Energy Agency has enacted a state plan which will save the state 9.5 percent of its projected energy demand in 1980.

1. In 1977 the state adopted the ASHRAE 90-75 energy code.
2. All homes must be retrofitted to meet these standards before transfer is permitted.
3. $80,000 has been allocated toward the study of load programs for housing unit owners for retrofitting on tenants.
4. A law has been enacted to discourage fraudulence on the part of retrofitting and alternative systems materials salesmen.
5. Legislation is under way for establishing solar access rights and easement.
6. There has been enacted a law which establishes efficiency ratios for home appliances and enforces adherence of these standards for all appliances manufactured, sold or transported within the state.
7. A demonstration project has been begun for the setting up of two solar energy systems for public display.
8. Since 1977 the state has performed aerial infrared roof top surveys in twenty-eight cities across the state. Seminars are set up to give explanations of results and information on retrofitting and conservation. The surveys appear to be financially self-sustaining in that sales tax from retrofitting materials exceeds the cost to the state of the aerial surveys.
9. There exists a law requiring disclosure of utility costs on all homes for which ownership is being transferred.
10. Legislation provides that homes with solar, wind, or methane energy devices do not receive property tax increases.
11. The Energy Conservation Information Center was established. It disseminates printed materials on conservation and provides a list of publications available; writes TV and radio programs on conservation techniques and services available; and provides a toll-free hotline for citizen use.
12. The energy agency in conjunction with the State Education Department has devised a comprehensive public education program—a public school curriculum exists for all grade levels

from kindergarten through high school. An annotated bibliography of other states' public school energy conservation curricula has been prepared and is available; an assessment has been made of teacher involvement with these curricula and their opinions of existing programs and future needs. An audio-visual library of energy conservation instructional materials is available from the state. Funds are available for state college instructors to provide energy curricula in local school districts, to provide in-service training to teachers, and to hold college instructor workshops to offer energy education workshops for the coordination of energy courses across the state. The Education Department has developed HEATLOSS, an interactive computerized home energy audit for high school students, which is available with a workbook through the Minnesota Educational Computing Consortium. Vocational schools provide courses in energy conservation and have organized 4-H groups to implement projects within their communities; through the Vocational Education Division and the energy agency, curricula for adult education extension courses have been prepared and are taught in adult education extension courses.

13. $400,000 per year is available to local communities and cities for projects geared at finding solutions to energy problems peculiar to specific areas.

14. The Local Services section of the Conservation Division plans and carries out conservation outreach programs on the local level. The primary function at present is the dissemination of infrared flyover information and the establishment of energy awareness programs. A local government energy awareness handbook was developed. Ninety cities and counties have state energy programs. Examples of activities are energy fairs, block parties, home energy audits, and award presentations for energy-efficient homes. The groups also serve to coordinate the efforts of service organizations in their projects.

Mississippi

Mississippi has not done anything beyond the barest EPCA requirements. The state indicated by letter that it offers no incentives for conservation. Building codes will have to be amended by law in 1979 but presently do not reflect any concern for residential conservation. The state does plan to create a public awareness program but has not yet done so beyond a program run by Mississippi State University.

Missouri

Missouri is in the process of creating a state building code to comply with a portion of ASHRAE 90-75 as required by EPCA. To this effect the Department of Natural Resources has submitted legislation to the Missouri assembly to establish statewide standards for all new and renovated buildings. There is presently no state building code. The state has also encouraged utilities to offer weatherization programs, but these are not required by law. Also, Missouri is developing a state education program.

Montana

Montana has adopted a new state building code patterned after ASHRAE 90-75 guidelines and has established workshops to retrain local inspectors. The state program for public awareness appears to be targeted on primary and secondary schools, for which courses and energy workshops are planned. Beyond this, no broader education program was described in Montana's report. The state has conducted at least one poll on conservation and one on knowledge about solar energy. Results were not included.

Nebraska

Nebraska Energy Office is complying with EPCA Conservation guidelines in attempting to decrease its 1980 expected energy needs by 5 percent, by means of enacting mandatory programs and a few optional ones—dealing mainly with transportation and agriculture.

1. A film which describes the state's dependence on fuel imports and identifies specific energy problems was made.
2. A free Homeowners Handbook on conservation, entitled "In the Bank or up the Chimney," was distributed upon request to 3,000 inquirers.
3. A telephone hotline was established to provide personal counseling on construction and retrofitting; over 500 consumers used the service.
4. A series of organizational and informational meetings was held across the state to give a local flavor to the ideas and services available to homeowners; over 2,000 people attended. The state strove for strong community, utility and

service club support in encouraging conservation on the local level.

5. An intensive advertising campaign at the local level was encouraged for the meetings; promotions included newspaper and TV coverage, advertising of materials and services from local businesses, radio interviews, and the distribution of conservation brochures.

6. The state will enforce the ASHRAE 90-75 lighting and thermal efficiency codes as prepared by ERDA. As one of twelve pilot states in a program to encourage home retrofitting in 1976-1977, Nebraska enacted five programs.

7. A personal audit service has been planned to replace the Project Conserve mail-in forms. This audit will be geared to low-income families, those in mobile homes, and those in older homes.

8. The utility companies in nine cities are carrying out an infrared scanning program.

9. Several cities are holding neighborhood meetings to assess and use the results of infrared scannings, and in some municipalities there have already been bulk purchases of insulation materials.

10. There is a full-time staff person available on the state level to coordinate volunteer efforts geared at promoting homeowner participation, arranging conferences, and answering questions.

11. A series of experiments is proposed on peak load pricing; these would be carried out by utility companies in conjunction with the state energy office.

12. A survey was carried out and published by an Omaha newspaper to monitor the success of President Carter's request for citizens to turn down thermostats.

Nevada

Nevada's Energy Management Division of its Public Service Commission developed a plan which would achieve a 5-percent reduction in energy consumption by 1980.

State-tailored lighting and building efficiency standards were designed by the state Public Works Board. A public awareness campaign was designed which included dissemination of printed material to households by persons going door-to-door and/or in utility bills; billboard notices; radio and television spots; and newspaper notices. Slide shows were prepared, and a speakers' bureau was established.

Home energy audits are given out in do-it-yourself form, with follow-up assistance and advice provided by the Department of Energy.

On a larger scale the state joins with local professional and special interest groups in providing biannual energy conservation expositions on the local level.

In operation is a public education program which provides teacher workshops, printed curriculum material, suggested projects geared toward training school children in conservation principles.

Various programs have begun to reduce homeowners' energy consumption through revised energy systems. State property tax credit is given up to $2,000 annually for the use of renewable resource heating and air conditioning systems. Utilities are encouraged to provide special loans to customers for the installation and addition of insulation to their homes. The state is also assisting community agencies in assisting low-income residents in the weatherization of dwellings. Legislation is being proposed in 1979 to eliminate open gas pilot lights on gas appliances.

New Hampshire

In October 1977, New Hampshire received $165,000 from DOE to carry out its EPCA plans. Its program included the five required programs and eighteen discretionary ones. Extending for FY 1979 is $513,000. The plans provide for a 7.67-percent savings by 1980.

1. As fulfillment of the mandatory requirement of building codes, the Governor's Council proposes to promote adoption of standards based on ASHRAE 90-75. The council will provide training sessions on interpreting and enforcing the code in municipalities, and will furnish education and advice to builders and contractors.
2. The Retro-Tech program will establish teaching teams at each of the seven vocational technical colleges to conduct free home winterization courses. The council will develop and provide course materials similar to DOE's Project Retro-Tech.
3. For those who cannot attend courses, a widely publicized hotline will be available for people who have questions and seek course material. A videotape version of the course will be prepared by Public Television. An energy extension service is also provided.
4. Two programs deal with improving the efficiency of oil

burners. Project "ACE" is a series of paid media ads to advise homeowners on the benefits of instrumentation testing of oil burners to increase efficiency. There is also a program which provides free oil burner checks and funds for major systems repairs for low-income and elderly persons.

5. The home winterization for low-income and elderly persons is provided by trained CETA workers who use the principles and materials recommended in the Retro-Tech program.

6. Most utilities in New Hampshire use a declining block-rate pricing structure. The council offers the concept of peak load pricing as an alternative.

7. The council will conduct an annual phone survey of household fuel wood use and procurement as part of its Wood Energy Program, which is aimed at encouraging forest owners to practice woodlot management and promote the use of wood as a home heating supplement.

8. 200 families were chosen by lottery to receive $400 toward the purchase of solar domestic hot water systems; this money came as a grant from HUD. The families must select a system approved by the P.I.N.Y. study.

9. In an effort to assist homeowners in retrofitting, the state encourages the loaning of money at a lower rate. Two lending institutions are presently offering these loans at 2 percent lower rates.

10. The New England Regional Commission, through the computerized New England Energy Management Information System, provides information on building heat loss and transportation to facilitate decisionmaking on energy matters.

11. The NERA has developed a $3,000 collection of books on solar energy at the state library.

12. The New England Solar Energy Center has provided funds to the state for promoting solar energy.

13. Two noted attempts to measure program effectiveness are the annual wood usage survey and the monitoring of the state procurement program by the Energy Monitoring Committee.

New Jersey

New Jersey has a ten-year master plan, the first state energy plan in the nation to be adopted. It takes into consideration the economic growth of the state and especially attempts to deemphasize the "technological fix" solutions.

1. A state energy hotline has been established at Kean College; it serves to give information to and get feed-back from the public.
2. The Tri-City Citizens Union for Progress and the Office of Conservation, a non-profit organization fostering planned urbanization projects, provide data on housing conditions, usage of energy, and feasible conservation measures for urban housing, and will train community personnel and maintenance workers in weatherization. They will also conduct workshops to urban housing residents to educate them on conservation measures.
3. The Office of Conservation sponsors in one county a pilot program which offers audits, information, workers, and materials for the weatherization of the homes of senior citizens who do not qualify for low-income weatherization. (The senior citizens themselves pay for the work performed.)
4. VISTA has funded the New Jersey Public Interest Research Group for two community organizers who will weatherize 100 homes and provide conservation information and services to 900 families in a low-income neighborhood. This is in part a feasibility study for a statewide energy conservation program.
5. The state awards prizes on the residential and community levels for novel ideas toward the conservation of energy. Awards are also given in a poster contest for school students.
6. The Office of Conservation has helped to establish local energy offices in some counties. Services from these offices will include information services, lectures and displays, the coordination of community services with state services, and residential workshops and audits.
7. Workbooks for homeowners on the subject of insulation have been provided statewide. These include a walk-through audit, working instructions, and an inspection manual.
8. A workbook enabling citizens to audit their homes and lifestyles is available. Another workbook explains how the public can inspect their homes and calculate\specific energy and dollar savings.
9. The state publishes a monthly newsletter which disseminates information and advertises programs, services and workshops on conservation measures. Readership includes 20,000 citizens.
10. The Office of Conservation will conduct a study on how to motivate citizens to retrofit; they will administer five types

of home audits, distribute questionnaires to evaluate resulting retrofitting measures, and conduct pre- and post-audit fuel usage tests.

11. Thermograph surveys will be done on a limited basis (perhaps only as part of the above-mentioned retrofitting survey).

12. The state will sponsor a 100-residence survey of attitudes, understanding and behavior in energy conservation. The Eagleton Institute of Politics of Rutgers University will conduct the survey.

13. The state will provide a traveling exhibit of alternative energy sources and conservation techniques, and will try to integrate it with specific local savings developments as it travels across counties. The vehicle is to be a 40-foot donated trailer.

14. The Public School Education campaign includes a curriculum for grades K through twelve, a glossary of terms, and a bibliography of energy-related readings.

15. The state DOE and the Jewish Federation of Community Services co-sponsors a take-home Junior Energy Inspector Quiz for children in grades one through five to work on with the help of their parents. There is one for homeowners and one for children.

16. The state is undertaking a study of the fuel subsidy components of HUD's energy conservation in subsidized housing; suggestions for a program of incentives for both tenants and management will be provided.

17. Certain lending institutions offer low-interest retrofitting loans to homeowners.

18. Legislation provides for both local and state property tax exemptions for alternative systems equipment.

19. In an effort to encourage alternative systems, the Office of Alternate Technology keeps a listing of installers and dealers of such systems, a reading list, tax incentive information, and information on codes and standards.

New York

The New York program supposedly ranks with California, Massachusetts, Wisconsin, and Minnesota as one of the best state programs. The state requires that gas and electric utilities offer energy audits and arrange for the financing of various conservation measures. It also publishes do-it-yourself guides for retrofitting and auditing. These publications are distributed through banks, public interest groups, realtors, schools, and so forth. Among the publications that we reviewed, these were possibly the best in terms of understandability and comprehensiveness.

In accord with EPCA requirements, the state upgraded its building code, effective October 1, 1978. The state has also conducted an exhaustive survey of residential insulation, which found among other things that New York homes are better insulated than previously thought. Over 80 percent have attic insulation and 60 percent have insulation in the walls. Financing did not turn out to be a significant reason for not insulating.

North Carolina

North Carolina is outstanding not only in its range of programs but also in its continuing evaluation and monitoring of them. In 1976 the state received $106,000 from the federal government for its programs; in 1977 it received $520,000. The plans are designed for the conservation of 8.05 percent of the state's 1980 baseline predicted energy consumption. North Carolina's thermal efficiency standards for new and renovated buildings are at least as stringent as the ASHRAE 90-75 codes but are tailored for North Carolina's needs. Evaluation takes place by means of quarterly reports from the Building Codes Division and annual reports from the Department of Labor. The lighting efficiency standards are comparable to ASHRAE 90-75 and are included in the thermal codes.

The state energy office maintains an active hotline, the activities of which are recorded for subsequent program evaluation. There is a clearinghouse of information available by mail to citizens and organizations. The clearinghouse amasses literature from other agencies as well as producing its own pamphlets with information particularly pertinent to the state, such as one on the precautions to be taken in the purchasing of conservation materials. A separate energy library contains publications, films, and slide presentations. Some of the films have been developed by the state for use in workshops, training courses, and general special interest group presentations. A state energy newsletter is published and is available to schools, local governments, and agencies. A consumer protection program is being developed which will guard citizens against unfair and deceptive practices in the sale of alternative sources of energy materials. A large-scale energy exposition is designed to increase public awareness of conservation needs on all levels. In addition, smaller energy fairs assist in the public exposure of private conservation programs across the state. Furthermore, a special energy exhibit is presented at the annual state fair. All of the aforementioned services are monitored and evaluated by the Energy Office by means of records of citizen usage of services and a sample survey on popular interest in conservation issues as a possible result of the promotion of state issues and programs.

The State Economic Opportunity Office administers a low-income family home weatherization program. Weatherization processes vary from house to house and are primarily carried out by community action agencies at local levels. Ongoing program evaluation is carried on by means of the monitoring of each weatherized dwelling and by subsequent quarterly reports.

The state's home retrofitting program is multifaceted. A computer-assisted home energy audit was made available to citizens in the form of Project Conserve questionnaires. A do-it-yourself home audit workshop is currently available. The state is developing its own audit to be scored on a portable programmable calculator. North Carolina conducts an accompanying publicity campaign of the audits via mass media presentations. In coordination with this effort, workshops called "Saving Energy at Home" were carried on in several community colleges for public attendance. The Energy Division now operates its own workshops on home energy conservation and on solar and wood heating, both on a request basis. Another retrofit workshop for presentation to bankers and other lenders addresses the importance of providing alternative energy systems loans to citizens. An infrared thermograph survey of homes in ten North Carolina cities was conducted for the purpose of evaluating building styles and retrofitting programs. In the area of home retrofitting, the state will evaluate the results of a questionnaire sent out from the utility companies to assess voluntary home retrofitting activities. This program is one example of the state's efforts in the ongoing evaluation of conservation attitudes and practices.

The state's program of public education is extensive, and the evaluation and updating of it are equally comprehensive. A written curriculum is offered from kindergarten through twelfth grade. A 16mm film is presented to the children, and various slide shows are available. A program of twenty or more multidisciplinary school activities on energy is available, and an awards program accompanies the activities program. Teacher training for the energy curricula is presented through the following programs:

in-service training classes
film presentations
summer workshops
a clearinghouse of available programs and materials

a periodic newsletter on activities
occasional seminars
an extension service correspondence course.

On the college level, workshops, short courses, and full-year courses on retrofitting and alternative energy source equipment are offered in some community colleges.

In 1978 the state's 145 Local Education Agencies will be encouraged to submit proposals for the funding of energy education projects on a local level. The Energy Division will cooperate with other agencies in administering this program.

In the area of alternative sources, the state secondary education vocational training program offers a curriculum in solar energy components and systems. Ten local programs have been designed to fulfill an exemplary as well as an educational purpose.

The state legislature encourages the use of alternative energy sources for residential heating and cooling by means of two pieces of legislation. A state tax credit of $1,000 or 25 percent is given for the costs of the purchase and installation of solar equipment. An additional tax credit provides that new solar equipment added to residences will not be assessed until 1985. To encourage retrofitting, the legislature has guaranteed loans to low-income residents for the purchase of conservation materials.

North Dakota

North Dakota has passed a new statewide building code that meets ASHRAE 90-75 standards. The state does apparently offer incentives for conservation but does not have a tax credit of an undetermined amount for solar or wind devices. For public information, the state has developed several excellent brochures, but the respondents did not indicate that they had developed an active public education program. As of June 20, 1978, North Dakota had not attempted to monitor builder-homeowner attitudes about energy conservation but indicated that this would be part of plans for the future.

Ohio

Ohio has amended its building code to coincide with the standards set by ASHRAE 90-75 applying to new and renovated housing. A modest tax credit of sixty-five dollars for home improvements including insulation is offered. Public education programs are equally modest, but the State Department of Energy planned a major campaign this fall to "sell" their services. The main thrust of the energy department, however, would appear to be toward the production side.

Oklahoma

Oklahoma lists twenty-four programs to be carried out by its Department of Energy. The 1978 cost of implementation is $538,000 and aims at a 9-percent reduction in the expected energy needs for 1980.

1. Oklahoma presently uses the FEA self-audit for homeowners but feels it is not well received. Through the OSU extension service, county extension services, and libraries, the state has distributed 65,000 brief audits geared to stimulate homeowners on retrofitting. An Oklahoma-specific self-audit is currently undergoing approval.
2. Aerial thermograms have been performed in twenty-four cities through cooperation between the State Energy Office and the Grand River Dam Authority. The findings are given to the cities, which pledge to develop a system for interpreting the results to citizens on a one-to-one basis. For the first month after the aerial photos, citizens go to their city hall for interpretation; then they may go to local banks, libraries, or other organizations in which staff members trained by the cities will interpret photos and distribute literature. In the last six-month period from 4 percent to 25 percent of citizens viewed photos of their homes; those cities where interpretation was done in banks had the highest percentages.
3. The most successful program is the Demonstration Van, which is a rotating speakers' bureau and information center. Local mass media are used to promote interest in displays, slide shows, speeches and literature which are available. The van appears at fairs and public gatherings around the state as well as at schools and shopping plazas.
4. There is a comprehensive public education information program, through joint cooperation of the Department of Education at Oklahoma State University and the State Department of Education. There is an energy conservation curriculum for grades one through twelve. Also, the Department of Home Economics at Oklahoma State University, in conjunction

with their extension service, has a university-level curriculum on energy conservation and problems.

5. County extension services are the major mechanism for outreach into the communities, particularly the rural ones. In the two primarily urban counties, the state is attempting other mechanisms for contact with citizens.

6. There are hotlines available—one through which all citizens in the state may get answers to their questions and make requests for written information; one for the program of the demonstration van; and one for requesting the public school curricula.

7. In regard to building codes, a bill has been introduced which would allow municipalities to enforce their own building codes or to adopt the NICKBICKS code. Another bill will allow municipalities to adopt either the Massachusetts lighting code or to adopt NICKBICKS code.

8. Oklahoma State University conducts builder/contractor workshops which provide information on retrofitting, new construction, and alternative systems for the conservation of energy. At present these are awareness programs, but after new building codes are established, they will inform contractors of the new standards.

9. The University of Oklahoma is contracted to coordinate the efforts of the various levels of government and organizations in carrying out programs. Most important, the university is responsible for setting up the analysis mechanisms for each program so that each organization can monitor the effectiveness of its own program. For 1978, $48,000 was allotted for the evaluation of programs.

Oregon

Oregon has one of the more comprehensive state energy plans, most of which is covered by state law. The new building code, which requires an increase in ceiling and floor insulation values to R-30 and R-19, respectively, and double-glazed windows and vapor barriers, went into effect on January 1, 1979. Public information and weatherization services are available by state law from utilities and energy suppliers. These include audits and information about low-interest loans subsidized by the state and available at 6-½ percent from lending institutions. Oregon also provides a weatherization tax credit up to $125 for the cost of materials, passed a solar tax credit of 25 percent of the cost up to $1,000, and provides special benefits for veterans.

The Oregon Department of Energy has done some modeling to determine the effect of these programs. On the basis of present incentives it is estimated that 60 percent of single-family residences will take advantage of conservation programs by 1985. Only 37 percent, however, will have adopted either solar hot water or space heating by 1997.

Other aspects of the Oregon program include a flyover program using infrared photography supervised by the Bonneville Power Authority in cooperation with participating utility companies. Photographs are to be displayed at local utility offices. The state's public information program is heavily weighted on the electronic media—there are spot ads and PBS programs. In addition, the state has developed a publications program of information on weatherization and solar installation.

One of the novel features of the Oregon program is the use of coordinators to channel information to communities, to catalyze energy awareness at the grassroots, and to serve as a liaison between state agencies and the local government.

Oregon has also developed a program through public schools and junior colleges to provide instruction about the basics of energy and the alternative sources of it. The State Department of Energy indicated that it would begin to assess the effectiveness of the program in the fall of 1978 but did not indicate how this would be done.

Rhode Island

Rhode Island responded to our inquiry only by letter. The indication was that presently there are no incentives or disincentives affecting residential conservation. The state has complied with EPCA by upgrading its building code. In terms of public education, little beyond the preparation of a "curriculum for a two-hour energy workshop" has apparently been done. The state has conducted a survey of energy use but did not enclose the results.

South Carolina

South Carolina did not send a copy of its state plan but did indicate that no incentives for energy conservation or alternative sources are offered. The State Energy Management Office does not issue an annual report and has not attempted to survey public attitudes.

South Dakota

South Dakota's plans will be coordinated through the Office of Energy Policy, whose goal is to reduce the state's projected energy usage in 1980 by 9 percent. Some features of the state plan are as follows.

1. A state building code is in effect which in all its parts is at least as strict as the ASHRAE 90-75.
2. In an effort to reduce peak electrical demands, the utility companies have a block load policy. They also manage a consumer re-education program to reduce peak load. A peak-time price increase is proposed by the state.
3. The South Dakota Home Weatherization Program administers the retrofitting of low-income and elderly persons' homes. In a nine-month period, 1,300 homes were weatherized. Federal monies assure the continuation of the program.
4. Some utility companies offer lower utility cost incentives for homeowners who retrofit homes. Other utility companies sell retrofitting equipment to their customers as an encouragement to weatherize. Still others offer free insulation evaluations and estimates, and finance weatherization on the monthly utility bills at very low rates.
5. Infrared photography has been provided by the Remote Sensing Institute of South Dakota State University. The results were evaluated by means of citizen questionnaires, and the project was deemed popular.
6. Project Conserve is a computerized home energy audit program given out by the state OEP. The state prepared a manual for utility companies, which includes suggestions and materials for a mass media advertising campaign, instructions for the soliciting of the help of community organizations, copies of the audits, pre- and post-audit press releases, and details on the acquisition of referral lists of contractors and suppliers to pass on to customers. The OEP performs a three- to six-month follow-up survey to determine the effectiveness of the audits in getting citizens to retrofit.

Tennessee

Tennessee offers free energy audits by mail to homeowners, along with an energy hotline and an infrared aerial scanning service. The state did not describe other conservation programs except a property tax exemption for solar or wind power heating, cooling, or electrical generation systems. Tennessee also has a loan program for energy-saving home improvements, but the details were not available. In addition TVA sponsors its own program for home insulation and solar development which is not supervised by the state.

Texas

Texas does not have a uniform building code but rather has over 900 local codes. The state exerts little influence over these beyond the power of suggestion. Assistance in the form of thirty workshops for builders and financiers to increase knowledge of and familiarity with conservation techniques has been provided. The state has encouraged, but not required, utilities to offer retrofits and financing for customers. A do-it-yourself energy audit and energy hotline for customers are also offered. Beyond this, Texas had not provided financial incentives for solar or conservation equipment. We could find no evidence of attempts to survey public opinion or monitor energy use in the residential sector.

Utah

Utah's Energy Office manages a program designed to reduce the state's 1980 energy needs by 7.6 percent. Particularly noteworthy is the evaluation and ongoing assessment which is built into each program.

1. The state has its own code for thermal and lighting efficiency.
2. An assessment of public understanding of conservation has been done, and a more extensive survey this year will provide baseline information for ongoing evaluation.
3. The Utah State University extension service maintains a statewide hotline.
4. The extension service provides printed information and messages for distribution. All information is pre-tested before it is mass-distributed, although materials are prepared as specifically as possible for the populations for which they are used.
5. The extension service has set up an energy information network through its county offices. It also attempts to expose people to conservation efforts on a local level through car tune-up programs and designated energy months, portable displays, an awards program for local conservation projects, neighborhood forums, and a roster of speakers. A "Home

Energy Saver's Program" is run by the state to call public attention to the advantage of energy conservation. The extension service performs continuing evaluations of all its programs.

6. Utah has established an Energy Conservation Advisory Committee specifically to review and coordinate conservation efforts across the state.

7. Although no state-sponsored retrofitting programs exist, Utah coordinates all public and private retrofitting programs, including those run by the power companies.

8. The State Board of Education is developing a curriculum of energy conservation for kindergarten through grade nine. It offers teacher training and manages an ongoing program assessment.

9. The State Department of Community Affairs carries on a weatherization program for elderly, handicapped, and low-income people.

10. Class "C" audits are available to homeowners and renters through the state hotline and local energy offices.

Virginia

The Virginia Energy Office has set up an Energy Management and Training Program to reduce 1980s energy consumption by 5.18 percent. The overall program has five areas, each having its own manager and evaluation procedures. Two areas deal with the residential sector. General Public deals with personal acceptance of conservation, and Training and Support Services is responsible for dissemination of information to the public.

1. A program on retrofitting promotes the purchase and use of appropriate material by means of mass media campaigning.

2. An extension service is maintained through the State University and VPI.

3. A variety of energy audits for home dwellers is available through the State University Extension Service.

4. The extension service also provides an energy consumption analysis for individual residents to aid in the selection of retrofitting materials and more energy-efficient lifestyles. The Energy Office coordinates this computerized program.

5. Seminars and workshops provide homeowners with technical instruction in retrofitting. A "Rate Your Energy Efficiency" program helps them classify their personal usage of energy (lifestyle audit).

6. The state has adopted its own building code.
7. A Buyer Training Program provides homebuyers with the ability to rate new homes on their energy efficiency.
8. The Energy Office publishes a composite of energy tips in the form of monthly "Consumer Comments." It prepares a bi-weekly column for newspapers entitled "Your Energy Matters." Radio spots are also prepared for distribution.
9. A weatherization training program for low-income families is provided.
10. The state promotes the use of infrared photography in representative regions. The Training and Support Services Area is responsible for educating personnel in the technical aspects of residential conservation programs, and also for the preparation of material for the seminars and workshops held for the residential sector. In addition, it provides for other programs.
11. A Speakers' Bureau on energy matters is maintained.
12. Audio-visual training materials are prepared and kept on file.
13. The state sponsors evening courses in area high schools and colleges.
14. Virginia has enacted a law that suggests making solar energy equipment exempt from local taxes.

Washington

Washington has upgraded its building code to coincide with EPCA requirements. In addition, the state is attempting to provide energy audits in 160,000 homes before 1980. Homeowner workshops are being offered through the state community colleges. Washington expects to reach 60 percent of single-family homeowners by 1980 and to effect a 20-40-percent reduction in energy use. More broadly, the Energy Office expects to use these workshops to establish a network throughout the state that might be used in the future. To encourage the development of public information, the state uses an energy hotline, public service announcements, notices in major publications, an energy road show, and an energy display program. The state does not offer any tax incentives for conservation beyond exempting alternative energy devices from property taxes.

West Virginia

West Virginia presently has no state incentives for either conservation or solar. The Fuel and Energy Office indicated, however, that three utilities and several banks offered low-interest energy conservation loans. The state participates in Project Conserve and has accordingly established a home audit program that had reached some 40,000 homes by June of 1978. The state was in the process of conducting an attitudinal survey but its design was not indicated. An annual report is not published.

Wisconsin

Wisconsin has presented a plan designed to reduce the projected 1980 energy needs by 10.04 percent—the highest percentage savings of any state in the nation. The total 1978 cost of implementation is budgeted to be $865,041. The state's 1978 implementation grant was $1,025,300.

1. New thermal and lighting efficiency codes were enacted in 1978, which set a maximum for various areas. State programs have been initiated for the training of inspectors in the new rulings, and for informational seminars for consumers and contractors.
2. The state has adopted a new air conditioner efficiency bill, separate from the federal legislation.
3. A "Municipal Outreach Program" of technical assistance for local governments is provided. Functions within the program include the performing of energy audits, development of a municipal energy conservation workbook, and the presentation of seminars. The locally based "Regional Planning Commission Outreach Program" will bring similar conservation programs to small cities, villages, and towns with populations under 10,000.
4. The city of Madison "Model Energy Conservation Program" attempts to demonstrate the feasibility of city governments to serve as coordinators for a packet of energy conservation programs for their residents. Funding for 1977 and 1978 is $46,600.
5. Madison has developed a model insulation code and a consumer insulation guide.
6. Through the home weatherization program, 7,000 low-income homes will be weatherized. Funds will be received from the Community Services Administration, DOE, and the state.
7. A home energy disclosure bill has been enacted, requiring disclosure of past utility bills upon transfer of residences.
8. There is a home loan energy conservation program specifically designed for Wisconsin veterans.

9. The state has implemented a program for homeowners which gives state income tax credits of 8 to 20 percent of the costs of solar energy system equipment and insulation.
10. Legislation has been enacted which sets standards for solar equipment and guidelines for solar rights.
11. Energy audits are available to homeowners through utility companies and certain banks; such audits are required before any building reconstruction may be made. The state is developing a manual showing how community action agencies and public utilities can provide audits using municipal monies.
12. The Community Energy Conservation Planning and Implementation Grant was initiated in 1977 on a pilot basis in one county. Beginning in 1978, the state assisted in organizing the local conservation centers in other areas and funded several initial short-term programs; $80,000 was budgeted for 1978.
13. The "Hands On" energy intervention program is an effort to involve youth in the conservation effort by training fifty high school students from the Youth Opportunities Unlimited Program to give home audits on the computer home energy audit model. They are to conduct 4,000 audits. Also, fifteen high school teachers will train 150 students in conservation services, and they in turn will disseminate information on these services to at least 2,500 homeowners and renters. State law provides for tax credits for homeowners who install alternative energy systems in their homes.

Wyoming

Wyoming will use the $700,000 given to it by EPCA to achieve a 5-percent reduction in projected energy needs by 1980. Its state energy office has outlined a mixture of mandatory and secondary programs which it monitors and reviews for its quarterly newsletter. The program stresses direct individual contact and includes a large degree of local level participation.

1. The state will adhere to the ASHRAE 90-75 thermal lighting codes. There exists a state conservation coordinator who sponsors meetings to explain the standards and promote their adoption at local levels.
2. Wyoming encourages local utility companies to promote conservation by including in their monthly billing flyers, insulation programs, and reports of previous year consumption for the same time period.

3. The Energy Conservation Committee will sponsor workshops at universities and community colleges to give homeowners a first-hand opportunity to analyze their energy usage. Civic organizations and energy-related businesses are encouraged to co-sponsor the programs. FEA's Project Conserve questionnaire will also be given out.

4. The state will take aerial photos of entire towns, which will be given to homeowners and which will also be used in workshops for the evaluation of their effectiveness in getting households to retrofit. Local utilities and financial institutions will be encouraged to help finance the photos, explain the results to citizens, and absorb the cost of recommended improvements. This program is specifically earmarked for evaluation.

5. A low-income home weatherization program is being carried out with the use of federal funds. By 1979, 3,000 homes will have been weatherized at a cost of $250 each. The program is administered through the Division of Public Assistance and Social Services, and is implemented through the Community Action Programs.

6. Much attention has been given to the public school education program. A specific curriculum, developed by a non-profit educational corporation, is used at all levels of education. Workshops on conservation are held for secondary school and community college personnel and students. A goal is to have the schools serve as models for community conservation action.

7. The state is attempting to guarantee loans and give tax incentives for retrofitting.

8. A "Community Grants Project" has been implemented which provides seed money for the establishment of local conservation offices; coordinates their efforts with those of state and federal governments; and sends out announcements to local citizens, organizations, and businesses to encourage their interest in such community centers and their projects.

9. The ECC has designed a traveling display on conservation for use at fairs in several counties.

10. TV interviews are periodically prepared for the promotion of projects at the local level; also, four television shows have been prepared in coordination with the state of Colorado.

11. Organizations such as Girl Scouts are contacted and supported in the carrying out of local conservation efforts.

12. The state has established a statewide solar advocacy group.

13. A pamphlet of free materials which are available through state offices has been distributed.
14. An ongoing newspaper column, which provides tips on conservation is prepared in conjunction with the Energy Extension Service. Also, bi-weekly radio spots are prepared for distribution.

CONCLUSION

State involvement in energy conservation in the residential sector has been limited by several factors. First, since this has not been an area of traditional concern, there has been confusion as to how to proceed. This is compounded by the difficulty of deciding whose turf it is—whether that of the state, local, or federal governments. Within state governments jurisdictional problems have occurred between planning resource management agencies and newer departments of energy. Many of these issues can be resolved only by trial and error. Beyond these organizational problems, there remain issues concerning the substance and process of the energy program itself. States have adopted a mixture of regulatory provisions (e.g. building codes), market incentives (e.g. tax credits, low-interest loans), and public information programs to encourage millions of homeowners to reduce energy consumption by increasing efficiency. It is not apparent which type of program or mixture of programs is most effective. Undoubtedly, effectiveness depends on particular situations and will vary from state to state. In all cases, however, the attempt to moderate energy use is hindered by the limits of what we know about consumer behavior. Finally, perhaps the greatest obstacle to innovative programs of residential conservation is the fact that few states have taken the issue seriously. There are many reasons for this, including the attitude that the problem is either a federal one or a private one. A more serious obstacle is the belief that the energy crisis is only a temporary supply problem.

Of the programs which we studied, the most common energy-saving measures were the following:

home energy audits done by the state, utilities, the homeowner, or trained energy experts

installation of conservation retrofits by utilities as requested by the consumer

low-interest loans through utilities or lending institutions

tax credits for conservation, solar, or wind equipment.

It is too early to determine what effect these measures will have. Most states have not established evaluation programs. Presumably, effectiveness could be judged in terms of changes in aggregate energy use, changes in household energy consumption, numbers of house units constructed or retrofitted to ASHRAE 90-75 standards, or numbers of solar units installed. Data for the latter two should be available from state tax forms in those states offering tax credits. A number of states have conducted surveys on both conservation know-how and actual energy-consuming behavior. It is not always apparent what purpose these serve, since they seldom are designed to measure response to specific state programs. In the design of state policy, surveys ought to be conducted which relate knowledge to behavior. Only two states specifically mentioned this as a reason for surveys.

APPENDIX

List of All State Energy Offices—1978

State Energy Offices

ALABAMA
Edwin G. Hudspeth, Staff
  Director
Alabama Energy Board
  Management
State Capitol
Montgomery AL   36130
205-832-5010

ALASKA
William C. McConkey
Alaska Energy Office
Division of Energy & Power
  Development
Department of Commerce &
  Economic Development
7th Floor, McKay Building
Anchorage AK   99501
907-272-0527
FTS: dial 8-399-0150;
  ask for 399-0111

ARIZONA
Brent W. Brown, Executive
  Director
Office of Economic Planning
  and Development
Energy Program Section
Capitol Tower, Room 507
Phoenix AZ   85007
602-271-5371
FTS: 762-5371

ARKANSAS
Mac B. Woodward
State Energy Coordinator
960 Plaza West
Little Rock AR   72205
501-371-1374

CALIFORNIA
Richard M. Maullin, Chairman
Energy Resources Conserva-
tion and Development
Commission
1111 Howe Ave.
Sacramento CA   95825
916-322-3690
FTS: 552-3690

COLORADO
Betsy Sturgis
State Fuel Allocation Officer
1313 Sherman Street
Denver CO   80203
303-839-2507

CONNECTICUT
Lynn Alan Brooks, Com-
missioner
Department of Planning and
Energy Policy
20 Grand Street
Hartford CT   06106
203-566-2800
FTS: 641-2800

DELAWARE
David L. Press, Assistant to
Governor on Energy Affairs
c/o Secretary of State
Townsend Building
Dover DE   19901
302-678-5644

DISTRICT OF COLUMBIA
George R. Rodericks, Director
Office of Emergency Pre-
paredness
300 Indiana Avenue, N.W.
Room 5009
Washington DC   20001
202-629-5151

FLORIDA
Dr. Carlos Warren, Director
State Energy Office
108 Collins Building
Tallahassee FL   32304
904-488-6764

GEORGIA
Ms. Omi G. Walden
Georgia State Office of Energy
Resources, Room 615
270 Washington Street, S.W.
Atlanta GA   30334
404-656-3874

HAWAII
Hideto Kono, Director
State Department of Planning
& Economic Development
Kamamalu Building, Box 2359
Honolulu HI   96804
Dial 8-556-0220;
ask for 808-548-3033

IDAHO
L. Kirk Hall, Director
Idaho Office of Energy
State House
Boise ID   83720
208-384-3182
FTS: 554-3182

ILLINOIS
Director, Energy Department
of Business and Economic
Development
222 South College
Springfield IL   62706
217-782-7500

INDIANA
William Sorrells, Director
Indiana Energy Office
803 State Office Building
Indianapolis, IN   46204
317-633-6753

IOWA
Rodson L. Riggs, Director
Energy Policy Council
707 East Locust St.
Des Moines IA   50319
FTS: 863-4420

KANSAS
Robert Robel, Director
(temporary)
State Energy Office
503 Kansas Avenue,
   Room 241
Topeka KS   66603
913-296-2496

KENTUCKY
Damon W. Harrison, Com-
   missioner
Kentucky Department of
   Energy
Capital Plaza Towers
Frankfort KY   40601
502-564-7416
502-564-7070

LOUISIANA
Raymond J. Sutton
Department of Conservation
P.O. Box 44275
Baton Rouge LA   70804
504-389-5161

MAINE
Gary R. Linton, Deputy
   Director
Office of Energy Resources
55 Capitol Street
Augusta ME   04330
207-289-2196
FTS: 868-2196

MARYLAND
John P. Hewitt, Director
Energy Policy Office
301 W. Preston St., Suite 1302
Baltimore MD   21201
301-383-6810

MASSACHUSETTS
Henry Lee, Director
Mass. Energy Policy Office
John W. McCormick Bldg.,
   Room 1413
1 Ashburton Place
Boston MA   02108
617-727-4732

MICHIGAN
Director
Michigan Energy Administration
Fourth Floor, Law Building
Lansing MI   48913
517-373-8250

MINNESOTA
John Millhone, Director
Minnesota Energy Agency
740 American Center Building
150 East Kellogg Blvd.
St. Paul MN   55101
612-296-5120

MISSISSIPPI
George A. Cochran
Mississippi Fuel and Energy
  Management Commission
Rm. 1307, Woolfolk State
  Office Building
Jackson MS   39202
601-354-7406

MISSOURI
Weston Fisher, Program
  Director
Missouri Energy Agency
P.O. Box 1309
Jefferson City MO   65101
314-751-4000

MONTANA
John C. Braunbeck
Fuel Allocation Officer
Capitol Station
Helena MT   59601
406-449-2860
FTS: 587-2860

NEBRASKA
George J. Dworak, Director
State Energy Office
P.O. Box 94841
Lincoln NE   68509
402-471-2867

NEVADA
Noel Clark, Chairman
Public Service Commission
505 East King Street
Carson City NV   89710
702-885-4180

NEW HAMPSHIRE
Marshall Cobleigh, Executive
  Vice Chairman
Governor's Council on Energy
3 Capitol Street
Concord NH   03301
603-271-2121
FTS: 842-2121

NEW JERSEY
Charles Richman, Acting
  Administrator
State Energy Office
101 Commerce Street
Newark NJ   07102
201-648-3290

NEW MEXICO
Fred O'Cheskey, Administrator
Energy Resources Board
P.O. Box 2770
Santa Fe NM   87501
505-827-2472

NEW YORK
Jeffrey C. Cohen, Acting Comm.
State Energy Office
Empire State Plaza
Swan Street Building
Core 1, Floor 2
Albany NY   12223
518-474-6691
FTS: 474-8313

NORTH CAROLINA
Brian Flattery, Director
Energy Division
215 East Lane Street
Raleigh NC   27611
919-733-2230

NORTH DAKOTA
William Robinson
Fuel Allocation Officer
Office of Energy Management
P.O. Box 1819
Bismarck ND 58501
FTS: 783-4011; ask for
  224-2250

OHIO
Robert S. Ryan, Director
Ohio Energy and Resource
Development Agency
30 East Broad Street, 25th Fl.
Columbus OH 43215
614-466-8102

OKLAHOMA
Richard G. Hill, Director
Department of Energy
4400 N. Lincoln Blvd.
Suite 251
Oklahoma City OK 73105
405-521-3941

OREGON
Dr. Fred D. Miller, Director
Oregon Department of Energy
528 Cottage St., N.E.
Salem OR 97310
503-378-4128
FTS: 530-4128

PENNSYLVANIA
William B. Harral
Executive Director
Governor's Energy Council
905 Payne-Shoemaker Building
Harrisburg PA 17101
717-787-9749

RHODE ISLAND
Director (vacant)
State Energy Office
State House
Providence RI 02903
401-277-3370

SOUTH CAROLINA
David S. Harter, Director
Energy Management Office
Edgar A. Brown Office Building
1205 Pendleton Street
Columbia SC 29201
803-758-2050

SOUTH DAKOTA
James A. Van Loan, Director
Energy Policy Office
Joe Foss Building
Pierre SD 57501
605-224-3603
FTS: 782-7000

TENNESSEE
Edward J. Spitzer, Director
Tennessee Energy Office
250 Capitol Hill Bldg.
Nashville TN 37219
615-741-2994
615-741-1772

TEXAS
Alvin E. Askew, Assistant to
  the Governor for Energy
  Resources
7703 North Lamar
Austin TX 78752
512-475-5491

UTAH
Joseph N. Waller, Administration Assistant, Petroleum Allocation
Department of Business Regulations
330 East Fourth South
Salt Lake City UT 84111
FTS: 588-5500; ask for
533-5511

VERMONT
Bruce Haskell, Deputy Director
State Energy Office
State Office Building
Montpelier VT 05602
802-828-2768

VIRGIN ISLANDS
Bruce Potter, Director
Virgin Islands Energy Office
Office of Budget Director
P.O. Box 90
St. Thomas VI 00801

VIRGINIA
Louis R. Lawson, Jr., Director
Virginia Energy Office
823 East Main St., Rm. 300
Richmond VA 23219
804-786-8451

WASHINGTON
Laurence B. Bradley, Acting
Director
Washington Energy Office
100 South Cherry St.
Olympia WA 98504
205-753-2417
FTS: 434-2417

WEST VIRGINIA
John D. Anderson, III, Director
Fuel and Energy Office
1262½ Greenbrier St.
Charleston WV 25305
304-348-8860
FTS: 924-1230

WISCONSIN
Stephen M. Born, Director
Office of State Planning and
Energy
Room B 130
1 West Wilson St.
Madison WI 53702
608-266-3382

WYOMING
John P. Goodier
Department of Economic
Planning and Development
Barrett Building
Cheyenne WY 82002
307-777-7284
FTS: 328-7284

GUAM
Clark E. Jewell, Administrator
Guam Energy Office
Office of the Governor
Government House
Agana, Guam 96910
dial 9-967-1221; ask for
477-9502 or 477-9639

AMERICAN SAMOA
Ray Coston, Special Assistant
to the Governor
Government of American Samoa
Pago Pago AS 96799
dial 9-967-1221; ask for 633-4116

**TRUST TERRITORIES
OF THE PACIFIC**
Koichi L. Wong
Director of Public Works
Office of the High Commis-
sioner
Saipan, Mariana Islands 96950
dial 9-967-1221; ask for
342-4246

PUERTO RICO
Frank Castellon, Director
Office of Energy
P.O. Box 41089, Minillas Station
Santurce PR 00940
809-726-3636

Index

C

About the Editors and Contributors

Raymond J. Burby is Assistant Director for Research at the Center for Urban and Regional Studies of The University of North Carolina at Chapel Hill and director of the Center's research program on energy and patterns of human settlement. He is the author of numerous books and articles on energy, environmental analysis, and community development. Most recently, he co-edited *Energy and the Community*, authored *Recreation and Leisure in New Communities*, and coauthored *New Communities U.S.A.*, *Health Care in New Communities*, and *Schools in New Communities*. Professor Burby has been conducting research at The University of North Carolina at Chapel Hill since 1968.

Mary Ellen Marsden is Research Associate with the Institute for Research in Social Science of The University of North Carolina at Chapel Hill and editor of IRSS Publications. In the Division of Research Programs at IRSS, she engages in program development in the areas of energy and criminology and criminal justice. Her current research involves factors influencing energy conservation and retrofitting of homes, testing causal models of crime and delinquency, and the impact of urbanization on crime rates.

Jeanne T. Hernandez is a research assistant with the Institute for Environmental Studies at The University of North Carolina at Chapel Hill, where she is engaged in the assessment of the physiological and psychological effects of environmental pollution on human populations. Her research specializations are community mental health and diagnostic testing.

William W. Hill is Assistant Professor in the Department of City and Regional Planning at The University of North Carolina at Chapel Hill. He has published a number of articles on environmental policy and environmental impact assessment. His research interests include analysis of institutional impediments to the implementation of solar and renewable energy systems, development of methodologies for community energy planning, and analysis of federal energy policy.

Edward J. Kaiser is Professor in the Department of City and Regional Planning at The University of North Carolina at Chapel Hill, where he teaches land use planning courses. He has been conducting research on public policy and various aspects of the urban development process for over fifteen years. He is author of numerous books and articles in the fields of planning and social science research, and he is the coauthor, with F. Stuart Chapin, Jr., of the recent third edition of *Urban Land Use Planning*.

Duncan MacRae, Jr., is William Rand Kenan, Jr., Professor of Political Science and Sociology and Chairman of the Curriculum in Public Policy Analysis at The University of North Carolina at Chapel Hill. He is author of *The Social Function of Social Science* and *Policy Analysis for Public Decisions*. His major research interest is the measurement of value-related social indicators and their use for policy choices.

Michael W. McKinney is Acting Director and Associate Professor in the Public Administration Program of North Carolina Central University. He is author of a number of articles concerning voting behavior and the survey assessment of consumer demand for publicly supplied goods. Current research activities include the viability of energy policy alternatives and the development of modular teaching packages in public administration for nontraditional students.

David W. Orr is codirector of the Meadowcreek Project, Inc., in Fox, Arkansas. The author of numerous articles on energy and environmental policy, he is completing a book about risk and social order.

He also is the co-editor of and a contributor to *The Global Predicament: Ecological Perspectives on World Politics*. His current research interests include the political economy of risk.